D0745932

The Buffalo People

*Prehistoric Archaeology on
the Canadian Plains*

The Buffalo People

*Prehistoric Archaeology on
the Canadian Plains*

Liz Bryan

 The University of Alberta Press

First published in Canada by
The University of Alberta Press
141 Athabasca Hall
Edmonton, Alberta, Canada T6G 2E8

Copyright © The University of Alberta Press 1991

ISBN 0-88864-220-2   cloth
ISBN 0-88864-221-0   paper

Canadian Cataloguing in Publication Data
    Bryan, Liz.
    The Buffalo People

    Includes bibliographical references.
    ISBN 0-88864-220-2 (bound). ISBN
0-88864-221-0 (pbk.)

    1. Indians of North America—Prairie Provinces—History. 2. Indians of North
America—Prairie Provinces—Antiquities. 3. Prairie Provinces—Antiquities. I. Title.
E78.P7B79 1991   971.2'01   C90-091377-0

Typesetting by Pièce de Résistance Ltée., Edmonton, Alberta, Canada
Printed by Quality Color Press Inc., Edmonton, Alberta, Canada

To my father, John Rodgers,
who first gave me a love of words.

CONTENTS

PREFACE

This book attempts to recreate the lives of some of the very first Canadians, the buffalo hunters who lived on the grasslands between the waning days of the great Ice Age and the coming of the first Europeans. It is also, almost as a byproduct, a brief history of archaeology in the prairie provinces. Who am I to try such a task? I am not an archaeologist, simply a writer with a great curiosity about the past. On the prairies I visited such places as Writing-on-Stone and Moose Mountain (their names alone were enough to tempt me) and intrigued with the potential for discovery, I volunteered to dig for three summers at the magnificent archaeological site of Head-Smashed-In Buffalo Jump in Alberta. When I walked the long lines of drive cairns; when I held in my hand a broken chert arrowhead, a chopped bison bone or a bird-bone bead; when I traced with my space-age fingers ancient dream-pictures scribbled on stone, I wanted to know more about the people who had made them so long ago. This book is a result of my search, a search that led me throughout the grasslands of Alberta, Saskatchewan and Manitoba.

One point I would like to make clear. In early diaries and in all subsequent literature except for academic reports, North American bison are called buffalo, a name bestowed by the first Europeans and one that has become firmly entrenched in the romantic vision of ancient life on the plains. It is, however, scientifically inaccurate. The animal which has the repetitious appellation of *Bison bison bison* is not related at all to the true buffalo or *Bos* of Asia. I have titled this book *The Buffalo People* in recognition of the widespread popular usage of this name and also because the Indians themselves, in historic times when they began to speak English, called the animals buffalo. But because the work is based on the discoveries of archaeologists, the text itself follows scientific precedent.

ACKNOWLEDGEMENTS

I acknowledge with gratitude help from the following sources: the Canada Council whose generous nonfiction arts grant funded travel and writing time; Jack Brink and his associates of the Alberta Archaeological Survey, Edmonton, who welcomed me as a neophyte excavator at Head-Smashed-In and provided both stimulation and encouragement for this book; archaeologist John Brumley of Medicine Hat who showed me the sites on the Suffield Military Reserve in Alberta and offered much insight and inspiration; Brian Spurling, Director of the Heritage Branch of Saskatchewan Parks, Recreation and Culture, Regina; Margaret Hanna of the Museum of Natural History, Regina; Leigh Syms, curator of the Winnipeg Museum of Man; Beverly Nicholson, Eldon Johnson, Ted Douglas, Terry Gibson, Laura Wright, Tim Jones and many other archaeologists, professional and amateur, who gave of their time and hospitality to show me sites and talk with me about my book. For advice and criticism of the work in progress I am deeply indebted, once again, to Jack Brink. The Alberta Foundation of the Literary Arts provided funds towards publication. Finally, my husband Jack kept the home fires burning during my several prolonged absences in the field. Without him, the project would have been far more difficult to accomplish.

INTRODUCTION

These Indians who reside in the large Plains are the most independent and appear to be the happiest and most contented of any People upon the face of the Earth. They subsist on the Flesh of the Buffalo and of the skins they make the greatest part of their cloathing which is both warm and convenient.

Daniel Harmon, North West Company fur trader; Journal of 1804.

P eople have lived for more than 12,000 years on the grasslands of Canada's prairie provinces. Touching only lightly on the land, they left behind few visible traces of their presence and many of these have been demolished by the demands of the twentieth century. The country is no longer untrammelled but curbed by fences, roads and railways. Its lovely wilderness, silent now to the hoofbeats of great herds of bison and antelope, has become fields of grain, sunflowers and sugarbeets, rangeland for domestic cattle. Its rivers have been dammed, its valleys flooded, its air polluted. Great cities of concrete and glass rise up in place of the tipi encampments and the buffalo hunters themselves have been diminished by the effects of an alien culture, their old ways mostly forgotten. Yet they are in a sense our ancestors; they were custodians of a large part of the land we now call Canada. They used it wisely and passed on a grand, unspoiled inheritance.

The people of Canada's grasslands were among the last in America to be "discovered" by Europeans. Immured in the vast heartland of the new-found continent, they remained distanced by time as well as space long after the peoples of the coasts and the fur-rich north had learned to live with the technologically superior invasion force. In parts of southern Alberta and Saskatchewan, some natives had not even seen a white man until the Northwest Mounted Police rode in to establish the Queen's law and order in the late nineteenth century, a good 400 years after Columbus' first footfall. They entered the history books late and briefly; before their indigenous culture could be examined and documented, it was all but gone.

Today's Plains Indian exists as a stereotyped image in feathered head-dress and fringed buckskin, riding over the grasslands to hunt bison with his Winchester rifle. But this is a false portrait from what we now call the equestrian years, the ephemeral last flowering of a culture revolutionized by the horse and coloured indelibly by the glitz and glamour of Hollywood. The reality of life on the prairies in prehistoric times, before Columbus and de Soto, before Kelsey, La Verendrye, Fidler, Harmon and all the spreading tentacles of European civilization, is far more difficult to grasp. Henry Kelsey was the first European to see the plains at "ye outermost edge of the woods" and after his first look in 1691 came a long procession of fur-traders, explorers, missionaries and scientists, many of whom described in letters and journals the people who lived there. These eye-witness reports provide some documentary evidence of the native way of life—but the written word, by definition, puts an end to prehistory. By the time the Plains Indians were encountered by Europeans, their basic culture was undergoing swift and dramatic change. For the effects of the European presence had preceded the explorers themselves, a kind of filtering vanguard that brought mixed blessings: social and territorial upheaval and disease as well as the horse, gun, iron kettle and warm blanket.

Clues to life in the long days of prehistory must be gathered from the earth itself, piece by tiny piece; lost or discarded fragments, abandoned traces, dead and buried relics—a mere fraction of the material remains of a strong and vibrant culture. We must examine these scraps and somehow make sense of them, breathe life into them. This, of course, is properly the work of archaeologists. Without them, there would be nothing to study. And so any examination of the prehistoric peoples of the plains, all of them united by a single strong thread, their dependence on the North American bison, also reveals the story of archaeology on the Canadian Plains, a science that here is scarcely thirty years old. The surface has barely been scratched; there are depths yet to be plumbed. And each turn of the spade, each careful scrape of the trowel and flick of the whisk-broom could very well reveal part of a very different picture than the one drawn here. For archaeology goes on; there are sites still to be found and dug, data to be analyzed, new scientific methods to be tried, space-age technology yet to be invented and applied. The applecart of the currently accepted archaeological scenario might very well be upset as early as tomorrow, making this book obsolete. But this is the nature of science, ever to push forward on its frontier, seeking answers for currently unanswerable questions—and finding new questions to ask.

Archaeologists have worked hard to reconstruct the past lives of the prehistoric peoples of the plains but, like other scientists, they tend to be specialists and to publish their findings in academic journals. This book is an attempt to synthesize and interpret for the layreader the theories and discoveries of archaeology on the grasslands of Canada's prairie provinces, and to bring to life an ancient and forgotten people.

The prehistoric Indians themselves deserve our admiration. They survived—and thrived—in the face of great odds: a harsh and often hostile environment that offered only one single life-sustaining resource: the bison. Almost totally dependent on this great animal, they remained nomad hunters to the finish, a people so well adapted to their way of life they had little reason to change. They were not, in this sense, uncivilized, though they had no writing, no elaborate social or political organizations and certainly no grand settlements. They moved on foot with dogs to help them carry their tents, and never discovered the use of the wheel — perhaps because the rough and roadless prairie was unfit for wheels. They made the most of what they had; like other people, they wrested food and shelter from their environment, cared for their families, mourned their dead, strove to understand the world around them and the stars above, worshipped what they could not understand, drew pictures and told tales—and aspired to immortality.

Like an untimely frost in the night, the coming of Europeans nipped the bud of this developing culture; before it could reach full flowering, its glory was gone. The prehistory of these first Canadians passed into the sad days of history: the astoundingly swift depletion of the bison herds, the arrival of European farmers and ranchers, the land treaties and the reserve system, the loss of an independent way of life. But the people themselves, deeply rooted in the grasslands for 12,000 years, survived. And their story continues.

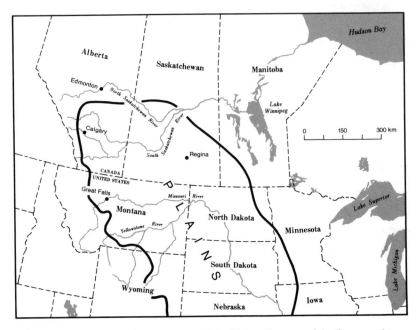

Map of North America, showing extent of the Plains. Courtesy of the Cartographic Section, Department of Geography, University of Alberta.

ONE

The Plains

Travellers driving east along Highway 3 through the dark enclosures of the Rocky Mountains cannot help but notice, as they swoop down from the Crowsnest Pass, that the land ahead is different. The precise landmark of change is difficult to pinpoint—perhaps it lies at first more in the mind than in the eye—but past the stark ridges of the Livingstone Range there seems suddenly to be more sky and the air is clearer, permitting a sharper focus. The valley reaches out, unfolding like the petals of the first prairie crocus and the land lies down, its thrust no longer vertical but horizontal. Ahead the road is straight and fast, the skyline clear. Soon the Rockies are only a picket fence fast diminishing along the western horizon; to the north lie the dark shoulders of the Porcupine Hills, the last defiant mountain outliers, and to the ever-expanding east the grasslands billow and beckon.

From the foothills of the Alberta Rockies to the Manitoba Lowlands, Canada's prairies sweep eastward for 1,200 kilometres, about a quarter of the total width of the continent. This enormous expanse of country is commonly thought of as flat because this is the dominant first impression, particularly if one has just journeyed through the mountains. But given a closer look, the land reveals a more intricate reality. From west to east the prairies descend in three large sloping steps, from 1,300 metres above sea level at the edge of the foothills to less than 300 metres at Lake Winnipeg. The Alberta Plains form the first step. Then gently over the Missouri Coteau the land drops down onto the Saskatchewan Plains, then down again over the steeper Manitoba Escarpment. Within these three major undulations, the prairies ripple with hummocky hills and valleys, wide plains and deep river trenches, rock escarpments, eroded badlands, sandhills and sinuous coulees. It is a landscape of many different terrains, each with its own distinct microenvironment but all subject to the overall discipline of continental climate.

Because the Rocky Mountains drain the moisture from the prevailing Pacific winds, rainfall on the prairies is scarce and unpredictable: never more than fifty centimetres a year, and usually much less. The climate is extreme: summers are short, hot and parched, winters long and cold. Severe frosts,

1

blizzards, hail, lightning, dust storms, tornados, floods and drought, all play their part in prairie weather, making this land some of the most difficult on earth for human occupation. The winters, in particular, are hard to bear; the cold is intense and uninterrupted, the wind bitter. Only in the extreme southwestern corner of the plains is there a possibility of reprieve from winter's long sentence: warm chinook winds from the west coast occasionally breach the mountain barrier, bringing a false and fleeting spring. Snowbanks melt overnight, exposing tracts of winter-brown grass and leaf buds are tricked into premature growth.

Ecologists divide the region broadly into three different biotic zones, ranged like a rainbow arching northward from the forty-ninth parallel. The shortgrass zone in the rainbow's heart covers most of southern Alberta and Saskatchewan. This merges gradually into an arc of moister mixed prairie where the native grass grows thicker and taller, and this in turn blends into aspen parklands, dotted with tight clumps of trees, like islands in a grassy sea. Beyond the grasslands, the dark boreal forests stretch into Canada's north. All three zones are dry but in the shortgrass country, which has poor soils and less than thirty centimetres of rain a year, near desert conditions prevail. Modern cultivation has failed to tame this land. Even today it is still sparse natural grassland sprinkled with sagebrush and cacti, eroded badlands and great desolate sandhills; what little agriculture is practiced must rely on intense irrigation. It was such forbidding territory to the first explorers that Captain John Palliser who journeyed through on an inspection tour of the Canadian west in 1857 pronounced it "desert-like, unfit for cultivation." Because of his report, it was many years before Europeans even tried to settle on "Palliser's Triangle," as the unpromising area was later called.

On the dry windswept reaches of the southern plains there are few native trees for shade or shelter, though cottonwoods and willows grow in the shelter of river valleys and coulees and pines speckle the few upland slopes. Wherever there is a damp dimple, tough shrubs such as saskatoons and wild roses, wolfwillow and snowberry, find a toehold. But it is—or was—primarily a world of grass, a hundred different varieties including the tough blue grama and spear grass, western wheat and bluebunch and red fescues, each one adapted to thrive in a particular microenvironment. Before Europeans came to curb and disturb the prairies, this huge sweep of grasslands and parklands provided ideal habitat for a large numbers of herbivores—countless millions of bison, vast herds of deer and antelope—and many other animals and birds. Here, too, the first peoples of the plains found their ecological niche, enduring the heat and the drought and the cold to forge for themselves a lifestyle that was to endure without major change for 12,000 years.

Geology

The underlying bones of the Canadian prairies are old, older by far than the Rockies to their west, though not as ancient as the obdurate granite of the Canadian Shield that defines their eastern edge. The bedrock of the grasslands consists of thick layers of sedimentary deposits accumulated over tens of millions of years, most of it when the land lay submerged under a midcontinent sea. But the land's physical appearance is mostly due to a comparatively recent geologic event in Earth's history, the Ice Age.

A million and a half years ago, the world climate gradually began to chill. Snow failed to melt, even in midsummer, and piled up like a thick blanket over the land: a metre, ten metres, fifty metres and more. The lower layers turned to ice and under the great weight of the snowy overburden, the ice began to march. In a giant pincer movement, the prairies were assaulted from two directions, the northeast and the west. Most of the ice advanced from the James Bay region of Hudson Bay but glaciers slipped down also from the western mountains and, at the height of the great freeze, the two ice fronts met and merged, encasing all the plains. Only the highest mountains and a few small upland areas escaped the icy occupation.

Canada was covered with ice for tens of thousands of years but in time the climate warmed and the ice retreated. The debris of rocks and soil churned up and carried by the glaciers was left stranded when the ice melted: tons of silt and sand, thick layers of stones, even enormous boulders were dumped often far away from their origins. And floodwater from the melting ice ravaged the landscape. Rivers swollen to ten times their former size cut deep channels through the glacial deposits and spilled out into valleys and plains, creating huge lakes and leaving behind tons of sediment. For a long while the prairies were awash. Until the waters drained and plants and animals recolonized the land, processes that took several thousands of years, it must have been a cold, bleak and sterile environment.

At least four times in the past million and a half years this dramatic scenario repeated itself. Each time, ice from the Western mountains (the Cordilleran advance) and from the Eastern sub-Arctic (the Continental or Laurentide advance) ebbed and flowed, stalled, retreated, melted and froze again, the later ice advances smothering and erasing traces of earlier ones. The most recent surge of glaciation, known as the Wisconsinan, held Canada in its grip for more than 60,000 years. Geologists can track its movements by following terminal moraines, the piles of rocks and soil that the ice fronts bulldozed ahead of them and then abandoned. They can pinpoint the positions of ice dams that impounded giant lakes and diverted rivers, identify meltwater channels, some of them gouged sixty metres deep into the sedimentary bedrock, and trace the origins of ice-borne boulders, known as glacial erratics, some of them as big as houses.

Wherever the ice went, it drastically altered the landscape, scraping down the highpoints and filling in the valleys. The prairies have been ice-free now for the last 12,000 years, but the effects of glaciation are still deeply etched. Everywhere the sedimentary bedrock of the plains basin is spread with thick layers of stony rubble scraped up mostly from the northeast and distributed unevenly, sometimes in the form of small hills, wherever the ice went. In the hollows of this hummocky till spring run-off collects to form seasonal lakes known as potholes, one of the most characteristic features of the plains landscape. The valleys of all the major prairie rivers are wide, deep canyons sliced down into the bedrock by rampaging meltwater. In some of these, notably the Red Deer and the Milk, the canyon walls have since been eroded by winds and rains into sculptured hoodoos and fantastic badlands, some of the most astounding scenery in Canada, while on the valley bottoms, sheltered from the wind, forested oases provide very different ecosystems from the prairie floor above. Some of the meltwater drainage channels were temporary; when the floods subsided, these were left as deep dry gashes in the earth, today's coulees. The sandhills are remnants of giant dunes, wind-eroded from the beaches of glacial lakes, and the flat plains areas are mostly the old dried-up lake beds themselves, their former shorelines often preserved as escarpments. The most prominent of these is the Campbell Strandline in southwestern Manitoba, a 400-metre height of land that marked the western edge of Lake Agassiz, the largest of all the glacial lakes in North America.

Everywhere one goes in the prairie provinces, the legacy of ice and floods is easy to see. But the deep and enduring impact of the Ice Age on the land is overshadowed by the critical role it played in the story of humanity in North America.

TWO

First Canadians

F or millions of years the continent of America was an island unto itself, separated by oceans from the rest of the world. This geological quarantine resulted in biological isolation. Species which evolved elsewhere and which could spread naturally throughout most of the rest of the world were prevented from entering America—until the Ice Age.

One of the effects of the worldwide Pleistocene chill was a drastic drop in sea levels. The oceans themselves did not freeze over, but without freshwater input they sank by as much as ninety metres and all the submarine margins of the continents became exposed. In the North Pacific, the shallow sea channels, low-lying coastlines and islands of today's Alaska and Siberia were joined together in a continuous stretch of land, a huge new temporary continent that scientists now call Beringia. And across this new intercontinental link, popularly known as the Bering land bridge, came a wide variety of land mammals from Asia. Among them were the first humans ever to set foot in Canada.

For much of the one and a half million years of the Ice Age the northern half of North America was mostly covered with solid ice, in places thousands of metres thick. But in a reversal of today's climatic patterns, large sections of Beringia, including parts of Alaska and the Yukon, were then a dry belt with only minimal snowfall and so escaped total glaciation. Scientists disagree as to ecological conditions in this ice-free refugium—some say it was covered with lush Arctic grasses, some that it was a bitterly cold and barren desert— but the fact of its existence is undeniable, given the geological record. Studies of fossilized insects and pollens not only substantiate an ice-free environment but make it possible to reconstruct Beringia's vegetation. According to geologist J.V. Matthews of the Geological Survey of Canada, the presence of grassland beetles and weevils and a high percentage of sagebrush suggest that it was an arid environment, likely a varied mosaic of grassland steppe and frozen tundra (Matthews, 1979). It was bleak, cold and dry, essentially a treeless country though a few river valleys provided shelter enough for woodlands of alder and dwarf birch. Nevertheless, this unpromising landscape supported large game animals—mammoths, giant bison, muskoxen, bears, elk, antelope,

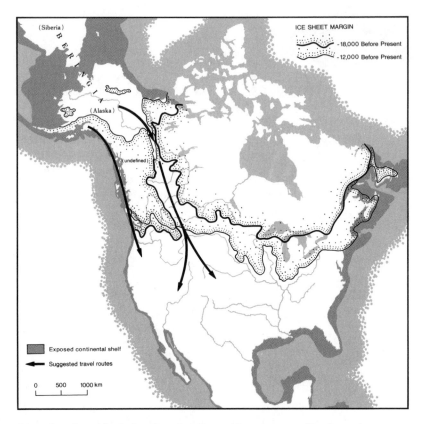

Map of northern North America, showing maximum extent of ice sheets, the Beringian ice bridge connecting Siberia with Alaska and the hypothetical "Ice-free Corridor" along the eastern slopes of the Rocky Mountains. Courtesy of the Cartographic Section, Department of Geography, University of Alberta.

caribou, deer, horses, sloths and tigers, as well as many smaller mammals, an Ice Age bestiary of surprising diversity. Scientists have found their bones, the dung beetles that lived in symbiotic relationship, even some of the giant beasts themselves, preserved in deep permafrost. From the stomachs of frozen mammoths unearthed in Siberia comes evidence of what they ate—cottongrass, sedges, moss and twigs from small trees.

The Asian Connection

While the evidence for the animal population of Beringia is plentiful and uncontested, proof of human presence during the Pleistocene is scanty, though by about 12,000 years ago, when the ice was well in retreat, traces of ancient hunters are found pretty well everywhere in the Americas south of the glacial ice. Scientists generally agree that the first human immigrants crossed into America through Beringia and that their genetic origins are Asian. There are obvious general similarities even today between the indigenous peoples of the two continents—their skins are dark, their cheekbones high, their hair black and straight, their eyes brown. These first impressions are validated by other less visible evidence. Native North American human blood is different from that of Europeans or Africans but similar to that of Asians. Studies of the A, B, O groupings, of blood antigens, proteins, red cell enzymes and antibody molecules all bear this out (Zegura, 1987).

More proof is found in teeth. Teeth preserve very well and are less influenced by diet, health and exercise than bones are. From an evolutionary point of view they are also very conservative—they change only very slowly through time—and thus provide ideal clues to biological affinity. Twenty-four separate human tooth characteristics, mostly of roots and cusps, have been identified. (Cusps are the bumps on the chewing surfaces of the back teeth.) In North Asians, these characteristics form distinct patterns known as Sino-dont (Chinese teeth) traits. These include such things as three-rooted lower first molars (Europeans and Africans have two roots), single not double-rooted lower canines, cusps on the tongue sides of the upper molars, and strongly shovel-shaped incisors, traits that seem to have evolved at least by 18,000 years ago and perhaps as early as 30,000 years ago.

A recent study of 200,000 prehistoric teeth from the New World (prehistoric teeth were chosen because they predated any possible European admixture) showed a high frequency of the Sinodont pattern in all American Indian groups, a clear indication that they all must have originated in North-east Asia (Turner, 1987). This study of tooth traits and evolutionary divergence not only fixes Northeastern Siberia as the ancestral homeland of the American native peoples, but suggests there were three separate migrations: of hunters who filtered east of the Rockies all across North and South America, of a separate maritime people who spread throughout the Arctic, today's Eskimo-Aleut populations, and later, of the people who settled interior Alaska and the British Columbian Coast and Interior. Recent research into variants in blood proteins appears to support this three-migration hypothesis. In the light of all the evidence, scientists generally concede that the collective family tree of all native Americans is well and deeply rooted in the Mongoloid races of Siberia and Northern China.

During the Ice Age, the neck of Asia stretched into Beringia with nothing to distinguish the boundary of a new continent. Scientists believe that Stone Age hunters tracking the great beasts of the Siberian steppes gradually wandered eastward into Beringia then across the land bridge to occupy the ice-free areas of Alaska and the Yukon. They stayed here perhaps for thousands of years. During warmer periods, when ice around the refugium retreated, some of the animals and the hunters who depended on them moved slowly south down the Mackenzie Valley into the Peace River area. But where they went from there is a matter for discussion.

For years it was believed that, as the glaciers receded, an ice-free corridor opened periodically between the mountain and continental ice sheets all the way east of the Rockies. It's an alluring—and well entrenched—prospect; one can just see those little bands of animals and hunters moving slowly down between the parting glaciers. Current research, however, seems to cast doubt on the theory. Studies of ancient continental and mountain ice margins in the middle reaches of the supposed corridor show that, rather than pulling back, the two ice sheets coalesced for centuries and that no continuous gap seems to have existed between them until very late in the waning days of glaciation, when mankind had already established a claim to the grasslands.

But if there were no ice-free corridor, how did the first Canadians move south? Some archaeologists suggest that they made their way down from the Peace River along unglaciated valleys in the interior of British Columbia, or came all the way down the partly ice-free Pacific Coast where, with sea level dropped, the flat continental shelf would have been exposed. Test drilling into this shelf has shown that it was above the sea for a very long period of time, long enough to support the growth of coastal forest (Fladmark 1978 and 1986b). However they came, these earliest immigrants undoubtedly wandered south of the great ice sheet eventually to colonize all of North, Central and South America, leaving traces of their presence just about everywhere.

This human immigration into North America was by no means a series of planned, continuous journeys but simply an accidental drifting of a nomadic people already on the move. The game animals expanded their territories through Beringia into America and the hunters simply followed, unaware that they were on the edge of a huge new unpeopled continent. The migration was also not one-directional, but rather an interchange of species between the two newly-attached continents. Humans, mammoths, bison, muskoxen and deer came into America and horses, wolves and camels crossed into Asia. It is also possible that humans also wandered back and forth between Asia and North America until rising seas towards the end of the Pleistocene epoch left them stranded in the New World, cut off from further Old World influences.

When the first Canadians arrived is as open to dispute as their travel routes. Some say they came early, perhaps as early as 70,000 years ago; others that they appeared only during the waning days of the Ice Age some 12,000 years ago. However, it is generally agreed that since no earlier skeletal types have ever been found here, the first humans to arrive in the Americas were thoroughly modern *Homo sapiens* and this fact alone helps in the dating conundrum. Mankind as a distinct genus first developed about three million years ago on the tropical grasslands of Africa where hundreds of early hominid fossils have been found. But today's humans with their large brains and ability to socialize and communicate did not evolve until about 40,000 years ago and it is these people who successfully colonized most of the warm and temperate areas of Eurasia and Africa, and apparently did so with extraordinary speed. Some archaeologists believe, however, that it took another 10,000 years for people to spread out into stringent northern latitudes which required warm clothing and shelter for survival. This hypothesis places people in Northeast Asia, poised for a possible crossing into America, no earlier than about 30,000 years ago. Archaeologists have found traces of these early people at sites in Siberia and Northern China where some of them made semisubterranean houses framed with mammoth bones. Ancient bone awls and needles show that they knew how to sew and presumably stitched clothing of animal skins. They also made large chipped pebble tools, shell and amber jewellery and carved stylized human and animal figures of ivory.

Between 60,000 to 25,000 years ago, there seems to have been a lull in the Ice Age, a period known as the mid-Wisconsinan interglacial. The climate warmed and the ice retreated to strongholds in the Western mountains and on the Laurentian Plateau, leaving most of North America open to comparatively easy land travel. Some archaeologists argue that the first human immigrants could have arrived during this time, crossing a narrower Bering Strait either in primitive boats or on foot over the winter ice (Fladmark, 1986b). Others believe that they—and the Asian animals—came only when the great cold of the Ice Age returned and the Bering land bridge was exposed, a phenomenon said to have happened several times between 25,000 and 14,000 years ago. In the latter school of thought, some favour an early crossing and others a late. Arguments can be found to bolster all theories.

Studies of native American languages seem to suggest a comparatively early migration. At the time of white contact, the native peoples of North and South America used at least 400 different and mutually incomprehensible languages, a linguistic diversity that argues for many millennia of cultural isolation from the Old World (Coe et al., 1986). On the other hand, evidence from teeth suggests a later migration. Christie Turner (1987) calculates that the amount of time needed to establish the microdifferences that exist today between Northeast Asian and native American teeth is not much more than 15,000 years.

What about archaeological proof? Unfortunately, there are very few excavated Early Man sites in the Americas where the evidence and the dating are universally accepted as valid, and this is not as strange as it may seem. The first immigrants, whether they arrived before or after 25,000 years ago, or only at the very end of the Ice Age, were Asian hunters who like all primitive peoples probably travelled in small family bands. Prehistoric nomads everywhere leave scant trace of their existence: their campsites are temporary, their possessions pitifully few. Generally speaking, only those items made of stone and perhaps bone might survive the centuries. In Canada, the odds are very much against preservation of this early material. The grinding advances of later glacial ice destroyed everything in their wake; torrents of meltwater and rising seas washed away more, and what little trace might remain would be today deeply buried in the frozen gravels of northern muskeg and spruce forest or under layers of till from later ice movement. Like needles in the proverbial haystack, clues to the presence of these first Canadians are staggeringly difficult to find, particularly since archaeologists are not sure where the haystack is, nor whether the needles even exist.

The best chances of finding clues to early people in Canada are believed to lie in the Yukon Refugium, where they likely lived for generations, and east of the Rockies in the area generally accepted as the first to be ice-free and capable of sustaining both human and animal life. In both these critical areas, the archaeological search is ongoing.

Bones of Contention

Even in lands to the south where geological and climatic conditions for preservation are far better than in Canada, few human remains or signs of ancient human activity have been discovered, and fewer still are accepted as serious evidence of Pleistocene occupation. Dating such ancient materials presents a major problem. Until the late 1940s, archaeological discoveries could only be given the age of the geological strata in which they were found, a method often infuriatingly imprecise, since the smallest increments of geologic time are measured in millenia. When the first crude stone artifacts (an artifact is anything made by humans) were discovered beside—and sometimes inside—the fossilized bones of extinct Ice Age animals, it was agreed that they were indeed very old, evidence perhaps of some of the first American immigrants. But the best age estimates were give or take a few thousand years—not exactly scientific.

Many of the firm dates of archaeology were determined only fairly recently by a nuclear age invention, radiocarbon dating. Carbon 14 atoms are present in microscopic amounts in all living matter. As the atoms disintegrate, others are absorbed from the air to keep the ratio, one part per million, constant throughout life. At death, there is no further absorption and the radioactive carbon atoms continue to disintegrate at a known regular rate. Half will be gone in 5,760 years, half of the rest in a further 5,760 years and so on. The age or year of death of a specimen is calculated on the amounts of residual carbon 14, the results being given in years B.P. which stands for Before Present with 1950 the commonly ascribed "present." (To translate B.P. into B.C., simply add 1950; for dates A.D., the B.P. dates must be subtracted from 1950.) Any organic material, such as wood, charcoal, bone, peat, fibre, or shell, can be dated by this method, but there are drawbacks. First, the specimen must be big enough for accurate measurement and much of it must be reduced to carbon before the tests can take place, a procedure out of the question for a rare bone or artifact. Test results can be skewed by even the tiniest amount of contamination from other organic matter, perhaps leached down into the soil by rains. Also, the amount of natural radioactive fallout in the atmosphere has varied considerably in the past, affecting the amount of absorption during the life of the material under study. Nevertheless, until very recently, this was the best that science could do.

With this admittedly imperfect tool, archaeologists set about attempting to date some of the intriguing but controversial "Early Man" sites that have been discovered throughout North, Central and South America. Many of these contained similar elements: the battered and charred bones of extinct Ice Age animals, modified pieces of stone and bone, concentrations of charcoal and, rarely, fragments of human bone. But were the animal bones butchered or torn up by carnivores? Were the stone and bone "tools" modified by humans or by natural causes? Was the charcoal from domestic hearths or from natural fires? The carbon 14 tests often gave incredibly early dates, but could the carbon have been contaminated? There seems to be no archaeological consensus here and most of this evidence has been set aside as ambiguous.

However, there are a few sites where the clues to a very early human presence in America seem pretty convincing. One of these is Monte Verde in the temperate rainforests of south central Chile, one of the most exciting discoveries made so far in the New World. Here, some 13,000 years ago, a group of people lived for a while on the banks of a small creek. When they abandoned the settlement, the site became swamped in a peat bog—a lucky event because peat is a great preserver; the constant humidity and general lack of oxygen retards the decay of organic matter. Excavating here in 1976, archaeologist Tom Dillehay unearthed the wooden foundations of twelve rectangular pole-frame houses, the oldest village in the Western hemisphere. Outside the houses there were two large communal hearths lined with clay, a dozen shallow clay braziers, wooden mortars, grinding stones and traces of forty different edible plants, including wild potatoes. At one end of the village was another larger building, shaped intriguingly like a wishbone, with foundations of banked sand and gravel cemented together by animal fats. Around this building which was perhaps a communal workshop for the preparation of meat and hides were found the butchered bones of at least seven giant mastodons, scraps of animal skin, and large numbers of wood, bone and stone tools, some still attached to their wooden handles by bitumen from nearby coastal oil seeps. Also identified here were a cache of salt and the leaves and seeds of several different kinds of medicinal plants, some from the coast eighty kilometres away, prompting Dillehay to suggest that the building had also served as a dispensary or a hospital. No human bones were found, but pressed into the clay around one of the hearths was the unmistakable imprint of a left human foot, probably that of a child.

The date of this early occupation of the Chilean rainforest seems firm— at least it has not been seriously questioned. But if humans were here, well down towards the toe of South America, by 13,000 years ago, at what earlier date did their ancestors first cross into Beringia? Further excavations at Monte Verde confound the timing question even more. In the earth nearly two metres below the village level Dillehay and his crew found evidence of another cultural occupation. And this gave carbon 14 dates of 33,000 years ago! Excavated here were three hearths filled with specks of beechwood charcoal and traces of charred edible reed, and more than two dozen stone implements, most of them fractured pebbles. Eleven of these showed clear evidence of human alteration by hammering or use (Dillehay, 1984 and 1987; Dillehay and Collins, 1988).

Other convincing evidence for the early presence of man was discovered on a part of the Appalachian Plateau in Pennsylvania which during the Pleistocene epoch lay just south of the icecap. Here, in a cave known as Meadowcroft Rock Shelter, archaeologists unearthed a long sequence of human occupation levels dating well into historic times. On the lowest level, well isolated from the one above by rock fall from the roof of the cave, archaeologist James Adovasio excavated flaked stone tools "of indisputable human manufacture," a charcoal-filled hearth and a charred snippet of bark, possibly from a basket. Seven carbon 14 dates from this level ranged from 13,300 to 19,600 B.P. The stratum immediately above the rock fall contained a well-made leaf-shaped spear point, plus other stone artifacts and the waste flakes from their manufacture. Charcoal from several fire pits here gave dates of between 11,000 and 15,000 years ago.

Archaeologists agree that this important site was very carefully excavated and most believe that the artifacts from the oldest occupied level are indeed of human manufacture. But the site is not without its anomalies. For a start, no remains of extinct Ice Age animals were found in the presumably Pleistocene levels of the excavation and the analysis of pollens indicated not the frigid conditions of tundra or spruce forests one would expect (the rockshelter was only fifty kilometres from the ice front) but a deciduous forest of oak and hickory. Critics also argue that the artifacts could have become mixed into earlier organic materials by the actions of humans or animals operating on the "floor" above, presenting a false picture of association. And they also hold out the possibility that the carbon samples were contaminated by older carbons from a seam of vitrinized wood. Adovasio has persuasive counter arguments for all these criticisms and at the moment, Meadowcroft's claims to great antiquity seem to be riding out the storms (Adovasio et al., 1978 and 1980; Adovasio & Carlisle, 1984; Fagan, 1987; Kelly, 1987; Mead, 1980).

Early Man in Canada

In all of the above sites, the presence of early humans has been inferred from their fire hearths, their tools, their buildings, their footprints. But in Canada, the most sensational "Early Man" discovery was human bones, those of the Taber Child, found by a geologist in 1961. Dr. Archie Stalker, head of a Geological Survey of Canada team, was investigating ancient glacial deposits in bluffs along the east bank of the Oldman River north of Taber, Alberta. It was 11 July, just another routine day under the hot prairie sun and Stalker was slowly working his way up the steep bank describing the deposits. His survey assistants were ahead of him, looking for features. One of them, John Nunan, spotted some bones in front of a hole about halfway up the bank. He immediately called to Stalker, for bones of any kind are always interesting. Stalker's diary entry for that momentous day is matter of fact: "In A.M. to cut on east side Oldman, north of Taber. Not too interesting but there John found some interglacial bones" (Stalker, 1983). No-one dreamed then that the bones were human or that their discovery would stir up controversy for more than twenty-five years.

The bones were mostly cemented in sand but as Stalker reported: "The thinness and fragility of the exposed bone indicated it was from a skull and because the specimen came from interglacial or inter-till deposits [I thought], the find might be important to glacial chronology. To avoid damage, the bone was left in its matrix [the surrounding soil] and later carefully packed in shavings, crated and shipped to Ottawa. It remained crated until it was turned over to the National Museum of Canada" (Stalker, 1983).

Whenever Stalker finds bones, he excavates the area thoroughly to see whether more bones exist and to determine the type and origin of the surrounding soil. He dug out a section two metres long by a metre high, extending 0.7 metres into the bank, as far as he could go without collapsing the upper soil layers, but no further bones were found. His field notes record that the surrounding sediments were sand, grit and fine gravel. He did not take photographs—as he explained later: "In those days pictures were not taken as readily as now"—but the area of the find was carefully staked for later recognition. The bones were believed to be very old. They lay beneath eighteen metres of soil deposits, including four layers of till from the last Wisconsin glacial advance. Conservatively, Stalker first estimated their age at around 25,000 years, based on their geological context. However, wood fragments from nearby comparable strata were later radiocarbon dated at 32,000 and 49,000 years, imputing a far greater age for the bones than Stalker had dared to suggest.

When the bone fragments, still firmly cemented into their sand matrix, arrived in Ottawa they were identified as human, those of an infant of undetermined sex between the age of four and nine months. The archaeological world went wild. Judging from their geological context, the human bones were the oldest found anywhere in the whole of the Americas! The child's skeleton was incomplete: only the bones from the skull, the left side of the face, including jawbone and teeth, two or three vertebrae and parts of the breast and shin bones had survived. How did the baby die? Stalker speculates that perhaps it fell into the river and drowned. Its tiny body was then washed downriver and stranded on a sand bar where it became partly covered by sand and grit. The bones left exposed were gradually broken up and carried away by the current but the rest remained to be further buried, first by river sand then by alluvium in the path of the approaching ice sheet. When the glacier overrode the area, its weight flattened the infant skull and its several readvances added further layers of glacial till. The site of this tragedy, and the pitiful remains were only revealed when post-glacial floodwater cut the present canyon of the Oldman River, exposing the old river bed (Stalker, 1983).

As soon as the bones were proclaimed human, efforts were made to date them directly. But they were too small and too precious to be sacrificed for radiocarbon dating, then the only direct method known. The bones remained at the museum, their age approximated from their geological context. They were preserved, catalogued and put away. It was an unsatisfying state of affairs. Most archaeologists were uncomfortable with the early dates and suggested alternative scenarios. Could the bones have somehow slipped into position from higher up or might the child have been buried in the river bank, its grave cut into the ancient deposits? Others wanted to believe but needed more proof. For ten years, the Taber Child occupied a prominent niche in archaeological

Fossilized tibia of caribou manufactured into a tool for scraping the flesh off animal hides. Found in permafrost gravels of the Old Crow Basin in the Yukon, it was at first believed to be 27,000 years old but was later redated. Close-up photo shows tiny teeth cut into the working end of the scraper. Courtesy of the Canadian Museum of Civilization.

and popular literature as the "oldest human remains in America." It had certainly put Taber, Alberta, on the map.

Five years after this controversial discovery, more possible evidence of the first Canadians turned up, this time on the banks of the Old Crow River in the northern Yukon. As before, it was not an archaeologist who made the find. In 1966, palaeobiologist Richard Harington and his assistant Peter Lord were probing the permafrost in search of Ice Age animals whose bones were unusually well preserved in the valley gravels. On 5 July, Harington wrote in his field notes: "Noticed unusual fractures of bone and chert." He told Lord to keep an eye out for anything that might seem to be an artifact. Five days later, Lord brought him the leg bone of a caribou, thirty centimetres long, fossilized to a deep brown, at first glance nothing special. But one end, its corner broken off, had been delicately chiselled into eight perfect little teeth. It was obviously a manmade tool, a "flesher" for scraping away the inside of fresh animal skins. Nearby were fossilized bones of Pleistocene animals that seemed to show signs of human alteration.

Camped downstream at a site a day's journey away by river boat, archaeologist William Irving was brought in to verify the find, a possible first clue to the presence of early human immigrants in the Yukon refugium. He found the site strewn with broken bones from mammoths, bison and horses, all species that had been extinct since the end of the Ice Age. The types of fractures showed that the bones had been broken while still fresh, yet many of them seemed far too large to have been cracked by animal carnivores. If humans were here during the Ice Age, he reasoned, maybe they had smashed the bones to obtain marrow.

The caribou flesher and two broken mammoth bones found nearby were sent to the National Museum of Canada for examination and radiocarbon dating. More than half of the precious artifact had to be destroyed to provide the test material (only the toothed end could be saved) but from it came an astonishing result—a radiocarbon age of 27,000 years B.P., the same age as the mammoth bones. The archaeological world was stunned and experts scurried for ways to substantiate or deny such incredible antiquity. They turned first to the geologists. Unfortunately, the flesher and the other bones all lay in gravels churned up and only fairly recently redeposited by the river. Twigs and branches found in the bone-bearing layers gave radiocarbon dates that ranged wildly over the past 40,000 years. The whole of the Old Crow Basin is a geological jumble of clays and silts from countless shifting and flooding streams. Only if the flesher had been found in soil undisturbed by natural events since the time it was dropped there could geologists have pinned down a time frame. There seemed no way to verify that unbelievably early date.

All the excitement, however, attracted more workers to the field. The search for traces of Early Man intensified. Scientists combing the frozen gravels of the Old Crow Basin found many more broken bone fragments of extinct Ice Age animals and some believe these to be tools, chipped and flaked by humans using the same basic technology required to fashion stone tools. In a dramatic butchering experiment using a dead zoo elephant as a mammoth substitute, it was shown to be possible for humans to break even thick leg bones by bashing them with large stones. In the same experiment, elephant bone tools were flaked using elk antler hammers and these were found to be excellent for cutting up the elephant flesh, though they needed constant resharpening. Bone tools are known to have been used along with stone by other primitive peoples throughout the world. Were the modified bone "tools" found in the Yukon proof of early human occupation of the north? The evidence is ambiguous. Other scientists have shown that most of the marks of apparent human manufacture can be duplicated by gnawing or trampling by animals, by turbulent water action, by freezing and thawing and by a variety of other natural causes. But no one has ever claimed that the Old Crow flesher is anything but manmade. For years, it remained an enigma (Harington et al., 1975; Irving et al., 1977; Irving, 1987; Stanford, 1987).

More enigmas came to light in 1976 on a point bar deposit in the Old Crow River. This deposit, under thirty centimetres of sand, was found to be piled high with the bones of Ice Age animals, some of them "modified," and among them were found two jawbones: one human, one a dog's. Dentition studies showed the human bone to be from an adolescent of eleven plus years; the dog bone from a domesticated species. Clearly the two jawbones were potentially too important to be destroyed for radiocarbon dating, but bones from a horse, found adjacent, were tested and gave a date of 13,000 years B.P. (Irving et al., 1977; Beebe, 1980).

Perhaps because of the excitement of the Old Crow finds, or perhaps because new scientific dating methods had lately been perfected, in 1976, ten years after they had been discovered, the Taber Child bones were reassessed. First they were sent to California for testing by a new method: one that measures postmortem changes in amino acid levels. But by then the bones were so heavily contaminated by preservatives and by the solvents required to loosen them from their sand matrix that the tests could not take place. In 1978 and 1979 new geological and archaeological investigations were carried out at the discovery site. The overburden (all the deposits on top of 300 square metres of the critical sand layer) was stripped off by dragline one summer, and detailed excavations took place the next. Geologists as well as archaeologists painstakingly went over the area but no further human traces were found. However,

Excavations at the site of the controversial Taber Child discovery on the banks of the Oldman River, plus other dating tests, resulted in an official redating, from the initial claims of more than 25,000 years old to less than 4,000. Courtesy of the Archeological Survey of Alberta.

scientific comparison (by a process known as X-ray diffraction spectrometry) of the material still surrounding the infant bones with all the other sands, tills, slope deposits and mudflows on the site appeared to show that the child had most likely been embedded, not in ancient preglacial deposits but in a much more recent sandy mudflow that had infiltrated the older sand (Wilson et al., 1983).

A couple of years later, the bones were tested for protein content. Bone protein or collagen is a highly stable material which remains in the bone long after death but which is eventually broken down into amino acids. Between 5,000 and 10,000 years after death, only about five percent of the protein remains; after 10,000 years, the amount is microscopic. The Taber Child bones were found to contain between five and six percent protein, far more than expected. This gave them an age of less than 10,000 years. To verify this surprising result, the amount of residual protein in the bones was then compared with that in human bones from Saskatchewan known to be between 3,000 and 5,000 years old and in various fossilized animal bones from the Medicine Hat area dated between 10,000 and 100,000 years old. The protein content of the Taber Child bones matched that of the human bones, although researchers cautioned that this inter-site and inter-species comparison dating was only "very approximate" (Moffat and Wainwright, 1983).

The scientists were not finished yet. Late in 1981, a portion of the child's legbone was cleaned of preservative resins and subjected to the latest form of radiocarbon dating using the accelerator at the Chalk River Nuclear Laboratories in Ontario. This method, known as accelerator mass spectrometry, or AMS process, directly measures the amount of carbon 14 by accelerating the carbon particles through electrical and magnetic fields. During this procedure, the carbon 14 ions are automatically separated from other types of carbon and counted. One of the advantages of this new method is that it requires only one one-hundredth the amount of material that the former carbon 14 method required: only a tiny fraction of a precious relic needs to be destroyed. The results of the AMS test on the Taber Child bones supported the protein comparison test. The infant was dated to 4,000 years plus or minus 750 (Brown et al., 1983). In 1982, the National Museum of Man, in whose charge the bones had been placed, was finally satisfied. It issued a statement relegating the age of the controversial bones to a mere 3,500 years.

Is this the final word? Most archaeologists regretfully agree that it is. But the bones still have their champions. Dr. Stalker remains adamantly convinced, even after the extensive excavations of 1979 in which he took part, that the Taber Child bones "are old and were laid down before the advance of the last glacier." He also asserts that the small amount of bone present, its porosity and the preservatives applied to it in the museum laboratory prevent accurate radiocarbon or protein dating. Archaeologist Robert Lee (1983) argues against the protein dates on the basis that environmental factors influence decay rates, particularly if bones were frozen for any length of time. Others (Moffat and Wainwright, 1983) criticize the Museum of Man for improper care: when the bones were received by the Canadian Conservation Institute for protein analysis, two were found to be painted replicas. The originals have never been located. Will future, more sophisticated scientific testing methods prove or disprove the antiquity of Archie Stalker's great find? Until the matter is finally resolved, to everyone's satisfaction, it seems that the Taber Child will not be able to rest in peace.

But what about the 27,000-year-old bone flesher from Old Crow? In 1986, tiny samples from it and three caribou antler tools of presumably similar age were all tested at McMaster University using the AMS method. Included in the analysis were an assortment of thirty-two other Pleistocene animal bone fragments from the same locality, some from known geological strata and others which had been collected from modern river banks. This time carbon from the flesher was extracted from bone collagen whereas the former test had used bone mineral or apatite, a material since found to be less stable. The tests showed all the samples of the animal bones to be of Pleistocene age, ranging from 25,000 to 47,000 years ago, and all four of the bone and antler tools to be Holocene, dating after 10,000 years ago. The flesher itself, which had raised so many hopes and spurred so much investigation in the Yukon, gave a date of only 1,350 plus or minus 150 years. How can the huge discrepancy between the two dates, the first 27,000 years old, the second a mere 1,350, be explained? Scientists believe that the bone apatite originally tested was probably heavily contaminated by older carbons in the groundwater (Nelson et al., 1986).

There is another possibly very ancient human site in Canada, this one discovered in 1968 in a commercial sand pit in the city of Saskatoon, though for some reason it was not so well publicized and raised far less controversy than the two preceding ones. Here, in a deposit of sand between layers of glacial till seven to ten metres below the surface were found hundreds of fossil bones of mammoth, horse, camel, bison and deer. A workmen hauling sand for a construction project noticed them and alerted the University of Saskatchewan. The next day, archaeologists were able to snatch a couple of the bones from under the blades of the bulldozers. These were quickly identified as the jawbone of a horse and a mammoth tooth—unmistakable signs of antiquity—and salvage work began immediately. The archaeological crew was given only ten days to rescue what they could from the Saskatoon Site before it was totally destroyed.

Their efforts paid off. Soon they encountered small pieces of chipped chert (a type of flinty quartz) and bones that appeared to have been butchered by human hunters. On the fifth day they found a large isolated section of mammoth tusk that seemed to have been deliberately altered. Because of the potential importance of this object, the whole block of earth in which it was found was transported to the university laboratory for meticulous excavation. The one-metre-long section of tusk had lain by itself, with no other bones nearby. A thin splinter, split from the tusk and scraped down to the ivory, was still lying across one end. There was no obvious natural explanation for this splinter and it was assumed to be of human manufacture. Other evidence for human presence included an abundance of worked and unworked small stone tools said to be "technologically similar to Middle and Upper Paleolithic traditions of the Old World," and the fact that the animal bones had been broken when they were still fresh, an indication of possible human butchery. Also found was a broad scapula (shoulder blade) that was heavily and apparently artificially grooved on its flat surface. In Northeast Asia, scapulae were often used as "table tops" for the cutting up of meat (Pohorecky and Wilson, 1968).

One of the large mammoth bones from the inter-till sand layer was radiocarbon dated at around 20,000 years ago. Wood found in an identical series of strata a few miles to the east gave dates of 34,000 for the till beneath the sand and 18,000 to 20,000 for the till above. The evidence seemed to point to the presence of humans in Canada at a very early date, yet archaeologists cannot agree that it is proof positive. Recent attempts to relocate the site for further evidence have failed. Again, the search for the earliest Canadians appeared to come to a dead end.

Luckily, the archaeologists did not give up, for evidence soon came to light that was not easy to dismiss. Just fifty kilometres south of Old Crow, at the base of a ridge-top outcropping of jagged limestone dolomite 250 metres above the valley of the Bluefish River, a team from the Archaeological Survey of Canada discovered two caves. Caves are prime targets for archaeological explorations. Not only were they often used by early humans for shelters and dwelling places but also the chances of finding undisturbed and well-preserved deposits are usually good. The Bluefish Caves were no exception. Excavating in 1977 and 1978, Jacques Cinq-Mars found the caves filled with layers of loess or wind-blown glacial silt, in places three metres thick, overlain by undisturbed rubble and modern soils. Fossilized pollen from the silt layer disclosed proof of tundra vegetation. Here were found bones of Ice Age mammoths, horses, bison, elk and caribou, some of them apparently butchered, and many with scrapes and cuts similar to those found on bones from Old Crow. Alongside were some unquestionably manmade tools of nonlocal stone, including a chisel-shaped engraving tool, a wedge-shaped core, several flakes and microblades. The latter are long narrow flakes like razor blades, three to six millimetres wide and 10 to 30 millimetres long, used as disposable cutting edges inset into wood, bone or antler hafts. These tiny blades were a customary part of the Stone Age toolkits of Europe and Asia and seem to have been brought into Alaska at least 11,000 years ago. From Alaska, they spread into the northern coast of British Columbia, though they are seldom found east of the Rockies.

Radiocarbon dates obtained from Bluefish animal bone collagen were definitely Ice Age: around 15,000 years B.P. for a "butchered" mammoth bone, around 13,000 years for a horse femur or thighbone. The stone tools were given, by association, a similar antiquity. So far, these dates stand firm as evidence for very early human occupation of Beringia (Cinq-Mars, 1979; Fladmark, 1986a; Fagan, 1987).

Men with Fluted Spear Points

Except for the Bluefish Caves, no unshakable archaeological evidence for the presence of *Homo sapiens* in Pleistocene Beringia has so far been found. Yet it is clear that by about 12,000 years ago mankind was widespread throughout the Americas, successfully adapted to a great diversity of environments, from Arctic ice to the tropics, from cold tundra to steamy jungles, from dense woodlands to grassland plains. By this date, the first people had travelled on foot to the farthest tip of South America, 16,000 kilometres from their Beringian point-of-entry. Just to reach there would have taken at least a thousand years, and successful environmental adaptation far longer than that. Logic alone points to a far earlier human occupation of northern Canada than current proof suggests, though new evidence might any day be found.

On the other hand, the shadowy people of 12,000 years ago left clues to their presence everywhere. It is almost as if they appeared overnight. Some archaeologists believe, in fact, that there was a sudden surge of human migration over the Bering land bridge in the final years of its existence and it is these later peoples whose remains are so widespread and seem so easily found. These first undisputed Americans are identified by a distinctive type of stone spear point, shaped like a leaf and with a fluted channel flaked from the centre extending about a third of the way up on both sides. This unprecedented form of stone point has the experts puzzled. Where did it come from? How did it spread so fast? Examples are found virtually all across North America and all can be dated to approximately the same time. Did the fluted point develop here, the first distinctive product of the New World, and if so, did it evolve from the crude unifacial (worked on only one side) tools discovered with possibly earlier traces of man (Adovasio et al., 1978)?

The enigmatic spear points (and by inference the people who made them) are called Clovis, after the site in New Mexico where they were first identified in 1932. It is quite common to apply the names of different types of stone points to the people who made and used them, mainly for reasons of simplicity and clear meaning. However, the practice can be misleading because it implies that the group of people in question attempted to distinguish their group from that of others and had a name for themselves. Even if they did, it is clear that we will never know what it was. In this book, whenever a group of people is labelled for the stone point they used, it is done solely to provide an easy means of identification. Nothing else is implied.

From archaeological digs mostly in the western United States, a fairly clear picture emerges of the people who used the Clovis fluted technology. They were nomadic hunters who roamed throughout North America generally

*Fluted Clovis point, first undisputed tool known to
have been manufactured in North America, appeared
suddenly around 12,000 years ago. The fluting
around the base enabled the point to be fitted into
spear shafts for the hunting of giant mammoths.
Courtesy of the author.*

east of the Rockies at a time when big game animals were plentiful. They may
also have eaten such vegetable foods as nuts, seeds, fruit and berries, but of
these no traces have survived. South of the glacial ice 12,000 years ago the
land was rich and grassy, speckled with trees and well-dimpled with lakes,
a perfect natural game preserve for such megafauna (giant animals—and they
were giants compared to modern species) as mammoths, bison, bears, camels,
horses, wolves and antelope. It was here that the Clovis people honed their
hunting skills and perfected their weaponry. Their quarry was mostly the huge
hairy mammoths which stood five metres high at the shoulders and had long
sharp curving tusks. With stone-tipped wooden thrusting spears Clovis Man
stalked these behemoths near watering holes, perhaps mired them in marshes
or trapped them in streams—and systematically killed and butchered them
for survival.

Archaeologists have excavated many Clovis kill sites and found many
butchering tools along with heaps of dismembered mammoth bones, some
still with spear points embedded in them. They have located ancient campsites with charcoal-filled fire hearths, scatterings of broken bones left over from
dinner, discarded tools—large flakes for cutting and scraping, hammerstones
for smashing open bones for marrow—and little heaps of stone chips, the waste
products of manufacturing. They have also found bone awls and needles for
sewing tailored skin clothes or shelters and surprising caches of stone tools
and fluted points. One such cache, found recently near Wenatchee,
Washington, contained a matched pair of giant Clovis points—nearly twenty-
three centimetres tall, the largest yet found—made of translucent white
chalcedony. And from an excavated burial of two children in Montana, laid
to rest with 120 beautiful stone tools and fluted points, archaeologists infer
that these ancient hunters believed in some form of life after death—and

obviously loved and mourned their children. The burial at the Anzick site was covered with red ochre, a mineral the colour of blood, which was used almost universally by ancient societies in rituals and ceremonies. Was this custom part of the cultural baggage brought over from Asia? Also found were bone rods believed to be detachable lance heads or foreshafts used for hafting the fluted points to the spear shafts and thus allowing the hunters to speedily reload a spent spear with additional stone tips. These inventions, say the archaeologists, "would have been sophisticated pieces of hunting equipment ideal for killing at close proximity" (Lahren and Bonnichsen, 1974).

Clovis people roamed widely; their traces have been found from Mexico to the Peace River and from eastern Washington State to Nova Scotia. But because in their heyday much of Canada was still under a coverlet of ice, their remains on the Canadian Plains are scarce. The handful of fluted spear points found here were mostly picked up from the surface of prairie fields and tell us very little beyond the fact that people using Clovis points were hunting here. A buried site can reveal much more. Archaeologists can usually tell when it was occupied, and by which group of people; they can deduce how many people there were, what they were doing, and how long they stayed; they can often decide what they ate for supper and even whether it was summer or winter. From tiny changes in their toolkits they can also track down the influence of new peoples, patterns of trade or a changing environment. By contrast, artifacts recovered from the disturbed surface of a ploughed field, though still important, have lost much of their information.

Clovis on the Canadian Plains

In 1980, for the first time on the Canadian prairies, fluted points were found in situ in an ancient excavated campsite. The site was discovered during an archaeological survey of a proposed new highway alignment through the foothills southwest of Calgary, eleven kilometres from the edge of the true plains. (In Alberta and Saskatchewan, provincial laws decree that such a survey may be required before land development, including the construction of new roads, can proceed.) The survey detected signs of prehistoric occupation near the new roadbed as it crossed the meadows of Sibbald Flats. A preliminary salvage excavation produced artifacts of great antiquity and highway construction was delayed, allowing more time for the archaeologists to dig further. The deeper they dug, the more they found. Soon they had unearthed evidence of a rich layering of cultures dating back thousands of years. And on the lowest occupation level, they discovered traces of a Clovis campsite, a find so important that the highway was rerouted around it (Gryba, 1983).

The Sibbald Creek site, though rich in cultural remains, suffered from a complaint well known to archaeologists on the plains—a lack of stratification. The textbook ideal is a site like a layer cake, where the different soil strata, including those occupied by humans, are thick, well-defined and preferably undisturbed. The study of soil deposits laid down over time, known as stratigraphy, can be of immense help in reconstructing both the geologic history and the human utilization of a site. But on the open plains, where precipitation is generally light, vegetation sparse and winds high, little soil is deposited that doesn't sooner or later blow away again. Over most of the prairies, the layers of post-Ice Age sediments are thin and as a result thousands of years of elapsed time and numerous layers of human occupation are compressed into a few centimetres of soil. Artifacts from cultures thousands of years apart can be found so close together that it becomes difficult to unscramble one culture from the other. At Sibbald Creek, 11,000 years of cultural remains were squeezed into less than forty centimetres of accumulated soil. The site was also disturbed, most likely by the uprooting of trees. However, archaeologists patiently uncovered a nearly continuous record of human life on the plains/foothills, from the Clovis hunters to the first white settlers.

Traces of the Clovis campsite were found in the deepest cultural level, between thirty-five and forty centimetres below the ground surface. Archaeologist Eugene Gryba first unearthed little heaps of stone flakes and chips suggestive of a tool manufacturing area. Then among the debris, he came upon a sure sign of Clovis occupation: a spear point of green crystalline siltstone fluted on both faces. Nearby was a fragment of a channel flake (a piece removed from the base to produce the characteristic flute) of the same material and the broken base of another fluted point of black pebble chert as well as several scrapers, choppers and knives. None of the material from this Clovis level could be directly dated (animal bones and other organic materials were sparse and poorly preserved), so it was assigned an approximate age of 11,000 years, an average derived from the dates of fluted points found elsewhere, a standard archaeological practice known as cross-dating.

The fluted point found at Sibbald Creek was not one of the "classic" Clovis points, seven to ten centimetres long, found extensively in the United States but one of the shorter versions that seem more common in western Canada. These are known colloquially as "stubbies" or basally-thinned triangular forms. Many bear the scars of extensive reworking and this has given rise to a theory (Gryba, 1985) that they are simply regular points which have been reduced in size through resharpening during winter months when new material was difficult to obtain.

More of these shorter Clovis points were later excavated in the Peace River country of British Columbia, an area that lies east of the Rockies, well within

Excavation pits in the parapet outside the mouth of Charlie Lake Cave in British Columbia's Peace River country.

Projectile point of grey chert found at Charlie Lake Cave is fluted, like Clovis, but far shorter and is known as a basally-thinned triangular point. This one was found with minute traces of preserved animal blood still on its tip.

Scraper and stone bead, found in association with the projectile point; grey-green schist bead is believed to be the oldest in North America. All courtesy of Knut Fladmark, Simon Fraser University.

the hypothetical "ice-free corridor." In 1983 archaeologist Knut Fladmark was digging on a ledge outside a sandstone cave overlooking Charlie Lake near the town of Fort St. John. The cave had been well used over the centuries as a hunting shelter and in deep sediments trapped in a gulley between the cave mouth and the lip of the ledge, Fladmark uncovered eleven distinct occupation levels, the deepest carbon-dated to around 10,500 years ago. At this time, judging from the kinds of animal bones found, the area had been grassland and the valley floor below the cave may still have been flooded by an arm of Glacial Lake Peace. Here, more than 10,000 years ago, ancient hunters had sporadically killed and butchered giant forms of extinct bison. Fladmark found signs of obvious cut marks on the bones and several stone artifacts, including a broken but complete fluted point of grey chert, well resharpened and still carrying minute traces of animal blood.

The fluted point was a find indeed, but more surprising still was the discovery nearby of a single delicate stone bead made of shiny grey-green schist with a central drilled perforation. This was the first stone bead ever found in direct association with a dated fluted point and it is believed to be the oldest in North America. It provides a tiny glimpse into the cultural life of a people who set aside time from the daily grind of survival to make items for purely decorative use. Radiocarbon dating tests on collagen from animal bone found with the artifacts gave firm dates of between 10,770 and 9,900 years ago. Fladmark believes there may be other cultural layers still to be excavated here for the work has not yet reached basal bedrock (Fladmark, 1986a; Fladmark et al., 1988).

Three years after the excavations at Charlie Lake Cave, signs of fluted point makers were discovered near Pink Mountain, also in the Peace River area of British Columbia. Found during a pipeline survey, the ancient artifacts include the base portions of two black chert Clovis points as well as a variety of other tools suggestive of a winter encampment. All these British Columbian Clovis points were stubbies, the distinctly northern variety, just like the ones from Sibbald Creek (Wilson, 1987).

Changing Styles

For a thousand years, hunters with fluted Clovis weaponry survived in the unique game-rich environment of postglacial America, from the plains of Texas to the Peace River. Then they vanished, or at least, Clovis stone points—the classics and the stubbies—disappear from the archaeological record and new styles of points are found in their place. How do archaeologists account for this? Did the Clovis people fail to survive the drastic environmental changes that followed the melting of the glaciers? Were they displaced by newcomers or did they simply change their toolmaking tradition—our only means of identification—for another? Do the Clovis "stubbies" represent a transitional technique belonging to hunters who followed their preferred prey north as the ice front retreated?

There are no definite explanations but the most likely scenario is this: in answer to the changing environment or because of different hunting techniques, the early people simply remodelled their weapons. They made their spear points smaller with channel flutes on both sides extending nearly the length of the blade, a process that made the weapons remarkably slender. Clovis points were probably fashioned by striking one stone with another, but the later, finer versions were made by applying pressure to the edges to peel off precise flakes. This pressure-flaking technique, most likely applied with a sturdy bone or antler tool, was definitely a New World invention: like the fluted technology itself, it has been found nowhere else. These instantly identifiable points, many of them far more beautifully made than they needed to be for utility, are known as Folsom, again named after the site in New Mexico where they were first found (Snow, 1980).

Folsom point differed from Clovis in that it was channel fluted on both sides almost the full length. Courtesy of the author.

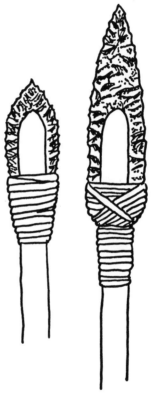

The channel flutes of both Folsom (left) and Clovis points (right) made them far easier to attach to the spear shafts. Courtesy of the author.

Removing a thin channel flake of stone from the centre of an already slender spearhead must have required a steady hand and much practice, a technique obviously very difficult to master (Frison, 1978). What was its purpose? Archaeologists think the fluted channel served to thin the weapon for maximum penetration and to enable the stone point to be securely fastened to the spear shaft (Coe et al., 1986). The shaft was split at the hafting end, jammed onto the stone spearhead to lie within the indented flutes, then bound with leather thongs. (To prevent the sharp edges from cutting the bindings, the lower sides of the point were ground smooth.) But from a purely practical point of view, fluting did not markedly increase the efficiency of the spear point and any advantages for hafting would have been far outweighed by the difficulties of production. This leads to a suspicion that the fluted tradition, which lasted for 2,000 years, served a more important purpose. It could have been a means of strengthening ethnic identity, perhaps the only means possible for a highly nomadic people, moving in tiny bands through a large and lonely land. Too, the fluting process may have been some kind of magic ritual to ensure hunting success (Frison, 1978).

Extinctions

While the Clovis hunters were slowly modifying their stone technology, the climate of North America was drastically changing as the ice sheets continued to melt. Arctic tundra gave way to new boreal forest; existing forests changed to grassland, the grassland in the south to semidesert. And along with this environmental upset came swift changes in the animal population: the giant mammals of the Ice Age began to die out. At the end of the Pleistocene epoch several big game species of the Old World—the cave bear and the European rhinoceros, the mammoth and bison of Asia—also became extinct, but in the Americas, the mass dyings were drastic. Three-quarters of all the large land mammals disappeared, including the giant mammoth and mastodon, the horse, camel, giant beaver and sloth, and even many of the smaller animals. They left their heaps of bones in the frozen muck of Alaska and the Yukon, in the gravels of Texas and Nebraska, the sands of Florida, the famous tar pits of California, and the glacial debris of Western Canada.

These sudden extinctions are very much a mystery. Were the great animals simply unable to cope with the sudden warming and drying trend which changed the vegetation and altered their diet (Guilday, 1967)? Some argue that this is unlikely, for most of the extinct animals had been grassland browsers and warmer conditions would have favoured grassland over forests. In any case, camels of all creatures should not have died because of desert conditions (Martin, 1967). Were their gestation periods, timed to the long Pleistocene winters, suddenly out of synchrony with the new climate (Slaughter, 1967)? Were they wiped out by disease? Or, most intriguing of all, were they pushed to extinction by a new and very successful predator: the human hunter? (For a review of theories, see Fagan, 1986).

It has been argued that elsewhere in the world animals and their predators, including the human variety, evolved together, thus adjusting gradually to their roles in the ecosystem. But in North America, where animals had roamed for thousands of years unchecked, fully modern *Homo sapiens*, complete with efficient stone weaponry, was suddenly thrust into the system. If, as it appears from the evidence, the human hunters arrived during a time of climatic change when the large mammals were already under environmental stress, and if they deliberately went after the more easily killed females and young, it is just possible that they could have delivered the coup de grâce. It is an intriguing thought: that mankind so early in his history could have disturbed the ecological balance of his world (Martin, 1967).

THREE

Bison Hunters

Eleven thousand years ago, when most of the Ice Age animals in North America were well on the road to extinction, there were some which prospered. One of these was the buffalo or North American bison which adapted quickly to the new postglacial conditions, finding its niche on the great plains in the rainshadow east of the Rockies. This vast sweep of grassland provided year-round forage, for many of the grasses retained much of their nutrients even in winter and the bison's hooves were well adapted to scraping away the snow. Biologists guess that this sustained feed may have led to a decrease in the winter mortality rate of the species, while a steadily ameliorating climate allowed a longer and more successful breeding season. The herds of bison flourished, becoming ever more abundant in the years immediately following the retreat of the ice until they were masters of the grasslands, a single species ascendency that does not seem to have occurred anywhere else in the world. It is estimated that in prehistoric times between 50 million and 60 million bison roamed the great American plains (Thompson Seton in Roe, 1951). Certainly when white explorers first came upon the great herds that blackened the prairie they were aghast: they had never seen such countless multitudes.

The early success of the bison, itself originally an immigrant from Siberia, is a critical component in the study of prehistoric peoples in North America. Seldom in the history of the Earth has a single animal species had such drastic influence on humanity. Without the bison, it is doubtful if people could have existed at all on the arid plains; certainly not in the way that they did. For the bison was much more than a food source; its hide provided shelter, clothing, shoes, bedding and blankets; its bones were made into tools for shaping stone, scraping hides, working leather and for sewing; its sinews and hair were twisted into cordage; its horns, bladder, paunch and scrotum were used as containers; its dried dung was indispensable as fuel on the treeless plains. Tied inexorably to the movements of the wild herds (bison were never domesticated), the people became nomads, following the source of their sustenance in daily and seasonal cycles from the high plains in summer to the shelter of foothills and valleys in winter. If the herds prospered, the people prospered; when the herds failed, the people starved. It is difficult to find other examples of such single species dependency.

To the Indians, the bison eventually became far more than a prey animal. It loomed large in their spiritual lives. Several creation myths attribute to the bison the essence of life itself while other folk tales of bison/human inter-marriage and transformation indicate a strong belief in the interconnectedness, even consanguinity, of the two species. Archaeologists frequently find bison bones, particularly skulls, in prehistoric human graves, possible indications of the hunters' burial rituals.

North Americans began hunting bison back in the days of the Pleistocene, though most excavated kill sites of this era contain the far larger Columbian mammoth. Is this simply because mammoth kills with their giant-sized bones are easier for archaeologists to find, or does it indicate a cultural preference for a slow-moving easy target with a huge meat yield? There are no sure answers. What we do know is that when the mammoth floundered towards extinc-tion along with other Ice Age animals, the hunters of the plains switched to the bison, a prey that was to sustain them through many succeeding cultures for the next 11,000 years.

The early hunters' distinctive Clovis fluted spear points are found mostly with mammoth kills; but the later and finer Folsom points are almost invariably excavated in association with bison bones. In the older sites these bones are monstrous: *Bison antiquus* and other extinct species were all far larger than today's animals, with flaring horns spanning nearly two metres. It was the immense size of these bones that led, in fact, to the finding of the first irrefutable proof that mankind was in America at the same time as Ice Age fauna.

Around the turn of the present century, a cowboy by the name of George McJunkin riding through the New Mexican desert in search of a lost cow noticed some huge, unusual bones eroding from the sides of an arroyo. Curious, he poked at the bones with his knife and unearthed a stone spear point. He took some of the bones and the point back to his home where they lay unnoticed until 1925 when they came to the attention of Dr. Jesse Figgins of the Denver Museum of Natural History. Figgins identified the bones as those of a long-extinct species of bison; but the finely fluted spear point, said to come from the same spot, was a mystery. It was unlike anything he had seen before. Could the bones and the spear point really have been found together, proving an incredible antiquity for American man?

The following year, Dr. Figgins launched a full scale excavation at the site of the cowboy's discovery, named for the nearby town of Folsom, and immediately found startling proof. There were many bison bones and several

Bison face pecked in the rock outcrop at Roche Percee near Estevan, Saskatchewan. The use of small dots rather than inscribed lines is unusual for prehistoric petroglyphs in Canada. Courtesy of the Saskatchewan Museum of Natural History.

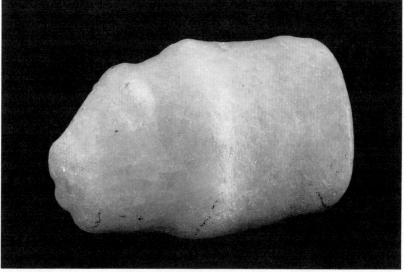

Small effigy figure formed in the shape of the bison may have been part of magic ceremonies to ensure hunting success. It was found near Melville, Saskatchewan. Courtesy of the Saskatchewan Museum of Natural History.

Folsom point found between the ribs of an extinct form of bison was the first real proof of mankind's antiquity in America. Courtesy of the Denver Museum of Natural History.

more of the fluted points, one lying right between two ribs, perhaps the very point that killed. This unique and convincing piece of evidence is still intact, for the whole block of earth around the ribs was excavated as a unit and remains on display at the Denver Museum of Natural History. Altogether, Figgins found the remains of twenty-three animals that had been deliberately trapped and killed in this deep gulley. When the bones were accounted for, most of the tail bones were missing, a good indication that the animals had been skinned and the hides removed, further proof that humans had been involved (Wedel, 1961).

Several excellent Folsom sites have since been excavated on the plains of the United States, most of them mass bison kills, but finds at a handful of small campsites have proved more interesting. Here were the implements of everyday life: flint scrapers, knives, drills and gravers, sandstone implements for shaping, choppers and hammerstones for butchering, bone awls and punches, carved bone disks that were probably counters or gaming pieces, stone and bone beads and chunks of hematite (red ochre) to provide colour for body paint or ceremonial use (Wedel, 1961).

Another group of ancient bison hunters used spear points almost identical to the classic Folsom but without the central flute. Some of these are known as Plainview from the Texas site where they were first found (along with the bones of at least one hundred slaughtered bison); others are known as Midland. These unfluted points, later found to be distributed widely on the plains, cause archaeologists problems. Technologically very similar to Folsom points, they are found above Folsom in some sites and below in others. Are the fluted or unfluted points the older ones? Or are they contemporary (Coe et al., 1986)? Several different variants are known, and the tendency is to lump them together as part of the Fluted Tradition.

In the United States, Folsom points are found across the country in far greater numbers than Clovis, and many Folsom kill and camp sites have been excavated there. This leads archaeologists to suggest that the human population had increased since Clovis days. But in Canada, the reverse seems true: there are more traces of Clovis than of Folsom. Only a scattering of Folsom points have been picked up from the surface, most of them the unfluted Plainview variant. Rod Vickers, Plains Archaeologist of the Alberta Archaeological Survey, has an interesting explanation for this apparent reversal. Perhaps, he says, the Clovis "stubbies" represent an entrenchment of later Clovis people who prevented the Folsom culture from expanding northwards (Vickers, 1986). Others give ecological reasons. The Canadian plains were still very much in environmental transition: 10,000 years ago, glacial ice still fingered the northern stretches while south of the ice, huge meltwater lakes and swamps covered much of the land. It was not a country that bison, or humans, would have favoured. Neverthless, Folsom people were here, perhaps only briefly, and sooner or later archaeologists may be able to uncover the details of their sojourn.

Finds in the Eastern Slopes

Recently, archaeologists have uncovered traces of ancient peoples in the mountain valleys of the Rockies' eastern slopes where, unlike the windswept plains, there are deep soil deposits from slope erosion and ancient campsites stand a chance of becoming quickly covered and preserved. When the Trans-Canada Highway was recently "twinned" through Banff National Park, extensive studies were conducted by Parks Canada to look for possible prehistoric sites in the land to be disturbed. And along the north shore of Vermilion Lakes (a popular tourist viewpoint where bighorn sheep cross the road for water), archaeological treasure was unearthed: a deeply stratified site containing 10,500 years of cultural remains. From dates obtained from radiocarbon tests on charcoal from probable hearths, it would seem that the three deepest cultural levels, all older than 10,000 years, are contemporary with the fluted point peoples, though none of their distinctive stone points were found. However, on the lowest living floor, among heaps of stone chips and the butchered bones of sheep, deer and possibly bison, archaeologist Daryl Fedje found postholes defining a circular structure, most likely a dwelling, the earliest yet found in Canada. To preserve this and other sites located nearby, the highway has been rerouted and Parks Canada plans an interpretive centre nearby.

Stone Clues

In any discussion of prehistoric people much emphasis is placed on lithics, which is the term archaeologists give to stone tools and projectile points. The reason for this emphasis is clear: stone is often all that remains. Most of the other products—wood, leather, basketry, feathers and textiles—do not last long in the damp northern earth. Luckily, projectile points (they are called this rather than arrowheads because archaeologists really do not know with what weapon they were used) can be made to yield a number of clues to the past. Because ancient humanity's survival depended almost totally on hunting, weapons had to be most carefully made. Once certain shapes and manufacturing techniques proved successful, the stone points were duplicated by others of the same culture and tended to change so little over time that archaeologists can now use them as temporal indicators in much the same way that geologists use index fossils. If a point of a particular style can be dated at one site, its age can be assigned to another site where identical points have been found. This form of cross-dating based on point typology is in common use.

New styles of stone points are often thought to signify the presence of a new people, but this is not always the case. Changes could also indicate new ways of attaching the weapon to the shaft, different prey animals, new technology, or the copying of foreign shapes and ideas from people of other areas. Sorting out the reasons for point style change is one of the more challenging tasks of the archaeologists.

Stone artifacts also provide a wealth of other clues to prehistoric life. Scientists can tell how they were made by studying and duplicating the flaking technology, how they were used by scrutinizing the worn edges. They can see how and how often they were sharpened or reworked, sometimes into new forms (broken spear points turned into knives) for different uses. Analysis of tiny preserved plant and animal fibres often still clinging to the cutting edges can indicate diet (Briuer, 1976) and ancient blood found on killing points and butchering tools can even identify the type of prey animal. If the blood is human, the scientists might well have in their hands an instrument of war or a murder weapon.

Surprisingly, blood preserves very well, often for thousands of years. As soon as it is shed, one of its major proteins, serum albumin, begins to break down and if the blood dries on stone, these albumin fragments bond chemically with the rock molecules, becoming almost as durable as the rock itself. Sometimes the blood leaves a faint stain on the stone but it is often invisible and can be detected only with tests and procedures pioneered in the crime laboratory.

Tom Loy, an archaeologist formerly with the Royal British Columbia Museum in Victoria, was among the first to work with prehistoric blood and has successfully identified the animals slain at several prehistoric kill sites in Western Canada. In his laboratory, he first inspects the stone tools with a low power microscope, then checks suspicious stains for blood using standard medical tests to detect blood in urine, tests that are sensitive to minute amounts of serum albumin and haemoglobin. Confirmed blood samples are then examined under a high-powered microscope to isolate such things as red blood cells, collagen, tissue, even fragments of feather and hair. The blood protein is then dissolved and the solution left to crystallize, a process that often requires weeks. For species identification, the haemoglobin crystals are then compared with those from known mammals, for each species has its own blood crystal form, as unique as a fingerprint. It has long been standard archaeological procedure to wash artifacts before cataloguing and analysis but extensive cleaning, Loy cautions, can destroy much precious evidence: as much as fifty percent of any blood residue may be chemically sequestered in the first 0.1 millimetre of soil (Loy, 1983).

Ancient blood holds other clues: it can be tested for antibodies to indicate the prehistoric presence of diseases; it can give information on genetic sources and evolution and its proteins can be used to fix the date of death.

Prehistoric Quarries

Because success at the hunt was critical to survival, the prehistoric hunters of the plains became experts at recognizing the types of stone that would make the best weapons. They needed material that would not shatter or crumble, was easy to chip, and which would keep a keen edge. But utility, it seems, was not the only criterion. Also important were such artistic values as translucence, colour and intricate veining, indicating an appreciation of beauty either for its own sake or for some magic property. Favoured materials included obsidian, chalcedony, argillite and chert, and for these the hunters were prepared to travel long distances. Bedrock deposits were visited repeatedly—perhaps on purposeful missions outside the hunting round—often for thousands of years. At these quarry sites, men came to manufacture finished or roughed-out tools (tool blanks) and they carried pieces of the precious stone back home with them, sometimes to give or trade to neighbours.

Several prehistoric quarries have been found; obvious signs of mining

Prehistoric stone quarries on top of a high ridge in the Crowsnest Pass area of the Rockies date back as far as 8,000 years. The chert was heat-treated to toughen it and was much valued for tool-making. Courtesy of the author.

operations and the litter of flakes from years of manufacturing identify them. One extensive site lies on top of a high ridge 500 metres above the Crowsnest Pass where ancient miners hewed out lumps of multi-coloured Etherington chert as far back as 8,000 years ago. Because the quantities of fire-broken rock around the nearby campsite indicated more than casual campfires, Margaret Kennedy, the investigating archaeologist, believes that the workers heat-treated the chert before use to make it harder and therefore sharper, as well as easier to work. And heat-reddened Crowsnest chert has shown up repeatedly in archaeological sites throughout the area. Another prehistoric chert quarry is spectacularly situated at Top of the World Provincial Park in the Rocky Mountains north of Fernie, British Columbia. Here Wayne Choquette found a workshop site with discarded rock from other areas—siltstone from the Purcell Mountains, argillite from Kootenay Lake and chert from Montana—indicating that people travelled to this mountain area from both sides of the Rockies (Choquette, 1980). Other important quarries are found at Knife River, North Dakota (dark honey-coloured flint), and at Yellowstone National Park, Wyoming (obsidian).

Scientific analysis of lithic artifacts (by several sophisticated methods, including neutron activation and X-ray fluorescence spectrometry) can sometimes reveal precisely from which quarry the prehistoric hunters obtained their rock. This information helps archaeologists establish patterns of ancient travel and trade. Several prehistoric trackways have been surmised: one leading a thousand kilometres from Alberta's Peace River area over the Rockies to a source of obsidian on Mount Edziza in northwestern British Columbia (Fladmark, 1986a); another to the quarries of the Crowsnest Pass and the Kootenays; others to sites in Montana, Wyoming and North Dakota. It seems that "primitive" peoples were not only skilled stoneworkers, familiar with the effect of heat on stone but they also were prepared to travel long distances to acquire their preferred materials.

The Plano People

In the archaeological record from the southern plains, pressure-flaked fluted points and the unfluted variants disappeared about 10,000 years ago, along with most of the big game animals of the Pleistocene. The Folsom hunters, or at least their unique point technology, were gone and new people seemingly moved onto the plains, in greater numbers than ever before. Well-stratified archaeological sites in the south enable the early stone-working traditions (and presumably the people who invented them) to be neatly dated: Clovis from 12,000 to 11,000 years ago, Folsom from 11,000 to 10,000 years ago, and the new Plano people (Spanish for plains) from 10,000 to 8,000 years ago. Dates for all three appear to get later with more northerly latitude of the sites, implying some sort of cultural drift, perhaps in response to the shrinking ice and changing ecological conditions. But the scarcity of excavated and dated sites makes validation of this sequence difficult in Canada.

Certainly as Canada became habitable, people moved in. By 10,000 years ago, the plains were well clear of ice and floods and the newly exposed earth had been quickly reclaimed, first by spruce forests, then by grassland. We know from the numbers of fluted points found in Canada that a scattering of people with Clovis and Folsom weaponry had already lived here, despite the unpromising terrain, and as the ecological conditions improved, Plano hunters with their different style stone points arrived.

Like the earlier weapons, Plano points are long and leaf-shaped (in technical terms lanceolate) but unfluted, some with narrower bases or stems. They occur in several different regional variants which have been divided into two main groups: unstemmed varieties (Agate Basin/ Hell Gap series) and stemmed (Alberta/Cody), perhaps indicating the presence of two separate tribal groups. On the southern plains, the unstemmed points seem to date from an earlier time than the stemmed points. Despite the contrast in point styles, which could

Agate Basin, one of the unstemmed Plano points, is leaf-shaped like Clovis, but unfluted. Courtesy of the Archaeological Survey of Alberta.

be due chiefly to different hafting methods, archaeologists believe the people who made them all were clearly related and in some areas contemporary. From an artistic point of view, some of the Plano points are perhaps the finest ever made. They are so delicately beautiful that it is hard to imagine they were made just for utility—they are certainly far more artistic than they needed to be. The Eden point, for example, is typically ten to fifteen centimetres long and less than three centimetres wide, with even horizontal flakes imparting a fine rippled effect.

As the climate of North America became generally warmer and drier following the retreat of the ice, the plains of the far south turned to semidesert, game animals became harder to find and the Plano hunters of the area were forced to adopt a new survival strategy. They became foragers, subsisting on small animals, plants, roots, berries and nuts. This is known not only because of the dearth of large mammal kill sites but because archaeologists commonly find in the ancient campsites the bones of birds, frogs, rabbits, snakes and other small creatures. They also find large grinding stones, the first sure signs that people prepared vegetable foods. Some of the Plano people lived or camped inside rock caves where desert conditions are ideal for preservation. Many otherwise perishable artifacts of the culture have come to light here: fragments of baskets, coarse fabric, string, and matting, some of the earliest examples of these crafts in the world. Amazingly, in Fort Rock Cave in Oregon, preserved under a layer of 9,000-year-old pumice from nearby erupting volcanoes, were found the remains of fifty pairs of sandals made of shredded sagebrush bark, the first hint of craft specialization or, as we would describe it, a sandal factory. At Hell Gap, a Plano site in Wyoming dated to 8,500 years ago, archaeologists found signs of a dwelling. Stains in the earth marked where posts had been placed in a six-foot diameter circle, similar to the older house at Vermilion Lake.

On the Canadian plains, however, which were still well watered (in places overwatered), the grasslands and parklands were green and lush, and the Plano peoples were bison hunters, though they left no signs of habitation and precious few clues as to the details of their lives. Some archaeologists believe that the Plano peoples drifted up into Canada from the southern plains, following the herds of bison into the expanding grasslands. Their tracks have been followed right up to the Northwest Territories where sites have been dated at around 6,000 years ago. By inference, if they left the south around 10,000 years ago and moved at a relatively steady pace, they would have been on the Canadian plains around 8,000 years ago, though there is a sorry lack of excavated evidence to confirm this estimate. However, studies of fossil pollens have shown that the land was right for bison: by 8,000 years ago the boreal forests had retreated north, and grassland covered the southern sections of the prairie provinces where Plano stone points are sometimes picked up in farmer's fields.

In Manitoba, Plano sites are limited to surface finds and the two basic kinds of points, stemmed and unstemmed, are geographically divided: unstemmed points are found more or less throughout the southern province, while the stemmed types are limited to the highlands of the southwest, above the ancient shoreline of glacial Lake Agassiz. Archaeologist Leo Pettipas explains this division as follows: Plano people (he calls them the Horner people) making stemmed points moved into Manitoba, probably from the west, when the Manitoba escarpment still marked the edge of Lake Agassiz; they occupied the only dry land and they left the province before the lake level fell. As the lake drained, Sister's Hill people making unstemmed points arrived, probably from the southwest, and they ranged widely through the province, the first known occupants of the Manitoba Lowlands (Pettipas, 1985).

No Plano sites have been excavated in Saskatchewan, but both stemmed and unstemmed points have been found, quite prolifically, on the surface, indicating a fairly major presence. At the Parkhill site (Ebell, 1980), a wind-eroding sandy glacial moraine south of Moose Jaw, collectors have picked up more than 300 prehistoric stone artifacts, nearly half of them defined as Agate Basin (unstemmed). Archaeologists think that this was likely a seasonal gathering area for nomadic bison hunters, a place where they brought in the raw materials for the manufacture of stone tools and spear points. When the items became broken or worn, they carefully reworked them into smaller or different tools because the sandy site itself offered little in the way of suitable stone. Most of the artifacts are made of chert brought in from several sources and Knife River Flint imported from North Dakota, a fact which reinforces the theory of migration from the south.

In Alberta, while most evidence of Plano occupation comes from surface finds, (the Alberta-Cody complex of stemmed points is the most numerous) several buried sites have been found and excavated. In 1963, Armin Dyck, an amateur archaeologist, decided to check out a new dugout (waterhole) that rancher Frank Fletcher of Purple Springs had recently bulldozed out for his livestock in the arid country southeast of Lethbridge. The new dugout tapped a spring beneath a long sandy ridge and in the earth around it Dyck saw bones— big bison bones deeply mineralized, a sign of great antiquity. Poking around among them, he found several spear points that he knew by their shape to be very old. He raced away to Calgary to report the find and show the points to archaeologists. Dr. Richard Forbis, then with the Glenbow Foundation, immediately recognized that the points belonged to the stemmed point complex of 9,000 years ago. Later excavations into the wind-deposited soil of the Fletcher site uncovered a deeply-buried site beside an ancient spring where a group of Plano people had ambushed and killed a small herd of bison. Found were stemmed projectile points (mostly of the style known as Alberta), as well as side-scrapers for working hides, spokeshaves, hammerstones and miscellaneous other tools. Mineral contaminants in the groundwater precluded accurate radiocarbon dating of the bone (Forbis, 1968).

More clues to the Plano presence have been found farther north, in the parkland of central Alberta, a transitional area between grasslands and forest

Alberta point, one of the family of stemmed Plano points; and Cody knife, a distinctive asymmetrical tool. Both date back to around 9,000 years. Courtesy of the Archaeological Survey of Alberta.

Layers of ash from the explosion of the Oregon volcano known as Mount Mazama provide archaeologists with a firm date line of 6,600 years ago. Artifacts found beneath this ash are older, those on top, younger. This photo shows a sequence of several volcanic ash deposits, including Mazama, from Sunwapta Pass in the Alberta Rockies. Courtesy of Alwynne Beaudoin.

that changed its boundaries with the changing climate. A prehistoric late summer campsite was excavated at the edge of a seasonally dry pond near today's Buffalo Lake. Charcoal from two hearths at the Boss Hill site (Doll, 1982) were dated to around 7,750 years ago, and the dating was substantiated from analysis of plant material below the occupation level, and by the presence of Mazama ashfall above. Around 6,600 years ago an Oregon volcano, known postmortem as Mount Mazama, blew itself to bits. The violent explosion which created today's Crater Lake showered a vast area of Canada and the United States with a thick layer of ash which shows up clearly in the layers of soil and provides a very useful firm date for archaeologists and other scientists. The Plano campsite found well below the layer of ash contained the butchered remains of bison, elk, fox, badger, beaver, muskrat, hare and waterfowl, pointing to a mixed diet. Among the lithics recovered were two leaf-shape points similar to those found at Saskatchewan's Parkhill site and three variants of corner-notched stemmed points typical of late stages of Plano. Also found were two pieces of sandstone identified as milling stones, possible clues to a southern hunter-gatherer heritage.

Another site where Mazama ash played a part in the dating process is Hawkwood (VanDyke and Stewart, 1985), found during testing for a residential subdivision on Nose Hill in northwest Calgary. Here, in a bowl somewhat sheltered from the wind, small groups of prehistoric bison hunters had camped for short periods of time. Six different occupation levels were uncovered, three of them beneath Mazama ash, the earliest dating to around 8,250 years ago. Here, hunters of the Plano era had killed and presumably eaten one bison, perhaps roasting its haunches over one of the two hearths. They left a couple of projectile points and a few small tools behind, as well as a pitted quartzite pebble, described as a possible grinder.

Mazama ash also effectively sealed and corroborated the dating of cultural levels above the fluted point discoveries at Vermilion Lake in Banff National Park. One of these contained an unstemmed Plano point and datable material supporting occupation at around 9,500 years ago.

Between 8,000 and 10,000 years ago, then, small bands of Plano hunters wandered the Canadian plains, probably keeping to the shelter of wooded valleys and foothills in winter and spending the summers on the open plains. We know they hunted primarily bison, tanned hides for clothing (and presumably for shelter), sought out the finest stone for the manufacture of their tools and weaponry, travelled and perhaps traded over a wide area. Of their artistic leanings (except for consummate skill in flint-knapping), spiritual beliefs and details of their day-to-day lives we know almost nothing. Did they bury their dead? Believe in some kind of supernatural being? Did the tribes have chiefs and medicine men? Did they use domestic dogs to help them carry their camp paraphernalia from place to place, as later plainsmen did? These are some of the questions that archaeologists have yet to answer.

Drawing of atlatl in action. This simple extension to the spear shaft greatly increased man's throwing power. Adapted from Fladmark, 1986a; courtesy of the Cartographic Section, Department of Geography, University of Alberta.

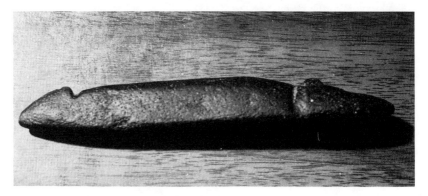

Atlatl weight in the shape of an animal, found near Meyronne, Saskatchewan. Courtesy of the Saskatchewan Museum of Natural History.

Advancing Technology

Little is known of the Plano people in Canada and not much more of the people who replaced them, except for one important thing: they carried a new type of weapon. Beginning around 7,500 years ago, at the start of the geologic period known as the Holocene, very different stone projectile points, smaller and widely notched at the sides, made their appearance, often alongside the older leaf-shaped ones. These radically changed points were used, archaeologists believe, on a mechanical invention known as the spear-thrower or atlatl, its Aztec name. Basically an extension about seventy centimetres long that hooks onto the end of a spear shaft, the atlatl is a simple but effective machine for increasing speed and distance. The additional thrust of its whiplike action makes the weapon far more deadly. How atlatls were used has been well documented by ethnographers, for the weapons survived (not in Canada but in other parts of the world) well into historic times. Some contemporary native peoples, including the aborigines of Australia, use them still.

In Canada, where conditions for the preservation of organic materials are poor, all that archaeologists can find of the atlatl are its stone points: the wooden shafts and the leather or sinew attachments have long since rotted away. But in dry caves in the desert areas of Nevada and southeastern Oregon (where the atlatl was used as early as 9,000 years ago) archaeologists have unearthed at least a dozen complete or nearly complete examples, with finger notches, deer and antelope hide wrappings and attached bone spurs for linking to the spear shaft itself. The wooden shafts of yew, juniper and mountain mahogany are in most cases carefully painted: one is tinted with red ochre with a series of white dots; others have spiral patterns in green and black (Hill, 1948; Jennings and Norbeck, 1964).

Where did atlatls come from? They were known in Europe during the Upper Paleolithic (our pre-Clovis of around 15,000 years ago) and thus could have been brought over by the first immigrants to America. Why then do they not appear until several thousand years later? It is possible, archaeologists caution, that some of the earlier points, even Folsom which were decidedly smaller than Clovis, were propelled with the aid of an atlatl (Snow, 1980; Kopper, 1986). The sudden switch to smaller, side-notched points would then represent not the start of a totally new technology but only a significant improvement to an existing one, perhaps the use of a thinner, flexible shaft with a stone weight attached to the centre to give added spring and power (Vickers, 1986, Snow, 1980).

For years these stone weights had archaeologists mystified. In most artifact collections they were listed simply as decorative objects because they were often beautifully fashioned and ground smooth into bird or boat shapes. Some thought they were magic charms; others that they were symbols of office: the winged examples with holes in their middles became generally known as bannerstones. The first clue to their real identity was a lucky find of a "ghost" weapon—all the durable parts of an atlatl, the handle, weight, socketed antler hook and stone point, in perfect alignment though the wood that once had joined them together had rotted away. Later, weighted specimens were recovered complete. Many of the weights seem to have been strapped on but others were perforated for slipping directly onto the shaft. The small size of the perforations, typically only about fifteen millimetres in diameter, meant that the atlatl shafts would have had to be very slender and for such slim shafts to be strong, tough resilient hardwoods were needed.

Would weighted atlatls be more efficient than unweighted ones? Field experiments suggest not. The weights increase neither the range nor the velocity of the weapon (Palter, 1976). Perhaps the power advantage of the weights was reckoned in magical rather than empirical terms. Atlatl weights are fairly commonly found in archaeological sites in the United States but they seem rare on the Canadian plains, although recently a possible weight of carved and polished green serpentine was excavated from a site near Grand Cache, Alberta (Brink and Dawe, 1986).

Whether they mean new technology or simply innovations to an existing one, side-notched projectile or atlatl points seem to have appeared first in the Eastern Woodlands of North America, then spread rapidly throughout the continent. Does their appearance on the plains represent an immigration—perhaps invasion—of Woodland people armed with atlatls (Husted, 1969; Reeves, 1978a)? Or did the Plains peoples simply adopt a clearly superior weapon from the Woodland peoples' arsenal (Vickers, 1986)? Archaeology is full of questions.

A Time of Drought

The smaller side-notched points that most archaeologists believe signify the advent of the atlatl appeared during a time of great climatic change throughout North America. Known as the Altithermal (more recently as the Atlantic) it was a hot, dry period that reached its peak around 6,000 years ago and caused widespread desiccation of the grasslands in the centre of the continent. Archaeologists are undecided just how severe this drought was in the northern plains: whether it was severe enough, in fact, to cause the virtual abandonment of the grasslands by both bison and men (Reeves, 1973). Certainly, very few sites from this period have been found in the plains heartland, but studies of past climate in the northern fringes of the plains— the aspen parklands, foothills and highlands—show that these areas were actually wetter during the Altithermal than they are today, a condition due to strong westerly air flow, and that here bison and humans could have continued to flourish (Buchner, 1983a).

Plains bison had been decreasing in size since the extinction of *Bison antiquus* at the end of the Pleistocene era. While this genetic change must have been due in part to the changing environment, there is also the intriguing thought that mankind may have also played a role by unconscious selection. Smaller, swifter animals were more likely to evade the hunter than larger, slower ones (Buchner, 1983a).

The first people on the Canadian plains to use atlatls on a regular basis are identified with the Mummy Cave culture, named for a cave in northern Wyoming where a 1,200 year-old mummified man was discovered, and where, in deeper levels, the type style of the Mummy Cave projectile point was first found. Due to the extreme drought in the south the people who inhabited Mummy Cave 7,000 years ago were nomadic foragers, like the Plano people before them, gathering vegetable foods and hunting small game. However, excavated sites in Canada from this time period seem to indicate that bison were still available here and that the basic big-game hunting lifestyles of the ancient plainsmen did not substantially change.

One such site is Stampede, at the northern foot of the Cypress Hills in Alberta, where a small group of hunters once camped beside a creek. They stayed for a time, using the site as a base for daily hunting forays. In the evenings, after their supper of roast meat, they sharpened their weapons and made new ones for the following day's hunt. Beside their shallow basin-shaped hearth (unearthed half-a-metre below a time-diagnostic layer of Mazama ash) archaeologist Eugene Gryba found five side-notched projectile points, along with miscellaneous tools and waste flakes, or debitage, from tool manufacture. There were also charred bones of bison and elk. The medium-sized projectile points (presumably for atlatls) were classified as Bitterroot, one of the many Mummy Cave series, and much of the stone debitage consisted of chalcedony and obsidian from quarry sites in today's North Dakota and Wyoming, suggesting the direction of early trade or travel (Gryba, 1975). Now the Cypress Hills, the highest point in Canada between Labrador and the Rockies, are known to snag down cool moist air flowing in from the Pacific and to have more temperate summers than the plains at their feet. Certainly, in times of drought, they would have provided a refuge for game and for people.

Buffalo Jumps

One of the most fascinating types of site on the northern plains is the buffalo jump, one that features prominently in popular accounts of prehistoric life on the plains. (It is, of course, more correctly known as a bison jump.) Described by early white explorers in the seventeenth and eighteenth centuries, some of whom were eye-witnesses to an actual event, it was such a successful method for the mass killing of bison that it remained basically unchanged for thousands of years. At first look, the procedure seems simple: a number of bison were driven or stampeded over a steep though not very high cliff. The fall itself killed or maimed most of the animals and the rest were finished off by hunters waiting below. (This was a gory job: the Blackfoot word for a jump was *pis-kun*, or deep blood kettle.)

But behind its apparent simplicity lies a whole set of complex strategies. Not only were great skills needed to drive the animals in the right direction and at the right speed to propel them over the cliff, but detailed knowledge of bison behaviour, herd movement and local topography was critical. Large numbers of hunters had to be positioned along the lines of the drive to keep the animals moving. Wind direction had to be just right, for bison have a keen sense of smell and would quickly steer away from human scent. Below some of the jumps, stout corrals had to be built to contain any animals not killed or crippled by the fall. And because often hundreds of animals at a time were driven over the cliff, much labour was needed for slaughter, butchering and meat preparation. In other words, a successful bison jump required a large number of people, many of them experienced and extremely skilful, and all of them well organized and strictly disciplined (Arthur, 1975; Verbicky-Todd,1984).

The people of the Canadian plains up to this point, at least as far as archaeologists can tell, were few in number and moved only in small extended family groups. But by about 6,000 years ago, arid conditions to the south may have promoted migration to the northern grasslands where the bison still roamed and the population of the Rocky Mountains foothills country of Canada may have increased. There could have been many small bands of Mummy Cave people here and seemingly the bands joined forces for large scale cooperative kills, probably in the fall.

Head-Smashed-In Buffalo Jump on the edge of Alberta's Porcupine Hills northwest of Fort Macleod is one of the oldest and best preserved on the North American Plains. (Many of the jump sites were looted and their huge stacks of bones shipped away to eastern fertilizer factories before people realized they were a precious part of the Canadian heritage.) So important is the Alberta site that it has been declared a UNESCO World Heritage Site and in 1987 a superb new interpretive centre was opened here. The jump has extensive and well-preserved bone beds that lie eleven metres thick and excavations show that it was used by four successive cultures over a period of 5,500 years, beginning with the Mummy Cave people, although a chance find of a Plano projectile point from possible outwash material may indicate that it was used even earlier. The oldest points recovered from the bone beds beneath the cliff are side-notched atlatl points typical of those from Wyoming's Mummy Cave, though made of distinctly local materials. These hunters were not recent immigrants from the south who just happened to be passing through but local groups who returned on at least four successive occasions to the jump, implying a sustained local presence (Reeves, 1978b).

Head-Smashed-In is a large and complex site in a scenically splendid location. From the top of the sandstone escarpment one has a fine view of the distant pickets of the Rocky Mountains, while below and to the east the plains stretch seemingly forever, scarred by the wooded meanders of the Oldman

Aerial view of the sandstone escarpment at Head-Smashed-In Buffalo Jump over which prehistoric hunters drove herds of bison to their deaths as long ago as 5,500 years. The ravine, now bushy with shrubs, covers extensive bone beds. Hunters camped on the flats, downwind. Courtesy of the Archaeological Survey of Alberta.

River. Archaeologists have studied the jump in order to reconstruct the mechanics of its use. In the Porcupine Hills directly to the west lies a huge high basin of some forty square kilometres, drained by Olsen Creek. It was here that buffalo runners were sent to scout out the herds and to lead them into one of several drive lanes which would funnel them towards the cliffs. The drive lanes, marked today by hundreds of small stone cairns, stretch for many kilometres in several different directions throughout the gathering basin. In historical times, these cairns, known as "dead men," were heaped up with brush or hides and served as stations manned by tribe members whose job it was to keep the herd moving towards the jump. But archaeologist Jack Brink, who headed recent investigations at Head-Smashed-In, thinks that the small cairns could also have been bases for upright tree branches which would flutter in the wind and keep the bison running in the right direction without the need for human help (Brink et al., 1986).

The main approach to the Head-Smashed-In jump runs through a low-lying area bordered on both sides by two low rock ridges, a natural funnel leading to the edge of the drop-off cliffs. On the tops of these ridges, the wind-eroded sandstone outcrops have been scratched into mysterious grooves, half-circles, crosses and crescents. Their strategic location leads archaeologists to suggest that these petroglyphs were somehow associated with the jump; perhaps they played a part in the magic rituals employed to bring the bison successfully in.

Judging from the extensive bone beds below the cliffs, Head-Smashed-In was a very successful killing machine. But after the Mummy Cave hunters abandoned the jump (just why and when we do not know), it lay idle for perhaps a thousand years and a layer of soil sifted over the ancient deposits. Above this sterile layer were found more bone beds and the distinctive projectile points of at least three other plains cultures that worked the jump right up to historic times. Excavations in the campsite area downwind from the reek of slaughter showed that many people throughout the centuries gathered here to organize the drive, butcher and skin the animals, strip the meat for drying and smoking, break open the bones to extract the marrow, boil the bones for grease— and perhaps to feast and make merry. A successful bison jump kill in the fall could mean the difference between survival and starvation in the bleak winter months ahead (Frison, 1978).

Excavated sites in Saskatchewan also serve to dismiss the notion of plains abandonment during the Altithermal. In fact this dry era caused an expan-

Beautifully made knife was excavated from the Mummy Cave level of a campsite at Long Creek, near Estevan, Saskatchewan. Blade is 10 cm long and is made of flint from the Knife River in North Dakota. Courtesy of the Saskatchewan Museum of Natural History.

sion of the grassland to hundreds of kilometres north of its present day limits and here it seems bison continued to graze, and man to hunt them, though perhaps it was not a time of abundance. The earliest Saskatchewan archaeological site from this era is Gowen near Saskatoon, which dates to 6,000 years ago (Schroedl and Walker, 1978). It was found in the fall of 1977 by heavy equipment operator Charles Gowen in a gravel pit on a terrace of the Saskatchewan River; excavation of the site, buried under more than a metre of sand, was carried out by the University of Saskatchewan shortly afterwards. From the evidence, very efficient food processing took place here. Bones from an estimated eight bison and at least two dogs had all been extensively broken and smashed to retrieve every last little bit of the grease and marrow. Were these people naturally thrifty or does the unusual amount of bone-smashing indicate a time of hunger, when even toe bones had to be split for the little sustenance they contained?

Another Saskatchewan site, at Long Creek in the southeast, was discovered during a 1957 survey of a proposed water reservoir (Wettlaufer/Mayer-Oakes, 1960). Unusual for the plains, it is a deeply stratified site, its nearly four metres of soil layers containing eight different cultural levels, some of them very rich. The earliest, probably an overnight camp by a single family of the Mummy Cave era, was dated from charcoal in the hearth to around 5,000 years ago. Found beside the hearth along with a scatter of bison bones was a splendid knife blade ten centimetres long and assymetrical in style, with one side rounded, the other straight. Archaeologist Boyd Wettlaufer surmised that such a well-made tool was not one to be discarded lightly but must have been lost, perhaps dropped at night when the family was sitting around the fire. Stamped into the mud—it was found a few inches lower than the hearth—it was not seen or handled again until he unearthed it.

FOUR

 Cultural
Expansions

F ive thousand years ago, with the climate of North America settling
down into more or less the pattern it holds today and with the grasslands
stabilizing along present boundaries, it seems that several new people
began to inhabit the plains. The pace of civilization appears to quicken: the
archaeological record reveals traces of far larger numbers of people, many
more artifacts, evidence of settlements, religious beliefs and rituals, art (perhaps
even astronomy) and increasingly sophisticated hunting techniques. These
new peoples, again identified principally by their distinctive stone points,
remained on the plains as separate cultural entities for hundreds of years.

First to make their appearance were people using what archaeologists
call the Oxbow stone point and traditions. Their centre of population seems
to have been in Saskatchewan, though they were also well distributed in Alberta
and southwestern Manitoba. Where did they come from? Archaeologist Brian
Reeves (1978a) believes from similarities in their projectile points that their
culture was simply an evolved version of the resident Mummy Cave peoples
and that they were astute enough to benefit from the appearance of immigrants
appearing on the plains 500 years later: the McKean. These, it is believed,
came into Canada from the Great Basin or Rockies of the United States
(Brumley, 1975). Evidence so far indicates that these two culturally distinct
peoples occupied the Canadian plains at more or less the same time, presumably
amicably, for at least the following 1,000 years, after which they both seem
to "disappear."

The classic Oxbow projectile point (first found at the Oxbow site in
Saskatchewan) is side-notched with a concave base and projections or "ears"
between the bases and the notches. The McKean point is lanceolate with
a deeply indented base. However, while point styles provide the main clues
to identify early prehistoric cultures (archaeologist Knut Fladmark of Simon
Fraser University calls projectile points "the cutting edge of the society"),

there are other distinguishing features to look for. These include differences in tools, ornaments, housing, hunting methods, fire hearths, burial practices and stone preferences. In archaeological parlance, these other clues are known as traits. When researchers find significantly different traits plus a new point style, they know they are on the track of culture change.

Clues gleaned from Oxbow sites can be pieced together to draw a new and different picture of life on the plains. The people were still nomadic hunters who, judging from the refuse they left behind at their campsites, relied almost totally on the bison for food and shelter. But there were more of them, at least archaeologists have found far more traces. Perhaps this apparent population increase was due to the ameliorating climate or to their skills as hunters. They seem to have believed in the supernatural for at least some of them buried their dead, indicating trust in an afterlife, and built complicated stone circular structures known as medicine wheels, the first solid architecture of the plains. They participated in a trade network which extended from the Pacific Coast to the Great Lakes and south into today's Dakotas, and had leisure time to make decorative purely artistic objects, such as pendants of shell and bone. They kept domestic dogs which they may have used as draught animals. In our terms they seem far more culturally advanced than the people who went before them, though this may be simply because they left behind many more clues. And these make it easier for archaeologists to reconstruct the everyday details and bring the Oxbow people to life. Earlier inhabitants of the plains, whose traces are fainter and more apocryphal, seem only shadows by comparison.

Stories in Stone

The grasslands of Canada's prairie provinces are, even today, after 150 years of cultivation, liberally sprinkled with prehistoric constructions made of stone, the visible, rather than the invisible sites of prehistory. They are not grand edifices like Stonehenge but seemingly rather simply made of small boulders laid out on the ground in the forms of men or beasts or geometric shapes. Found mostly in the northern plains, where a liberal supply of glacial boulders and tough shortgrass sod seem encouragement for their construction, most are simple rings of different sizes, found sometimes alone, more often in groups. At first they were thought to be of no great age.

Clues to their use are easily found in the writings of the explorers. Henry Youle Hind, Assiniboine and Saskatchewan Exploring Expedition of 1858 wrote: "On the high banks of the valley the remains of ancient encampments in the form of rings of stone to hold down the skin tents are everywhere visible . . . ."

Oxbow point is side notched with basal "ears" and a concave base. Courtesy of the Archaeological Survey of Alberta.

Tipi rings at the Lemsford Ferry site south of Kindersley, Saskatchewan. The area on the banks of the South Saskatchewan River was a popular camping spot—it contains 125 rings. Courtesy of the author.

Historically the Plains Indians lived in conical tents or tipis made of bison hides usually pinned down around the edges by pegs of wood or bone. But it seems that prehistoric campers found a sensible alternative to tent pegs. They used the stones available everywhere to weigh down the edges of their tents and to keep out drafts. When they moved camp, they simply pulled up the tipi, leaving the rocks behind. The term "tipi ring" has been coined to denote the remains of these encampments which are by far the commonest of the prehistoric surface features on the plains. It has been estimated that there are 600,000 of them in Alberta alone (Forbis, 1970)—and these are the ones that have escaped the destruction of cultivation. We don't yet know if the Oxbow peoples lived in hide tipis, or left tipi rings behind at their campsites, but it seems likely.

Some of the stone circles are obviously not tipi rings. They occur with other constructions such as rock cairns and radiating lines and are found in high and windy places unsuitable for camping. These are known as medicine wheels, mainly because one of the earliest configurations found in Wyoming was shaped very like a wheel, with hub, spokes and a rim, and because anything magical or mysterious in Indian culture was considered good or bad medicine. These medicine wheels are among the most spectacular aboriginal cultural features on the plains, constructions that are both varied (no two are identical) and mysterious. So far, some sixty to seventy have been found, most of them in Alberta and Saskatchewan, with a few sprinkled south of the United States border. Not very many of them look anything like a wheel. Some are double or single rings with radiating arms in number from three to twenty-eight. Some "wheels" have no hub; others have no rim; still others have neither rim nor hub. Few indeed are even symmetrical, yet they are all still known collectively as medicine wheels, a confusing lumping together of dissimilar forms. (The name itself is an unfortunate one, for none of the Indians of America ever used the wheel for transportation or pottery.)

While the stone circles themselves could be relatively quickly laid down, the giant cairns which sometimes form the wheels' hubs must have taken a considerable time to build. Once all the nearby boulders were collected and used, thousands of others would have had to be carried in from farther afield. Group effort and an overall plan would have been necessary. (Reviews: Brumley, 1985 and 1986).

Medicine wheels are among the most complex and therefore most intriguing relics of Canada's prehistoric past. By the time white men came to the plains, many of the Indians of the day denied all knowledge of them; their purpose and use had been long forgotten. "The Indians know nothing of the origins of these lines and cairns [at Moose Mountain] but state that they were made by the spirit of the winds" (Maclean, 1896).

Sundial Hill medicine wheel near Carmangay, Alberta, contains a central cairn, two concentric rings and an entrance path. Courtesy of the author.

Though a few were built in historic times as memorials to dead chiefs (Dempsey, 1956), their mysteries generally remain intact, provoking inquiry and speculation. Who built them and why? Were they boundary markers, direction finders, graves, calendars or astronomic observatories? Were they built as temples to celebrate the sundance or other ceremonies? As memorials to famous men or successful battles? Could they have been made by aliens from outer space?

Several of these possibilities (though not the last) have been seriously studied by astronomers and mathematicians as well as archaeologists. In some wheels, the arrangements of spokes and cairns appear to indicate not only the sunrise/sunset alignments of the summer solstice (a date thought to be important to the Plains Indians for their sundance ceremonies) but the risings of several bright stars, including Sirius, Rigel and Aldebaran. Interestingly, two of the wheels, one atop the Bighorn Mountains in Montana, the other on Moose Mountain, Saskatchewan, 675 kilometres distant, while dissimilar in shape and size, show an identical alignment of cairns and an identical celestial orientation. To astronomer John Eddy, it seemed as if they had each been built from the same set of plans. Several other medicine wheels also appear to show solstice alignments, including Roy Rivers, east of Empress, and Grassy Lake, Alberta, although most of them do not.

Medicine wheel astronomy is understandably controversial. Proponents point to a general similarity of ring shapes, and sighting cairns aligned not only

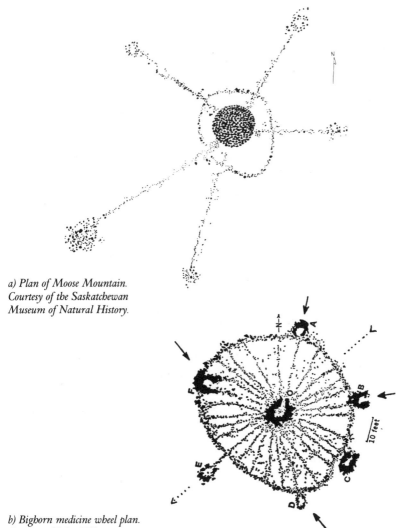

a) Plan of Moose Mountain.
Courtesy of the Saskatchewan
Museum of Natural History.

b) Bighorn medicine wheel plan.
Courtesy of John Eddy.

Dissimilar in shape and size and almost 700 km apart, these medicine wheels were found by astronomer John Eddy to show identical cairn alignments and identical celestial orientations. Were they built from the same set of plans?

to the summer and winter solstices but also to the risings of several bright stars (Eddy, 1974 and 1977; Kehoe & Kehoe, 1979; Vogt, 1983). Dissenters argue that the wheels' sighting cairns are not precise enough and pay no attention to such important considerations as the changing declination of the sun; that claimed stellar alignments are nothing more than random and in any case would have served no practical purpose (Ovenden & Rodger, 1981; Wilson, 1981; Haack, 1987). With the original builders long dead, their ideas and intentions unrecoverable, the speculations persist and astronomical research continues.

Other scientists have been puzzled by the medicine wheels' geometry. The not-quite-circular rings previously thought to be the haphazard designs of a primitive people have been found instead to be geometrically perfect shapes formed by series of carefully drawn intersecting arcs. Interestingly, these shapes are identical to those that the European builders of megalithic stone circles used and they also seem to have been built using the same standard of measure (2.72 feet, the Neolithic yard). Does this imply some trans-Atlantic connection, thousands of years before the Vikings? And were the ancient builders familiar with the principles of geometry long before Pythagoras (review: Ovenden & Rodger, 1981)?

In an attempt to bring order to the medicine wheel chaos (and perhaps to bring their studies back to earth) archaeologist John Brumley of Medicine Hat, Alberta, examined most of the wheels on the plains and found they could be divided into eight typological categories. He proposes that each of the eight basic configurations might indicate a different purpose and use. One of the categories, consisting of a tipi-ring-sized circle with radiating spokes, could be the remains of a burial lodge. Historically, a dead chief would be shut up in his tipi and the base weighed down with stones against predators. To denote funereal status or perhaps as a sign of respect, lines of stones radiating from the tipi ring were then added and the site abandoned, leaving the body and the leather tipi to rot. Once the tipi had disintegrated, the exposed human bones would likely be carried off by carnivores, leaving only the stones. The purpose of the other types of wheels has not yet been determined (Brumley, 1985).

Dating medicine wheels, or any of the surface stone features of the plains, must rely on the finding of artifacts or organic materials buried within them. It is just about impossible to tell from the stones themselves exactly when they were positioned: most lie on exposed, wind-swept hilltops or terraces and are unlikely to be buried very deeply by soil, no matter how long they have been in place. Dating by lichen growth is one possibility, for lichens grow infinitesimally slowly, their expansion rate determined by climate and

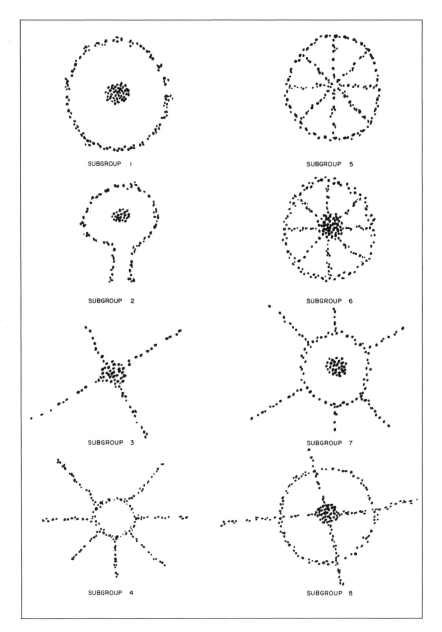

SUBGROUP 1

SUBGROUP 2

SUBGROUP 3

SUBGROUP 4

SUBGROUP 5

SUBGROUP 6

SUBGROUP 7

SUBGROUP 8

Eight categories of medicine wheel designs, formulated by John Brumley. He suggests that each type may have served a different purpose. Courtesy of John Brumley.

topography. Lichen growth can be measured at the site (the minimum time for meaningful measurement is ten years) and the rate extrapolated backwards to give age, assuming, of course, that the lichen started to grow on the stone after it was placed. Relative dating (whether one ring or line of stones is older than another) can also be done with some degree of success by examining changes in the soil beneath the stones. Rainwater flowing over the stones affects such things as soil colour, alkalinity and the amount of carbon, nitrogen and organic matter. The longer the stone has been in place, the greater the amount of change. This method was pioneered by Johan Dormaar, an Agriculture Canada soil scientist at Lethbridge, Alberta (Dormaar, 1976). Neither of these alternative methods has yet proved itself and the best chance of establishing dates still lies with the archaeologists.

The first medicine wheel in Canada to be given a full-scale archaeological investigation is one known as the British Block Cairn on a hilltop inside the Suffield Military Reserve northwest of Medicine Hat, Alberta. The reserve is a 26,000 hectare tract of prairie set aside by the military for weapons testing and manoeuvres and its closure to the public has preserved many prehistoric sites that otherwise would have been ploughed under: almost 2,000 have been found here, most of them stone circles and cairns. The medicine wheel, one of several on the reserve, is huge: its rim stretches 26 metres in diameter and the rocks in its enormous central cairn weigh an estimated 100 tonnes. Lying within the wheel perimeter is the well-defined human effigy marked out in prairie cobbles.

Many of the stones of the wheel had been rearranged by turn-of-the-century cowboys spelling out their initials or brands, but otherwise the site was undisturbed when the archaeologists set to work (Forbis, 1970). Many other medicine wheels have been so badly disarranged by people ignorant of their significance that they cannot be used for scientific investigation. The first farmers probably destroyed many without even noticing them. The wheels were, after all, just stones that had to be cleared before ploughing. Harder to forgive are the "pot-hunters" who selfishly dig into and destroy an archaeological site just for the loot, a few arrowheads, beads or other artifacts that are of little commercial value. Even the thoughtless rearrangement of a few rocks can tamper with precious evidence that archaeologists (or astronomers) might need and the ever-present threat of vandalism explains why these intriguing sites are so little publicized. They are difficult to guard: they lie for the most part on lonely outcrops. Often it is only their isolation that preserves them.

Excavations at British Block began in 1965. A crew from Glenbow led by Richard Forbis stripped down half of its massive central cairn layer-by-layer in the hopes of dating its construction. But the artifacts they found

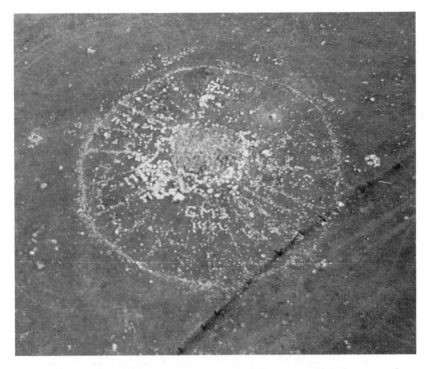

Aerial view of Majorville Cairn and medicine wheel. Excavation of the huge central rockpile indicated that construction began more than 5,000 years ago, 1,000 years before the building of Stonehenge. Courtesy of Brian Calder.

scattered throughout the cairn were of several different time periods; and in many cases, older pieces (the oldest were Oxbow) that should have been most deeply buried were on top, younger ones underneath. This archaeological scrambling could only be explained if the artifacts were offerings, prized possessions perhaps kept in the family for generations and left on the cairn as part of some ceremonial practice long since forgotten.

Excavations at another large cairn-centred wheel, also in Alberta, proved more rewarding (Calder, 1977). On top of the highest small hill south of the Blackfoot Indian Reserve, the site is known as Majorville after a nearby community. Luckily, this one too had survived more or less intact and it had not been looted for buried treasure. Archaeologist Jim Calder excavated the cairn in 1971, again stripping off the rocks in layers in an attempt to discover when it was built and if its construction was a single event or took place over many years. The time sequence was reconstructed from stone point horizon markers found in each layer and by other dating methods such as obsidian

63

hydration and carbon 14 tests. Nearly 3,000 artifacts were recovered, this time in chronological order, the oldest ones at the bottom, the youngest on the top.

Analysis showed that the cairn had been started more than 5,000 years ago by the Oxbow people (a good 1,000 years before the building of Stonehenge and 500 years before the Egyptian pyramids) and it was later used and added to by six other cultures right up to contact with Europeans. There was no hard evidence, of course, as to how the site was used, but Calder believes it was a centre for ceremonies to ensure the success of the hunt and the fertility of the bison herds. Among the artifacts recovered were more than 500 projectile points and such magic objects as concretions, bird bones and *iniskim* or buffalo stones: fossil ammonites whose shape resembles that of a bison and which in historical times were considered items of great power. Many of these were stained with red ochre, a sign of their mystical importance.

The Oxbow people who constructed this elaborate ceremonial feature, stone by patient stone, thus were found to have introduced a new cultural practice of theology and ritual, a ceremonial tradition that was to last on the plains for thousands of years. The stimulus for such activity, says Calder, apparently came from outside the plains, as there was nothing in the cairn to connect its construction with previous plains occupants. It must be remembered, of course, that these findings relate only to the central cairn, not to the wheel configuration surrounding it. No attempt was made to associate the age of the cairn with that of the wheel but as Calder says, nothing was found to suggest that they were substantially different.

Can we assume then, that all medicine wheels with central cairns were built by the Oxbow people? Apparently not. Excavation at Moose Mountain wheel in Saskatchewan (Kehoe & Kehoe, 1979) showed that it is a far later construction than Majorville, built between 3,000 and 2,500 years ago by a people who left only domestic utilitarian items (mostly scrapers and knives for the women's work of preparing hides) not magical artifacts behind. And several, including one at Manyberries, in southeast Alberta (Carter, 1967; Friberg, 1974), seem to have been burial cairns. Manyberries, its central mound of earth and stones shaped in the middle eighteenth century originally in the form of a turtle, contained the bones of a young woman, an interesting link with local indigenous tradition which ascribes to the turtle the spirit of female procreativity. (The turtle is native on the plains only within the Missouri River drainage.)

Turtle figure inscribed on a ground stone "plate" of unknown use and age was found near Oxbow, Saskatchewan. Among historic tribes, the turtle is a symbol of fertility and longevity. Courtesy of the Saskatchewan Museum of Natural History.

Effigies

Equally as puzzling and as difficult to explain and date as the medicine wheels are the prehistoric stone figures that lie scattered throughout the shortgrass plains. Also made of glacial boulders, these trace out the figures of men and women, turtles, snakes, bison and various geometric shapes. Surprisingly, given the importance of the bison to all Plains tribes, only one bison effigy has been discovered in Canada, at Big Beaver, Saskatchewan, but fifteen human male effigies are known, in such places as Rumsey and Grassy Lake, Steveville and Crawling Valley, Alberta, Cabri Lake and Wild Man Butte, Saskatchewan. Eleven of these are very similar, with box-outline bodies, upraised arms, heartlines and prominent sex organs. Six of them are aligned latitudinally, their heads to the west.

Many of the effigies have been tampered with over the years, a fact that makes investigations of any sort most difficult. The figure on Wild Man Butte in southeast Saskatchewan is a prime example. This man appears today to have a tail, a smiling face and a broken circle of stones above his right shoulder. He was already in place, deeply embedded in the sod, when the land was first leased in 1914 and had lain apparently untouched until examined by

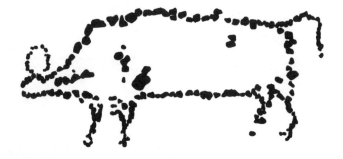

Figure of a bison laid out in stones on a prairie knoll near Big Beaver, Saskatchewan. Bison figures are strangely rare on the plains.

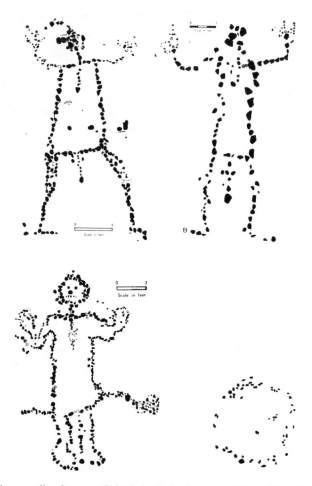

Three human effigy figures; at Cabri Lake, Saskatchewan (top left); at Steveville, near Dinosaur Provincial Park, Alberta (top right); on Wild Man Butte, in southeastern Saskatchewan (bottom). All plans courtesy of the Saskatchewan Museum of Natural History.

archaeologists in 1961. However, twenty years after this examination there came to light a document written in 1863 which revealed a very different picture. The report or "historical observation" on the hilltop effigies had been made by William Clandening, an Ontario man who had passed through the country on his way to the goldfields of Montana, and it described, complete with measurements, a man without a tail or a face carrying a bow-and-arrow in his right hand. It also detailed a second effigy nearby, this one of an elk not made of stones but cut into the sod in much the same way that the famous prehistoric white horses of England were cut into the chalk hills. The elk had long antlers and a round red-painted stone in the centre of its body around which were strips of red cloth. Since these early observations, grass has grown over the elk and the stones of the man have been rearranged, making the 1961 archaeologists' studies of little use (Dyck, 1981).

While several effigies are known or suspected to be alterations, few have suffered the indignity of deliberate, wholesale removal. Ted Douglas of Eatonia, Saskatchewan, farms land adjacent to the hillocky terrain where the Cabri Lake male effigy is located and he likes to keep an eye on it, from the air (he flies a small plane) and from his pick-up truck. One day when he took visitors to see it, the man was gone! Kidnapped! Only holes left in the sod marked where he had lain. Telephone detective work ultimately revealed his whereabouts: the figure had been exhumed by the Saskatchewan Museum of Natural History with the intention of placing it in a protected spot on the museum grounds. With help from local members of the Saskatchewan Archaeological Society Douglas made sure that the man was put back. Fortunately, he had been removed scientifically: each stone had been numbered and plotted onto a very exact map so that reconstruction was precise.

Most of the known turtle effigies are in Saskatchewan and Manitoba, the most famous of these being one atop a high knoll near Minton, Saskatchewan, overlooking the Big Muddy valley. This has four legs, a pointed tail, and a head with two Mickey mouse ears, eyes and mouth—in other words, a very questionable turtle. Some (Brace, 1987) think the outline better depicts a badger though others point to what they see as clear depictions of carapace plates. The "turtle" is about forty metres long with a nine-metre-diameter cairn in the centre. An outlying cairn and a line with a small sunburst design at one end mark the summer solstice sunrise and other astronomic alignments have been found to indicate possible ancient interest in the stars Sirius and Capella (Kehoe & Kehoe, 1979).

Perhaps the most amazing effigy or boulder mosaic site in all of North America is at Tie Creek within Whiteshell Provincial Park in southeastern Manitoba (Steinbring, 1970). Here the enigmatic mostly abstract designs sprawl

The most famous turtle effigy is near Minton, Saskatchewan. The creature has a face, ears, legs and tail, plus suggestions of a carapace. Central cairn is 9 m in diameter. Plan courtesy of Saskatchewan Museum of Natural History.

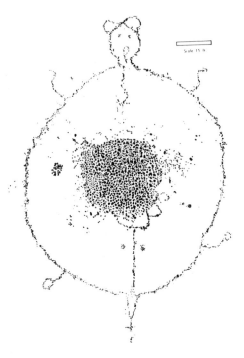

Photo of Minton turtle shows its scenic location, overlooking the Big Muddy river valley. Courtesy of the Saskatchewan Heritage Resources Board.

Aerial views of some of the figures in the extensive boulder mosaic or effigy site at Tie Creek, Whiteshell Provincial Park, Manitoba. Designs here are mostly abstract with the rocks placed directly on the glacially-scoured bedrock. Courtesy of Manitoba Information Services.

over fourteen hectares of glacially-ground Canadian shield bedrock surrounded by muskeg swamps; not exactly part of the grasslands, but worth considering here because of possible cultural influences. Placed for the most part directly on bedrock, the constructions cannot be dated except through measurement of lichen growth and this has yielded a minimum measure of 1,000 years. Because no evidence of habitation has been found nearby, though the formations must have taken several days if not weeks to build, archaeologists assume the boulder "mosaics" to have had a religious or magical purpose.

In the middle of these astoundingly large and complex boulder beds, archaeologist Anthony Buchner found indications that the site was used as a celestial observatory. Marked out in rocks was a direct sighting line to the summer solstice sunrise, complete with a small "viewing circle," and other patterns seemed to point to the risings of the moon and other planets. Intrigued by the notion of prehistoric astronomers, Buchner studied other effigy sites throughout the plains and found an amazing consistency of orientation. Effigies on the grasslands differed greatly in style from those of southeastern Manitoba, but similar shapes, sometimes hundreds of kilometres apart, tended to be aligned in similar directions. For example, ninety percent of all turtles face west, snakes invariably point south and ovals and lines point to the rising midsummer sun. Other features show almost a preoccupation with the cardinal points, some being aligned to true north, others to the west. All this might mean, Buchner says, that a single linguistic group of people could be responsible for all the effigy figures on the northern plains. If they did not actually build all the figures themselves, then they must have given the detailed plans to others. He proposes that the Tie Creek site, because of its immense size and complexity, was the point of probable origin for this phenomena throughout North America. Perhaps these artistic Woodlanders pushed west along the great maze of rivers and lakes into the plains, adapted to a plains way of life, and brought their effigy-building ideas along as part of their cultural heritage (Buchner, 1980 and 1983b).

Most of the rock constructions on the grasslands consist of small rocks moved from their original positions and deliberately placed to form the required shapes. However, a few large boulders, all of them quartzite transported by glaciers from the Canadian Shield, and all of them on the tops of hills, were not moved but altered by engraving. Because this work was mostly done in lines of parallel grooves thought to represent ribs, the boulder glyphs are called ribstones, though the designs are also richly embellished with circular pockmarks. A few have faces and others exhibit wavy snakelike lines. The face on the ribstone at Trochu, Alberta, also has horns and the whole creation is presumed to represent a bison. No-one knows when or why these

Ribstones near Viking, Alberta. The parallel grooves cut into the quartzite boulders are believed to represent the ribs of a bison. Courtesy of the Archaeological Survey of Alberta.

sculptures were made but archaeologists guess they played some part in magic ceremonies related to the bison and to success in hunting in much the same way as the far smaller and portable *iniskim* or buffalo stones.

Stories from Bones

Scientists can learn much about an ancient people by digging them up. The bones of their skeletons reveal far more than obvious things such as shape of head and average height: they can shed light on diet, health and way of life, indicate social customs and medical practices. Pathological studies can pinpoint diseases, abnormalities, how old the person was when he or she died, and often the cause of death. From mass burials, scientists can tell average life expectancies and the relative population sizes of men, women and children. Analysis of bone proteins can tell if the individual ate corn-on-the-cob, an important proof of early agriculture in America. How the bodies were interred and the kinds of artifacts buried with them (grave goods) are clues to such things as status, social structure, sense of values, even how the people thought about death and the possibility of afterlife.

Historically, Plains Indians did not bury their dead immediately but exposed the body to the elements, usually on a wooden scaffold, until the

71

flesh had rotted. Often the camp would move on before this happened, in which case the scaffold would be abandoned until the tribe returned some indefinite time later to bundle up the bones for burial. Archaeological evidence shows that sometimes relatives were not able to wait for the flesh to rot: they took down the bodies, chopped them up into manageable size, stripped off the remaining flesh and packaged them up for transport along with the rest of the camp paraphernalia. This bundling method was the only practical way for nomadic tribes to transport cadavers to a traditional burying ground. However, it seems that burial of the complete skeleton was not necessary; for the final rites, often a few token bones would suffice. Again, this tradition may have had a practical origin. Burial scaffolds often collapsed and the bones of the dead were scattered and scavenged. When the family returned, only a few bones were likely to remain.

Burial sites of the Oxbow era are rare on the Canadian plains, with one magnificent exception. In April 1963, Earl Gray was walking the fields of his family farm in southwestern Saskatchewan to see if the land was ready for seeding. On a south-sloping hillside, the wind had scooped out a depression in the sandy soil and here Gray discovered a human skull. He notified the RCMP in nearby Swift Current. (All human remains, no matter how ancient, must first be reported to the police who check for recent foul play.) A quick inspection showed the skull to be prehistoric so the police called in the Saskatchewan Museum of Natural History in Regina which immediately sent a small excavation team. From an area of about five metres square, the skeletal remains of twenty-one individuals were recovered. Later test excavations of a further twelve square metres unearthed another thirty-five skeletons. It was the first prehistoric mass graveyard found in Canada. To date the bones of more than 300 individuals have been exhumed from a hundred burial units in the main graveyard area, only sixty percent of which has been excavated. (Total population of the graveyard has been estimated at about 500.) And archaeologists have found the site was used for more than 2,000 years, beginning about 5,000 years ago in Oxbow times (Millar, 1972, 1978 and 1981a).

Analysis of the graves and their contents sheds light on the burial practices and preferences of the Oxbow culture and also on the people themselves. They were of varied stature, with broad high cheekbones and heavy jaws. The teeth of adults were well worn down and many suffered from abscesses and severe gum infections. Death rates seemed particularly high for newborn babies and children; there were no elderly people in the population and only a few over forty years old. Many of the younger women died during pregnancy or while giving birth and there seems to have been a high mortality rate among young adult males, probably from injuries sustained during the hunt.

Excavation of prehistoric burials at Saskatchewan's Gray site had to be done with extraordinary care since many of the bundle burials were very close together and several lay on top of each other. Courtesy of J.H.V. Millar, University of Saskatchewan.

The bones showed markedly different degrees of weathering and decomposition, a fact that seems to substantiate the historic tradition of exposure prior to burial. The arrangements of the bones also bears this out. They were seldom in anatomical position as they would have been if the whole body had been buried soon after death. Instead, the remains were bundled, sometimes with the bones of more than one person mixed together. The majority were token burials: only a few bones from each individual. While no evidence of the bundling material, most likely hide, was found, its presence could be assumed from the arrangement of bones, often with the long bones "stacked like cordwood" and with the skulls placed at one end. Rarely, the bones were arranged in patterns, sometimes with circles of skulls surrounding a heap of

73

Examples of bundle burials from the Gray site. a) Multiple secondary burial, the bones from several bodies bundled together before interment.

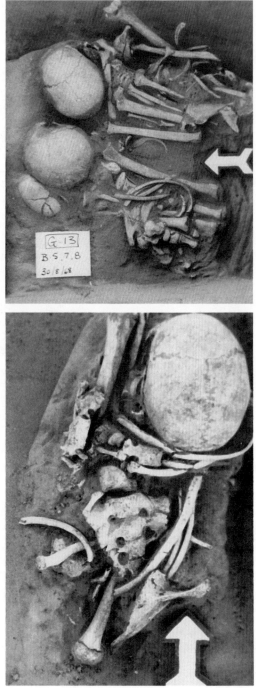

b) Single bundle burial. Both courtesy of J.H.V. Millar, University of Saskatchewan.

The Gray site also contained several primary burials in which the body was buried intact, soon after death. Courtesy of J.H.V. Millar, University of Saskatchewan.

bones, sometimes in linear arrangements. Only in a few cases were bodies interred soon after death. These primary burials, it is assumed, were of individuals who happened to die while the band was in the neighbourhood of the graveyard.

Fifty-eight percent of the burials were of infants or children, an indication of the high rate of infant mortality. There was also evidence that the children of this society had been loved and deeply mourned. Their bones had been lain to rest with a great deal of ornaments, including rare and precious shell and copper ornaments imported from great distances. Five burials included necklace sets of valuable eagle talons. Too, most of the children, including sixteen babies given primary burial, were interred with at least one adult, perhaps, to look after them in the other world. Adult bundle burials were accompanied by mostly utilitarian artifacts. These, say the archaeologists, were likely gifts from the mourners, not personal possessions, since women's tools such as scrapers were found with men and men's hunting points with women.

Burial ceremonies at the site included the liberal use of red ochre: it was scattered in the graves and rubbed on skulls and long bones, a prehistoric ritual of long standing and widespread distribution. Most of the human leg bones seem to have been deliberately broken at the ends. Was this a device to stop the wandering spirits from returning to earth? And many of the smaller bones of the body were deliberately smashed into heaps of tiny fragments, perhaps because of some belief, or perhaps merely to keep the final bundle burial as compact as possible.

Bones of bison, antelope, deer and other animals (mostly leg bones with the best meat), were placed in the graves as symbolic food for the afterlife journey. Also included were leg bones of domestic dogs to provide transportation. Dogs were used historically for hauling camp goods by means of a travois made of poles, a method that later tribes transferred to the horse. But the burial of an almost complete skeleton of a dog, liberally smeared with ceremonial ochre, has archaeologists mystified. Dogs in historic time were not well treated by the Plains Indians; they were fed with a miserly hand and made to haul heavy loads. Was this dog, buried by itself with such ritual, a favourite pet?

Once the Oxbow people had placed the bones and the grave goods into the prepared graves, the pits were filled with sand and sprinkled with ochre. Some graves were then covered with piles of cobbles brought to the site from a nearby coulee, presumably to mark the locations. However, over the years, the exact position of existing graves must have been lost, for in several instances new graves were dug on top of the old, and bones from more than one burial were scrambled together. Fortunately for archaeologists, once the cemetery was abandoned, its ancient surface, still scattered with miscellaneous bone,

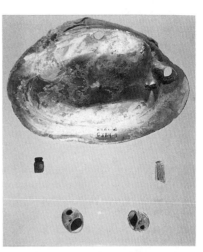

Some of the artifacts from
the Gray burial site included
a) large grooved stone maul
b) clam shell gorget
perforated with two holes;
shell beads and pendants
c) many stone projectile
points, indicators of the
Oxbow people. All courtesy
of J.H.V. Millar, University
of Saskatchewan.

cobbles, lumps of ochre and white clay (believed to be paint for the mourners' faces), was covered with a layer of wind-blown sand which effectively sealed off the site. Some twenty centimetres of brown soil then formed over the sand, further protecting the burial from the effects of twentieth century ploughing. But for chance erosion, this important site and its buried population would be buried still.

While the Gray burial site gives evidence of long-term cultural continuity and many leads in our inquiry into the lives and deaths of the ancient people of the plains, it raises serious questions. Why, after 2,000 years of continued use, was the community graveyard abandoned? Did the people move out of the area, change their burial practices, become extinct through disease or warfare? Did all Oxbow people bury their dead in mass cemeteries? The Gray site was used for two millenia and contains, at best estimate, 500 bodies. Where are the rest of the people who died during that period? Are there other graveyards yet to be discovered?

Oxbow Way of Life

It seems from the sites examined so far that we know more about the religious aspects of the Oxbow people than we do about their day-to-day lives. But this is not so. There is ample evidence, from excavations of several campsites in the prairie provinces, that these people continued the traditional hunting way of life that persisted on the plains throughout prehistory. For instance, above the slightly enigmatic Mummy Cave level of the Long Creek site in southeast Saskatchewan, archaeologist Boyd Wettlaufer identified two different Oxbow levels, the deeper one dated at around 4,700 years ago (Wettlaufer, 1960). This showed several interesting things. First, bison remains were so dominant that the people seemed to have been completely dependent on them. And there must have been a food shortage, for all the bones had been extensively split and crushed—many of them completely pulverized—for maximum food extraction. "Even the foot and ankle bones were split, a desperate measure, indicating near starvation conditions," commented Wettlaufer. A domestic dog, short-legged and heavy jawed, had also been skinned, butchered and presumably eaten. Does this imply severe drought conditions on the plains of southern Saskatchewan? The remains of several rough cherrylike pits, probably from the hackberry, were the only other source of food found among the household refuse.

Evidence was also found of Oxbow domestic activities. Along with weapons of slaughter and instruments for butchering were large numbers of polished and flaked bone tools, including many awls and scrapers, for cleaning and working bison hides. More evidence for this activity came from the

many fire hearths—ash was an important component in leather-working—
and from depressions found on the living floor which could have held large
stones to anchor hides for stretching and cleaning. Most intriguing was a ring
of small postholes and four larger ones positioned around a small hearth stain.
Wettlaufer thought that these likely denoted a construction of some kind used
in the tanning process. But he also suggested that the four larger poles could
have been used to suspend something, perhaps a bison skull, over a bed of
coals. "One can well imagine sweet-grass or other aromatic substances being
burned on the coals so that the smoke curled up around the central object."
The rest of the structure may have been "a miniature house type designed
as a small shrine" (Wettlaufer, 1960).

Another Oxbow bison hunter's camp, found after construction of a new
road had unearthed a pile of bones northwest of Saskatoon, was excavated
in the early 1970s. At this, the Harder site, archaeologist Ian Dyck (1977)
discovered traces of six to eight round packed earth dwelling floors suggestive
of circular tipis, though there were no signs of stone rings or other structures.
The occupation level, strewn with stone tools and quantities of butchered
bison bones, was dated at around 3,400 years ago.

Using historic reports of tipi population, estimates of daily meat
consumption—and some very basic arithmetic—Dyck was able to estimate
just how many people had camped here, and for how long. Each of the six
to eight tipis would have contained an average of seven people and five dogs,
giving a camp total between forty-two and fifty-six people and between thirty
and forty dogs. From the bones, Dyck calculated that between 93 and 138
bison had been butchered here. Each bison yields about 180 kilograms of meat.
Using calculations from the Olsen-Chubbock bison kill site in Colorado (Wheat,
1972), Dyck allowed daily rations of 4.5 kilograms of meat per person and
3.6 kilograms per dog—an astonishingly large amount. He then assumed that
only half of the meat butchered was eaten fresh, the rest preserved for winter.
Now he had all the parts of the equation. Half the total meat divided by the
total daily consumption equals between twenty-one and forty-two, the number
of days the site was likely occupied.

The campsite also contained quantities of large coarse stones which had
been carried to the site from glacial deposits at least nine kilometres distant.
The stones showed the effects of heating and sudden cooling—large, sudden
fractures and discoloration—and had likely been used as boiling stones in a
similar manner to that observed by William Francis Butler in 1872:

Their manner of boiling meat was as follows: a round hole was scooped
in the earth and into the hole was sunk a piece of rawhide; this was filled

Example of a bone-boiling pit, excavated at a campsite at Head-Smashed-In Buffalo Jump, Alberta. Archaeologists believe the Oxbow people were the first to use this cooking method and that it might indicate the first production of pemmican: dried meat mixed with rendered fat and berries. Courtesy of the Archaeological Survey of Alberta.

with water and the buffalo meat placed in it, then a fire was lighted close by and a number of round stones made red hot; in this state they were dropped into or held in the water which was thus raised to boiling temperature and the meat cooked.

Apparently cracked bones were also boiled in this manner to extract the grease and marrow. This type of boiling pit is typical of Oxbow sites. Archaeologists think the Oxbow people were the first to use this method of cooking and that it might indicate another technological advancement: the first preparation of pemmican, a mixture of dried meat pounded together with rendered fat and berries that stored well over winter.

Archaeologists know the Harder site was not a kill site because only selective parts of the bison carcasses, those rich in meat, marrow and grease, were found here. The animals must have been cut up into sections elsewhere and only the best meat portions carried back to camp. So far, no kill sites of the

Oxbow people have been found in Canada so we do not know their hunting methods, though from the large quantities of bison bones found at their camps they were extremely successful hunters and probably used some form of mass kill.

One researcher believes they may also have been, if not farmers, then at least primitive gardeners. During a pipeline survey in west central Saskatchewan, Oscar Mallory discovered thirty-four Oxbow habitation sites that were, at first glance, all located in most unlikely spots: on the tops of windy ridges, where no trees had ever grown. Nearby sandhills would have offered much better shelter and hunting opportunities. Yet the sites contained well compacted living floors, complete with fire pits, lots of ash and charcoal and fire-cracked rock, though only few remains of stone tools and hardly any animal bones. All these sites had one thing in common: maximum groundwater which gathered in the shallow loess-filled depressions on the hill tops. Loess (wind-blown soil) acts as a sponge, to hold water. In these naturally irrigated garden patches, Mallory suggests that the Oxbow peoples and their successors gathered in spring the green salad leaves of Amaranth (pigweed) and Chenopodium (lamb's quarters), returning in summer to harvest the seeds for grinding into meal and perhaps also to dig the roots of the Psoralea (Indian Turnip). The seeds ripen when the Indian hunters were likely to have little other food, the time of the bison rut when hunting was difficult and dangerous. The many fire-cracked cobbles could have been used as a heat source for loosening and separating the seeds from the stalks. It is a fascinating scenario (Mallory, 1977).

Man's Best Friend

The native fauna of North America is deficient in one respect of tremendous importance to the understanding of the lifeways of its prehistoric peoples. The mass extinctions of the Pleistocene left no large mammals such as the horse, ox and camel of the Old World that could easily be domesticated for hauling and transportation. There were huge herds of bison, but these animals are notoriously intractable and probably could not have been tamed. The only animal aid the Indians ever possessed were domestic dogs—and even these were likely not native. Scientists believe that *Canis familiaris* came from Asia and that some time prior to 12,000 years ago accompanied man on his intercontinental trek to North America. The Asian dogs were like small wolves with foreshortened muzzles and short, stocky bodies, but once here they undoubtedly cross-bred with both the native wild wolf and the coyote to produce the typical "Indian" dogs described in early historical reports (Walker & Frison, 1982).

Ironically, all members of the canid family, including the ancestors of the

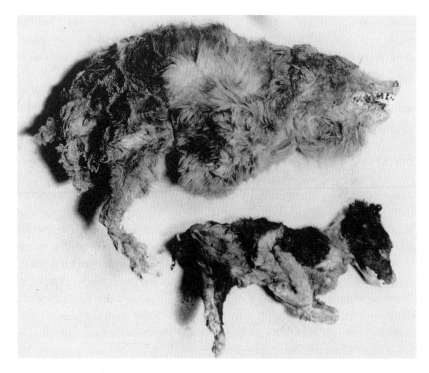

Mummified dogs were unearthed from a cave in the Arizona high desert. Collie-sized dog had buff-coloured hair; the terrier type was piebald, a black and white colour combination common only in dogs that have been domesticated for a long time. Dogs are about 2,000 years old. Courtesy of Peabody Museum of Archaeology and Ethnology, Harvard University.

domestic dog, originated in North America probably some fifteen million years ago and reached Asia during one of the earlier openings of the Bering land bridge, joining several other species such as the horse and the camel on an east-to-west migration. In Asia, a small variety of wolf, *Canis lupus*, whose remains have been found alongside those of Pleistocene hominids in China, is believed to have fathered the first domesticates of the species (Olsen, 1985).

Traces of domestic dogs occur remarkably early in the North American archaeological record. The earliest, found in Agate Basin, Wyoming, was dated to 10,800 years ago. At Jaguar Cave, Idaho, two others were excavated from an occupation level dated at 10,300 years ago. Both these examples are close to the most ancient household dogs found anywhere in the world: only a 12,000-year-old specimen from a cave in northeastern Iraq is known to be older. In Canada, the oldest dog yet found, represented only by its jaw, was unearthed in a site in the Crowsnest Pass and dates to 6,400 years ago (Driver, 1976). In the grasslands, where in historical times thousands of dogs were kept around the Indian camps, the earliest dog bones all date from the Oxbow era no earlier than 5,000 years ago.

Of great interest to animal lovers are the finds in White Dog Cave near Kayenta in the high semidesert of Arizona. Here archaeologists unearthed two dog mummies, complete with skin and hair, dating to about A.D. 1. Both animals had erect ears and bushy tails. One was about the size of a small collie with a coat of a pale buff colour, the other was smaller, with a short muzzle like a terrier's and a black and white or piebald coat. This colour pattern is common only to dogs that have been domesticated for a long time. The dogs were found with human mummies wrapped in fur robes; with them was a finely woven tumpline and pad made of dog hair. (The Indian tumpline, known historically, was worn across the forehead to take some of the weight of a backpack, enabling heavy burdens to be carried.) (Olsen, 1985)

How can archaeologists distinguish between the bones of a domesticated dog and those from a wild coyote or wolf? Apparently it is fairly simple. Dogs living and breeding in captivity rather than in the wild are subject to different pressures of natural selection and these result in genetic changes to their bones. The most useful bone for identifying domestication is the jaw, one that fortunately preserves very well. Generally speaking, domestic dogs have smaller teeth in larger, stouter jaws than coyotes; their premolars tend to be crowded and their teeth show more wear. This last attribute is due mostly to diet: Indian dogs were fed only bones and gristly scraps, but sometimes the dogs' canine teeth were deliberately broken or blunted to minimize the effects of their aggression and this resulted in heavier tooth-to-tooth wear (Driver, 1976).

From the excavated bones of prehistoric Indian dogs experts can reconstruct the approximate sizes and shapes of the living animals, whether their legs were long, their shoulders muscular, their muzzles long or short. They can also often tell whether they died naturally or were skinned and butchered for eating. We know dogs were used as pack and draught animals in historic times and we assume that they played a similar role in the lives of prehistoric peoples. Perhaps one day scientists may be able to prove this, and also to find some way of identifying different indigenous breeds. What we shall never know is how the dogs were treated, though from historical accounts they were overworked and kept submissive only through cruelty—far from the loving pets of today (Wilson, 1975).

Yet the Plains Indians depended on their dogs. Before the spread of the horse from southern Spanish settlements during the early eighteenth century, dogs were the only means of cartage the native hunters possessed, apart from their own backs. Dogs were trained to pull travois, a kind of sled made from two or more long poles tied to make an A-frame with a carrying basket in the middle. A medium-sized Indian dog could probably haul about twenty-five kilograms. A family tipi, made of several bison hides and housing six to eight people, must have weighed about 185 kilograms. At least seven dogs would be needed to carry it, with others required for bedding, food and other domestic paraphernalia. At the very minimum, each family would need eight working dogs; a small tribe of five families about forty dogs.

All these dogs had to be fed. Allowing a minimum consumption of 3.5 kilograms of meat per animal per day and the average amount of meat from a bison as 180 kilograms (Dyck, 1977), forty dogs would consume the equivalent of more than three-quarters of a bison a day—a sizable drain on the meat supply. These dogs would likely have fifteen puppies a year, which would aggravate the feeding problem—except for one thing: in times of want, the dogs themselves were a source of food. Butchered dog bones are quite commonly found in prehistoric plains campsites. At the Long Creek site in Saskatchewan, they were second only to bison in numbers, suggesting either that bison were scarce, or that dogs commonly formed an important part of these hunters' diet (Wettlaufer, 1960). Historical reports confirm this practice and suggest that hunger was not the only reason for the slaughter: the eating of specially-bred puppies accompanied certain rituals and even mature dogs were sometimes roasted to feast an honoured guest.

FIVE

Immigrants from the South

Archaeologists deal with scientific layers—of dirt and of time—and it is often only within this exacting framework that the story of life on the plains can accurately be told. In the earth above, and about 500 years later than the first appearance of Oxbow artifacts, field-workers find signs of change. There are sudden differences in stone points, hearths, tools, burial practices—enough new traits in fact that one might easily ascribe them to an entirely new group of people. Archaeologists however, are more meticulous. They point out that it has never been proved that different point styles equal different peoples, and they tend to talk instead about new complexes, phases and traditions, terms that tend to obfuscate rather than enlighten. It is possible, though, bearing in mind the archaeologists' cautions, to arrive at a simpler scenario.

Several centuries after the appearance of people with Oxbow traits and traditions, a new group of humans using a style of projectile point known as McKean arrived on the grasslands, probably bringing their dogs with them. They came, or so it is believed, from the semidesert country of the American Great Basin where arid conditions and scarcity of game had made necessary a forager tradition. For meat they trapped small mammals and snakes and they collected seeds and vegetable products which they ground on stone slabs, similar in principle to our kitchen mortars and pestles. But as they moved out of the desert environment into the game-rich plains of the north, foraging became very much a secondary pursuit. Like other peoples to inhabit the Canadian grasslands before and afterwards, they became primarily bison hunters, though they did not completely abandon their old reliances.

The Oxbow people, their traditions strong and well established, were seemingly unaffected by the newcomers. Archaeologists have found separate Oxbow sites and McKean sites which date from the same period and occur in much the same areas, suggesting that the two cultural groups lived side

McKean projectile point (left) has pronounced concave base; Duncan (centre) and Hanna (right) are believed by some to be simply variants of McKean, while others believe they denote separate cultures. Courtesy of the Saskatchewan Archaeological Society.

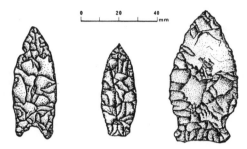

By side, sharing the same resources of the land. Their relationship was presumably amicable, at least there is no evidence to suggest otherwise, and it was sustained for some 1,000 years. Some sites even show a mixing of Oxbow and McKean points, evidence for direct interaction between the two groups. The cultures are differentiated archaeologically mainly by the markedly distinct forms of projectile points—Oxbow has obvious basal "ears," McKean a deeply indented or concave base—and by other traits.

So far, no direct evidence has been found on the Canadian plains to show how the Oxbow people hunted bison, though the large quantities of bison remains found at their camps show that they were efficient hunters and probably used some form of mass communal kill. (Near the Harder site, Ian Dyck (1977) found the remains of a possible pound.) However, current findings indicate that the McKean people stalked their prey by ambush, usually at watering holes, a strategy that suggests they lived in very small bands and lacked the social organization for communal pursuits.

Perhaps the best Canadian McKean site is Cactus Flower, a riverside camp that was occupied on at least seven separate occasions between 4,500 and 3,500 years ago. Here, there is good support for the theory that the slightly different forms of the McKean projectile point, known as Duncan and Hanna, are simply variants and do not indicate separate cultures: at this site, all three types of point are often found together (Brumley, 1975).

The Cactus Flower site has a beautiful name, descriptive of the masses of barrel and prickly pear cactuses that were in pink and yellow bloom during the first weeks of excavation in 1973. Its location is also singularly scenic: on the top of the bluffs along the southwest margin of a narrow-necked oxbow of the South Saskatchewan River upstream of Medicine Hat, Alberta. Almost surrounded by the deeply sinuous curve of the river, the land inside the meander is known locally as the Bull Pen, and it lies just inside the protective fence of the Suffield Military Reserve.

The site was first discovered by geologist Archie Stalker (of Taber Child fame) who was conducting surveys of the river deposits. He noticed a

Excavation of Cactus Flower site, a McKean campsite beside the South Saskatchewan River near Medicine Hat. The site was used by prehistoric bison hunters on at least seven occasions over a thousand-year period.

Ash-filled basin-shaped hearth at the Cactus Flower site is one of the diagnostic signs of McKean occupation. Both courtesy of John Brumley.

A typical McKean basin-shaped hearth, this one with heat-fractured stones still in position.

Some of the artifacts recovered from the Cactus Flower site. (Top, left to right) stone disc fragment, stone pipe, ammonite septa (possible buffalo stone or fetish) and a piece of fossil shell; (centre) circular polished stone disc, piece of burnt red shale, possibly used for paint; (bottom) an array of bone awls. All courtesy of John Brumley.

prominent ash-filled basin-shaped hearth exposed in the steep river bank four to five metres below the surface and filed a report in 1969. The site was relocated and tested in 1972 and results were encouraging enough to warrant full-scale excavation under the direction of archaeologist John Brumley during the two following summers. It proved a particularly rewarding, well-stratified site where the separate occupation levels had been sealed and separated by layers of soil and sand from a series of ancient river floods. In all, Brumley unearthed nine different levels; the seven lowest were all McKean campsites. Artifacts found around the basin-shaped hearths (features typical of the McKean culture) showed that a variety of activities had taken place at this riverside camp, including manufacture of stone projectile points and tools, cutting and smoothing of spear shafts, scraping and working of hides, sewing (a dozen bone awls were found), and various kitchen jobs such as butchering, cooking meat and extracting bone marrow and grease. Missing in the kitchen were the grinding stones traditional to these people back in their homeland, suggesting that already their adaptation to a hunting way of life was complete.

Also excavated was evidence for possible forms of McKean housing. On one living floor the cultural debris was spread out in a circle around the hearth, stopping abruptly as if to indicate the edges of a round dwelling, though no evidence of its construction was found. On another occupation level and also centred on a hearth, were many unbroken stones arranged in a circular arc suggestive of a partial tipi ring. Both of these "circles" were of acceptable size for a classic Blackfoot tipi of around three metres in diameter.

Other artifacts gave intriguing hints of McKean social and religious life: part of a tubular stone pipe, probably for smoking tobacco; bone and shell beads, the latter from the West Coast; part of a fossil ammonite, used as a buffalo stone fetish or *iniskim*; pieces of naturally burnt red shale, perhaps used for paint, and a fragment of a polished stone disc believed to be a die or gaming piece. A different kind of die attributable to the McKean people was unearthed at the Long Creek site in Saskatchewan. This was the canine tooth of a dog, the root end of which had been carefully incised with precise rows of thirty-one tiny dots (Wettlaufer, 1960).

Most of the butchered animals in the Cactus Flower camp were bison— the bones of at least forty were identified—and the remains of five domestic dogs about the size of coyotes were also found. One puppy had been skinned and butchered, presumably for food, though perhaps for some ritualistic purpose.

From these few fragments, John Brumley was able to reconstruct the events that took place at Cactus Flower thousands of years earlier. The remains of the McKean hunters' camps were those of only a single family or at best a

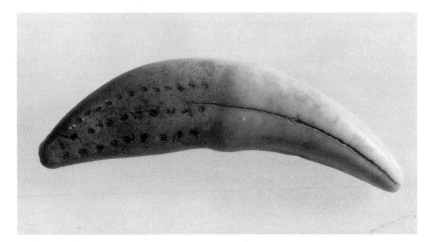

Dog's canine tooth with thirty-one dots inscribed on its root end is believed to have been used by McKean people as a gaming piece. It was excavated from the Long Creek site. Courtesy of the Saskatchewan Museum of Natural History.

few family groups. There were not enough people to attempt a communal bison kill so instead the hunters hid themselves behind the brush on the river bluffs and waited until the animals came down to the river to drink. Then they crept stealthily nearer until they were close enough to launch their weapons. The Bull Pen oxbow is surrounded by steep river banks except on the west and north where the land slopes gently down to the river, attractive watering spots for game animals, even today. The Indians skinned and butchered the slain animals where they fell at the water's edge and hauled back to camp only the meatiest portions of the carcasses—only certain bison bones were found in the camp refuse. Brumley guesses that the same small band of people returned to Cactus Flower every summer, year after year. They put up their tipis, tethered the dogs, built fires and settled down on the high cactus-covered bluff well away from the river flies. When they had enough meat, they folded their tents and went away, leaving the camp litter where it lay until river floods washed over a clean layer of silt (Brumley, 1975).

Nomadic Architecture

The hide tipi, used by the Plains Indians in historic times and believed to date back at least to the Oxbow era, was a form of architecture ideally suited to the windy plains environment and to a nomadic people. The wood poles of its structure and the bison hide covering were easy to obtain and to transport. Its conical shape made it simple to put up and take down, while its low

90

Modern Peigan tipi photographed at Head-Smashed-In Buffalo Jump in 1989; an example of traditional Plains architecture that has remained virtually unchanged except that the covering is canvas, not hides. Courtesy of the author.

volume-to-floor-area ratio made it economical to heat in winter by means of a small central fire. Protruding smoke flaps at the top of the tipi, held open by two exterior poles, could be shifted to catch the wind and closed in heavy rains. In summer, the height of the tipi tended to keep the interior cool and air flow could be increased by rolling up the hide perimeter. With its tough hide walls well anchored to the ground, it remained snug and stable in the worst prairie storm, pegged down for extra safety by a central interior guyline. Perhaps the fact that it could not be improved upon explains why the form has survived for more than 5,000 years (Adams, 1978).

The base of the tipi was often held in place by boulders placed upon the skirt of the hide covering. This is so well documented historically that archaeologists can be reasonably sure that this was the function of most of the stone circles that still lie scattered over the prairie. Even without the historical evidence, the use of stones for tent anchors seems valid, if only because it makes such good sense. The plains are well supplied with quantities of melon-sized rocks of glacial origin, all of them well rounded and therefore unlikely to damage a tipi cover. The rocks were available, easy to place, easy to remove and did not have to be carried from camp to camp since local supplies were always nearby.

Were these tipi rings used more than once? Archaeologist Gary Adams believes not. He tried erecting a tipi around an existing ring with a central hearth and found it impossible to obtain an exact alignment, far more trouble than starting from scratch. Each tipi ring or encampment of rings represents, therefore, only a single occupation, a fact that helps to explain the huge number of rings still in existence (Adams, 1978).

Where there were no stones, the Indians had to hammer pegs into the ground, a laborious task, particularly on the prairies where the unbroken sod is tough and unyielding. Archaeologist Michael Wilson has excavated several pegs from a tipi ring site in the foothills of southern Alberta. They were made from bison ribs which had been sharpened at one end into points; the other ends bore impact scars from repeated heavy blows (Wilson, 1977).

Historical observers noticed that the doorways of Indian tipis usually faced east and this was ascribed to some religious belief in the power of the rising sun. However, there could also be a practical explanation: an east-facing doorway would be in the lee of the prevailing—and unceasing—westerly winds. The high winds on the plains may also partly explain the apparent absence of hearths from many of the tipi rings. Once the wind protection of the tipi cover was removed, the ashes and charcoal of any domestic fire not contained within a tight circle of rocks would soon be blown away. This seems obvious, but how can it be proved? During a survey of tipi rings near the Red Deer

Aerial photo of the British Block Cairn near Medicine Hat, Alberta, and the adjacent camp circle of tipi rings, believed to have been the communal campsite of about 200 McKean people gathered at the site for ceremonies. Courtesy of the Archaeological Survey of Alberta.

River in southeastern Alberta, Gary Adams noticed that only half of the eighty-eight rings excavated contained any sign of a central hearth. In most of the others, however, he found tell-tale bits of charcoal lodged in the crevices of the tipi ring rocks—where only the wind could have scattered them (Adams, 1978).

For most of the Prehistoric era the plains peoples lived in small, family related bands averaging twenty-five to thirty people. This number, based on historic models, would need accommodation in three to four tipis; and it is exactly this clustering that occurs most frequently on the grasslands. However, larger groupings also occur. Sprinkled on the hillocky highland around the spectacular British Block cairn and medicine wheel northwest of Medicine Hat, Alberta, lie fifty-one stone tipi rings arranged into ten different clusters. Most are in groups of three to five, representing the camps of small bands of people who came to this lofty site over the years because they believed it to be a place of great power. In historic times, Plains Indians believed that stone weapons made in the vicinity of medicine wheels and other sacred places would absorb some of the magic and become strong and powerful themselves. Archaeologists believe this practice to be long-lived: within several of these prehistoric camps are small heaps of stone chips, the residue from spear point manufacture.

Just north of the medicine wheel, in a remarkable exception to the normal group size, a large arrangement of nineteen tipis spreads out in a giant horseshoe-shape, its arms open to the north. Archaeologist James Finnigan, who researched the tipi rings at this site, concluded that this was the remains of a communal camp of four to eight bands—perhaps nearly 200 people— gathered together for ceremonial purposes. This camp circle, an observed historical form of tipi arrangement, was dated by soil mineral analysis, radiocarbon tests, and depth of tipi ring rocks to around 2,700 years ago; and projectile points of McKean style were found (Finnigan, 1982). It seems from this study that medicine wheels may have played a part in the ceremonial lives of at least some of the McKean hunters and that, perhaps late in their occupancy of the plains, they gathered here in multi-band or tribal groups. At British Block astronomers have noticed a cairn alignment pointing to the summer solstice sunset, so it is possible that the McKean rituals were related to the sundance, the great annual ceremonial gathering of the Plains Indians that has persisted to the present day.

No evidence has yet been found that the McKean people buried their dead in a single large graveyard like their contemporaries, the Oxbow—indeed, there is little evidence that they buried their dead at all. Only one McKean burial has been found so far in Canada—the cremation of a single individual south of Saskatoon which has been described as "unusual to the point of being enigmatic"; the others, all found beneath the floors of their dwellings, were in the United States (Walker, 1982a).

Old Copper in Manitoba

While the prehistoric peoples of the western plains were forging for themselves a nomadic way of life dependent on the buffalo and using chipped stone for tools and weapon tips, Canada's first mining industry was underway around Lake Superior to the east. Thousands of ancient mining pits have been found along the south shore of the lake and on Isle Royale, opposite today's city of Thunder Bay. From these pits, as early perhaps as 7,000 years ago, native copper was mined and made into heavy spear points and tools of all kinds, including mysterious crescent-shaped objects that could have been knives but which some archaeologists believe were religious items used in a moon worship cult. Metalworking techniques included cold hammering and annealing (heating the copper to strengthen it) and, later on, forging at the high and critical temperatures of between 1,000 degrees and 1,038 degrees Centigrade, hot enough to soften but not melt.

The Old Copper Culture flourished primarily in Ontario and Minnesota but also made its appearance in the prairie provinces; at least fifty Old Copper

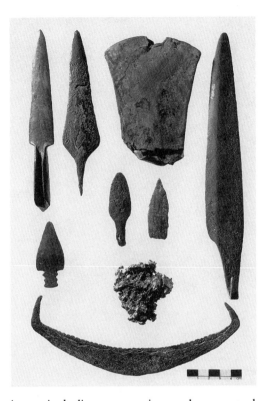

Old Copper artifacts, including axe head, projectile points, a lump of raw native copper and a large crescent-shaped knife, possibly a religious item used in a moon worship cult. While the Old Copper culture flourished mainly in Ontario, where copper was mined as early as 7,000 years ago, a copper crescent was found as far west as Castor Creek, in central Alberta. Courtesy of Leigh Syms, Manitoba Museum of Man.

items, including spear points and crescents, have been found in southern Manitoba, a few others in Saskatchewan and at least one, a crescent, has turned up as far away as Castor Creek in central Alberta (Forbis, 1970). Were these copper items merely trade goods imported from the east, or did people possessing copper technology migrate onto the plains? Undoubtedly some of the items were traded, but from at least one excavated site (in Nopiming Provincial Park, Manitoba) evidence has been found that some Old Copper forest people did move northwest, most likely at a time when a shift to a cooler climate brought the boreal forest treeline farther to the south (Buchner, 1983a). They began their migration about 5,000 years ago, making their way slowly up the Winnipeg River. From Lake Winnipeg, the migrants could then have continued into the Saskatchewan River system, which would have led them naturally westwards (Steinbring, 1980).

Curiously, even in the heartland of the Old Copper Culture, metallurgy did not develop beyond the first simple stages. The principle of mixing molten metals together to form alloys was never discovered. Bronze (an alloy of copper and tin) is far harder than copper and takes a far finer cutting edge; it would have been much more useful in the manufacture of tools and weapons

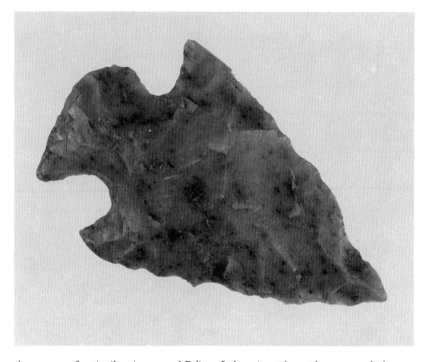

A new type of projectile point named Pelican Lake, triangular and corner notched, appeared on the plains around 3,300 years ago, indicating possible immigration of a new group of people. Courtesy of the Archaeological Survey of Alberta.

as the Bronze Age smiths of Europe discovered. On the other hand, finely honed flint knives are said to be sharper than the finest steel and have been used even today in delicate human surgery. Unalloyed copper could not compete with such crisp and long-lasting cutting power and its use for tools gradually declined. In later years it was used almost entirely to make ornamental objects. The heyday of the Old Copper Culture in Manitoba extended from 5,000' to 3,000 years ago and traces of it are found mainly in the forests and forest fringes of the southeast.

Renaissance People of the Plains

The technical revolution of metallurgy which the Old Copper people in the East were beginning to exploit had little effect on the prehistoric Plains Indians and they continued their nomadic "Stone Age" way of life. Around 3,300 years ago, another new type of projectile point, strongly triangular and corner-notched, made its appearance. At about the same time, the diagnostic points of the McKean and Oxbow peoples disappeared. Once again, it is an

96

archaeological puzzle: did the resident tribes who had lived together for so long maintaining their own cultural identities both suddenly start making this different type of point? Or did a wave of new people with their own distinct traditions and traits slowly engulf them? Archaeologists are not sure (Reeves, 1983b, Dyck, 1983) though some see the new points, known as Pelican Lake and first identified in Saskatchewan, as a natural evolution from the slightly corner-notched Hanna variants of the McKean culture (Joyes, 1970). Others believe they were brought in by newcomers from the south and east. The facts seem to support the latter opinion.

First, the new points are found right away at mass bison kills, particularly at jumps, suggesting that the people who used them, unlike the McKean, were experienced at this type of communal kill. Archaeological sites throughout the plains testify to the new people's prowess. After the Mummy Cave hunters stopped using the jump at Head-Smashed-In, it was deserted for about a thousand years, including all the years of Oxbow/McKean occupation. People using Pelican Lake points were the first to reuse it, leaving their tell-tale weapon tips in the hundreds of carcasses that piled up at the base of the sandstone cliffs. They were also the first to recognize and use the jump cliffs at other locations, including Old Women's in the foothills of Southern Alberta (Forbis, 1962) and Walter Felt (Kehoe, 1973) in Saskatchewan.

The average size of the Pelican Lake campsites indicates that, like native plainsmen both before and after them, the people lived and travelled generally in small family groups of twenty-five to thirty people. For communal bison hunts, which evidence suggests were mostly held in the fall, these groups must have met at a prearranged place and time and organized themselves into a mass killing and butchering corps, presumably under some kind of leader. This type of community organization suggests a far more disciplined society than that which went before. While McKean and perhaps Oxbow also met communally it was seemingly only for ceremonial purposes.

Another different trait shown by the Pelican Lake people is that they did not seem to use medicine wheels—at least the ones that have been excavated show no trace of their presence. And they buried their dead not like Oxbow or McKean but in rock-covered shallow graves on hilltops.

One of the most interesting of the Pelican Lake burials is Bracken Cairn in southwest Saskatchewan. On the top of one of the River Hills, it overlooks the deep glacial spillway now occupied by the Frenchman River. A lonely and scenic spot, it is utterly peaceful even today. Agriculture has worked only the river valley, leaving the steep dry hills along its southern edge untouched except for a few fences and some grazing cattle. Here can be found many undisturbed tipi rings and prehistoric stone alignments. The cairn was discovered

High on the River Hills overlooking the Frenchman River in southwestern Saskatchewan, these stones of the Bracken Cairn once covered a 2,500-year-old Pelican Lake burial tomb. Today, it is still a lonely, peaceful place. Courtesy of the author.

in 1936 by Mrs. Laura Wright and her younger brother Mel Bakken who were on a family outing to collect agates in the river. Climbing up into the hills, they noticed some broken pieces of worked shell in the backdirt thrown up outside a gopher hole beside a large pile of stones. These pieces fitted together into a handsome pendant in a head-and-shoulders shape, known as a gorget. They took the pendant and resolved to come back and dig for more "Indian treasures." But it was twelve years later, in 1948, that they finally found the time to do this.

Back then, there was little official interest in archaeological sites, and no laws against digging into them. But Mrs. Wright nevertheless decided to keep records and to make sketches of what they found. Digging with only crude tools—a penknife and a screwdriver—they unearthed beneath the rocks of the cairn two groups of human bones, each with a skull facing west, placed at either end of a shallow pit. The bones and the earth were deeply stained with red ochre and there were a great many grave goods. The finders kept the two skulls and the artifacts and reburied the rest of the bones.

It was much later again, in 1957, that the Saskatchewan Museum of Natural History began a scientific enquiry into the burial. The finders willingly cooperated with museum staff, giving them the skulls and artifacts and

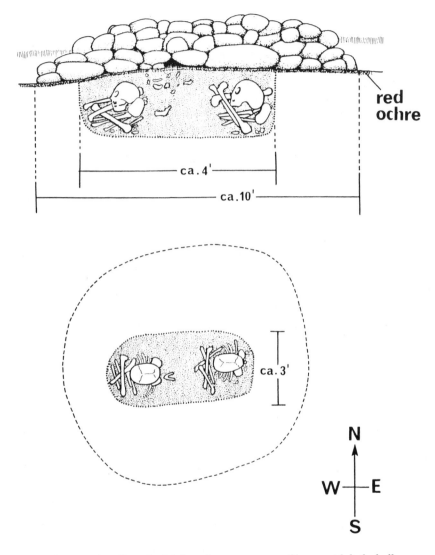

Plans of the Bracken Cairn burial show the arrangement of bones, with both skulls facing west. Courtesy of the Saskatchewan Archaeological Society.

the sketches they had made (King, 1961). Retrieval of the rest of the bones, many of them still stained with red ochre, made possible a complete reanalysis of the grave and its contents by archaeologist Ernie Walker, at the University of Saskatchewan, in 1981 (Walker, 1982a).

The Bracken Cairn grave, carbon dated to around 2,500 years old, had contained two secondary bundle burials with the remains of five individuals, a man aged about forty-one, a woman of about forty-seven, two children and one extra adult leg bone. The children were mere infants, one about twelve months old, the other a newborn. It is easy to jump to the conclusion that this was a family group, parents and children, but Walker believes this unlikely for in primitive societies, it was rare for women over forty to bear children. Instead he proposes that the five individuals just happened to die at around the same time, prompting a group burial. Cause of death of one of the adults was diagnosed as an aortic aneurysm, possibly caused by syphylis or tuberculosis.

Accompanying the human remains were a large number of bird and animal bones, mostly those of the swift fox, a species now extinct in Canada. Some of the animal bones had been shaped into pear-shaped decorative pendants—imitations of elk teeth—and beads; others, including the canine tooth of a bear and a beaver's incisor, into polished tools. And there were two nearly identical large carved gorgets made from clam shells native to the Gulf of Mexico. Among the many flaked stone tools was one clearly identifiable Pelican Lake projectile point. There was also a well used stone pestle ground from some stalagtitic material and a tiny piece of rolled copper. The exotic items among the grave goods provide important clues to Pelican Lake ancestry and lifeways. The pestle may very well denote a place of origin where vegetable foods formed an important part of the diet while the copper and the clam shells indicate trade connections with the Old Copper Culture to the east and with the southern United States.

Another Pelican Lake burial was found south of Calgary, Alberta, in 1980, when a few of the bones began to erode from the edge of a ploughed field on the lip of a high sandy ridge overlooking the Highwood River. Excavated by an archaeological team headed by Jack Brink in 1980, and dated to 2,700 years ago, the grave was found to contain the remains of a ten-year-old child, along with a few extra infant bones. The burial pit had been liberally sprinkled with red ochre and contained many grave goods, including shell beads, some from West Coast dentalium and olivella shells, a set of eleven perforated grizzly bear claws, and sixty-six drilled young bison teeth, all part of one or more necklaces, or perhaps originally sewn onto clothing. (Grizzly bear claws were prized by prehistoric people since the animal was believed to possess great supernatural as well as physical power). Like the Bracken Cairn, the Highwood

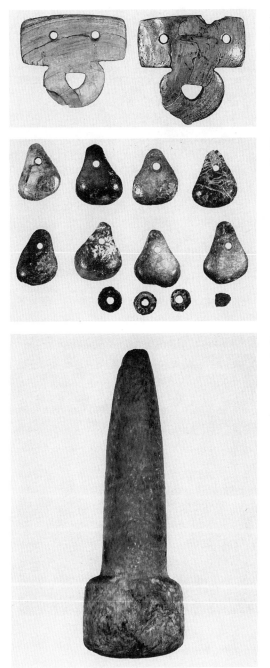

Artifacts from the Bracken Cairn included
a) two clam shell gorgets

b) animal bones cut into pear-shaped pendants and beads

c) a well-used stone pestle.
Courtesy of Ernie Walker,
University of Saskatchewan.

Bones and artifacts, including bison teeth, grizzly bear claws and shell beads, eroding from burial near the Highwood River, Alberta, before excavation.

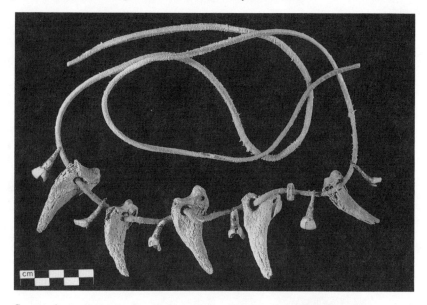

Suggested reconstruction of necklace using bear claws and bison teeth from the Highwood River burial. Both courtesy of the Archaeological Survey of Alberta.

burial contained a single Pelican Lake projectile point and a small piece of native copper. Because the grave goods were rare and valuable items, Brink speculates that the dead child must have been a person of some importance, perhaps the son of a chief (Brink and Baldwin, 1988).

All the evidence of differences between the Oxbow, McKean and Pelican Lake cultures seems to confirm that the new side-notched triangular points that make their appearance about 3,300 years ago represent a new wave of migrants coming into the prairies. First, the Pelican Lake point itself is radically different in size and shape and many were made of stone imported from great distances. In today's Saskatchewan and western Manitoba the new points were made mostly of Knife River flint from North Dakota; in Alberta, of Rocky Mountain cherts and chalcedonies (Reeves, 1983). The people's habits, too, seem different from previous prairie residents. They hunted bison communally, mainly by driving them over cliffs; they seem to have held dissimilar spiritual beliefs (they buried their dead on hilltops and apparently knew or cared little about medicine wheels); and they engaged in wide-reaching trade with people from the West and Gulf coasts, from the south and from the Eastern Woodlands.

Pelican Lake points and tipi encampments are found in great numbers throughout the northern grasslands and this suggests that their population was large and mobile. They have been called "the Renaissance people of the plains" because they revived and perfected the lost art of the buffalo jump, probably the most effective killing machine then known. Their culture with its sophisticated social and political structures lasted on the Canadian plains for at least a thousand years (based on carbon 14 dates from Head-Smashed-In and Long Creek), and ultimately spread into the parklands, the mountains and the Boreal forest.

However, it seems possible that the Pelican Lake people were not the only ones hunting on the grasslands of Canada during this era. Two other types of projectile points, both very dissimilar to the side-notched triangular points that typify Pelican Lake, show up at several of the very same bison jumps. One of these different points, as yet unnamed, shows similarities to those used by people in the Eastern Woodlands of Minnesota, Illinois and Ohio; the other, called Sandy Creek, seems typologically indistinguishable from Oxbow, though it dates to much later times. So far, archaeologists have little to say about them, or the people who made them.

SIX

Influences

S everal culturally distinct peoples moved onto the Canadian grasslands during the thousands of years before Europeans arrived but the harsh environment forced them all, eventually, onto the same narrow path of survival: that of the nomadic bison hunter. Around them, other environments encouraged different lifeways. To the east and southeast, the Indians of the Woodlands hunted smaller game, made canoes of birchbark to navigate the waterways and gathered roots, berries and grains, including wild rice. To the south, the Plains Village Indians eventually settled in semipermanent villages and grew crops of corn, squash and beans in riverside gardens. On the West Coast the people lived off the bounties of the sea while far to the south and in the Arctic, still other very different cultures flourished.

But as time went on and populations throughout North America increased, inter-area trade and travel accelerated. Ideas spread; technological inventions were passed along to be adopted or adapted for current use. Even the most isolated of the bison hunters ultimately came into a sphere of influence and culture change. And the archaeologists' job of interpreting this sudden melting pot becomes at once tremendously exciting and very difficult.

Two brilliant technological inventions, pottery and the bow and arrow, herald the era of change on the Canadian plains, an era which began, conveniently, about A.D. 1. Physical traces of these innovations are found buried in the dust of almost 2,000 years: small notched arrowheads, delicately made, and broken sherds of clay pots. But the people who first used them are harder to identify. Tiny clues gleaned from many sites throughout the Canadian and the American plains have helped piece some of the puzzle together and archaeologists now attribute the two inventions to two separate origins.

In deposits dating from this watershed of change archaeologists find new and very distinctive large side-notched atlatl points, sometimes along with a few rough sherds of clay pottery. The two traits seem clearly associated with a people who lived on the plains when the makers of Pelican Lake points were gone. This new culture is called Besant. Where did it originate? Again, archaeologists are in debate. Were the people immigrants from the Middle

Missouri region or the northern Boreal forests? Or were they originally residents of the parklands and forest fringes to the east whose "new" point style merely evolved from the late Oxbow phase called Sandy Creek (Reeves, 1983b)? The fact that they knew how to make pottery lends credence to the latter theory, for the peoples of the Eastern Woodlands were the first in Canada to posssess a ceramic technology. However, in several excavated kill and camp sites of this era, Besant and Pelican Lake points have been found side-by-side: this could indicate a different scenario altogether.

Whatever its origins, the Besant culture spread fairly rapidly throughout the Canadian plains in the wake of Pelican Lake and seems to have lasted some 700 years. So far, the earliest sites are Garratt and Melhagen in southern Saskatchewan (Dyck, 1983). Interestingly, some of the Besant sites contain side-notched points that are markedly smaller in size. Known as Samantha points, these are diminutive enough to be arrowheads (Reeves, 1983b). Were the newcomers (if they were newcomers) the first on the plains with both pottery and the bow and arrow? Archaeologists concede them one, but not the other.

Most researchers currently believe that the bow and arrow originated in the Old World and first reached the Western Arctic of North America from Asia about 4,000 years ago. The new weapons system infiltrated British Columbia during the next 1,500 years (it appears in archaeological sites in the Fraser Canyon and on the Interior plateau) and gradually spread eastwards to emerge onto the plains by about 1,800 years ago or A.D. 200 (Reeves, 1983b; Fladmark, 1986a). There is no suggestion of actual invasion and conquest by bow-and-arrow hunters: the idea was revolution enough and passed readily between cultures. Prehistoric peoples from both sides of the mountains are known to have crossed the Rockies to hunt, visit quarries and trade. The Crowsnest Pass for one shows unmistakable signs of their passage.

Most archaeologists attribute the first definite arrowheads on the Canadian Plains not to the Besant newcomers but to a people known as Avonlea from a site in Saskatchewan where signs of their culture (and the distinctive arrow tip) were first unearthed. No one can say for sure just where the Avonlea people came from, either, though most believe they are simply the descendents of the people who made the Pelican Lake points (Byrne, 1973; Adams, 1977; Reeves, 1983b). This could explain why these corner-notched atlatl points disappear so abruptly: all the people who used them quickly switched over to the new bow-and-arrow technology. Some, however, see affinities between Avonlea and the upper Mississippi Valley of the United States (Husted, 1969, Morgan, 1979).

While it is generally agreed that Besant were the first on the grasslands with pottery and Avonlea the first with the bow and arrow, both cultures

Projectile points of Besant (left), and Avonlea. The larger Besant point is believed to have tipped a spear used with an atlatl, while the far smaller and finer Avonlea is believed to be the first arrowhead on the Canadian plains. Courtesy of the Saskatchewan Archaeological Society.

ultimately possessed both. For in another classic example of peaceful coexistence, the two groups appear to have lived side-by-side on the Canadian plains for more than 700 years, each retaining its own identity, yet following virtually the same way of life. Both relied almost totally on bison, killing them very successfully it seems at both jumps and pounds, and moved camp seasonally to follow their food supply from the open plains in summer to the shelter of river valleys and foothills in winter.

Clearly their experience of life on the plains would have been nearly identical. So how do archaeologists know there were two different groups of people? And just how did the two cultures differ? Again, projectile points provide the chief diagnostic. The small, exquisitely-crafted notched arrowheads immediately differentiate an Avonlea site from a Besant, for it seems that the latter were stubbornly loyal to the atlatl and never adopted the bow and arrow whole-heartedly. Nor did they ever match the superb flint-knapping skills of Avonlea: by comparison their points are crudely made.

Archaeologists can also distinguish between the two cultures on other grounds, in particular their pottery, tool kits and lithic preferences. Besant assemblages contain pentagonal and triangular drills and a high proportion of imported Knife River chalcedony while Avonlea sites typically include cobble, core and flake choppers and show a distinct bias in favour of local stone. At Besant sites, excavators occasionally find bison bones hammered upright into the earth, tipi rings and sometimes the remains of wood poles indicating a form of housing akin to the mat-covered wigwams of the Woodlanders, additional evidence for eastern origins. Avonlea campsites reveal only tipis. The Besant culture is spread throughout the Canadian plains and parklands, while Avonlea seems concentrated on the shortgrass plains of southern Saskatchewan and Alberta. The fact that both peoples occupied the same area at the same time, yet were able to maintain their strong cultural differences over such a long period of time has archaeologists puzzled. For this pattern of coexistence breaks all the rules of social behaviour: such close proximity should result in either assimilation of one by the other, or a complete melding of cultures.

The New Weapon

Certainly the bow and arrow had clear advantages over the atlatl. Not only were the smaller arrow points and shafts easier to carry but the bow assured a longer range, more accurate aim and more rapid fire. Proficiency with the new weapon was also easier to attain. Use of the bow and arrow involved no violent movement; it could be drawn quietly and secretly from a hidden position (Frison, 1978). In the forests and mountains of British Columbia, the new invention probably encouraged a greater reliance on individual stalking and ambushing of small animals (Fladmark, 1986a), but on the grasslands it was used very successfully indeed against the great herds of lumbering, thick-thinned and shaggy-coated bison.

Archaeologists know that the tiny stone points they find with Avonlea and later cultures were definitely arrowheads because they are similar in size, weight and design to those used in historic times. But were they really the first arrowheads on the plains? Arguing that the prototype arrow, like the atlatl shaft, was probably unfeathered, Owen Evans of the University of Oklahoma began a series of practical field trials in 1957. He used a reproduction of a native bow and he fired unfletched shafts tipped with a variety of arrowheads. The results were interesting. He found that the shafts had to be used with heavy (and therefore large) arrow points, and the heavier the point the farther and more accurate its trajectory. The efficiency factor of an unfletched arrow was a matter of balance between the size of the shaft and the weight of the point. Obviously, a heavier shaft needed a correspondingly more powerful (and therefore larger and heavier) bow, the only negative in the equation. Even projectile points up to 125 millimetres long and 90 milligrams in weight, previously considered too large for arrowheads, could be accurately propelled with a bow, while diminutive arrowheads were almost useless when attached to thin, light unfletched shafts (Brennan, 1959).

Evans' experiments offer the possibility of a very different weapons chronology for the plains. The sudden appearance of small arrowheads could herald, not the first bow and arrow, but only the first use of feathered shafts. This would be innovation enough, for feathered shafts, and the bows to propel them, could be far lighter and more portable. The bow and arrow, then, might be considerably older than generally believed, and many of the larger stemmed and notched points assigned to spears and atlatls could very well be jumbo arrowheads.

However, Evans's field trials have had little influence on the fairly entrenched notion that the Avonlea arrow points were the first on the Canadian prairies. These points were tiny, less than 20 millimetres long, thin and delicate, sharp as a needle, far smaller and lighter than the British Columbia versions from which, presumably, they were copied. It has been suggested (Kehoe and McCorquodale, 1961) that the knob-and-kettle topography of the grasslands formed natural impounding pens and that Avonlea people developed their miniature projectile point specifically to kill impounded bison at close range. Hidden behind the stakes of the corral, hunters could take careful aim for the heart and slip their tiny arrows between the animal's ribs to strike home. Once they had made the switch to bows and arrows, Avonlea hunters never used the atlatl again, as their excavated kill sites throughout the plains show.

Yet archaeologists say it was the Besant people with their atlatls who first perfected the pound, building wooden corrals to pen the trapped animals for slaughter. The Besant hunters are acknowledged masters of the mass bison kill. George Frison (1978) talks of a "cultural climax in terms of bison procurement that was never reached again on the Northwestern Plains," while Ian Dyck (1983) calls them "masters of the pound hunting technique." Certainly the massive piles of bones they left behind at corral kill sites throughout the prairie provinces attest to their organizational ability and their hunting prowess. Does their seeming preference for the atlatl indicate a technological conservatism? Was their use of the more traditional weapon an attempt to preserve their cultural separateness? Or did the atlatl possess technical advantages that today we cannot perceive? And of course, if Evans' theory has merit, it is possible that the Besant people did use the bow, but with unfletched arrows and large arrowheads.

Impressions from Clay

By the time the first crude sherds of Besant pottery appeared on the Canadian grasslands, ceramics were already an established tradition of the Plains Village peoples of the Missouri to the south and had been in use for at least 200 years in the Canadian northeast. The earliest pottery of the forests, known as Laurel, was coil-formed into conical shapes, its smooth surface decorated, if at all, by designs made by notched sticks or by lines of small round indentations known as punctates. It is markedly different from either Besant or Avonlea (Syms, 1977a) an argument against Besant's Woodland origins. And Avonlea and Besant are sufficiently distinct that one can hardly have derived from the other.

At first, the Besant culture was believed to be aceramic, at least west of the Missouri Coteau (Byrne, 1973). But gradually, the evidence for pottery piled up at several sites in Saskatchewan and southwestern Manitoba. Besant pottery at the Garratt site near Moose Jaw, Saskatchewan, has been dated at 1,990 B.P. (about 40 B.C.) making it the earliest pottery—and the earliest Besant site—yet recorded anywhere on the northern plains (Dyck, 1983). Admittedly, at all these Canadian sites, the pottery finds are minimal—at best a few sherds. Greater quantities occur in sites south of the United States border, particularly in the Dakotas, and here archaeologists have pieced together enough sections of individual pots to discover the shapes and certain other characteristics of Besant pottery. It was found to have been made by lump modelling not coiling (no North American potters ever took advantage of a wheel) and was shaped into a neck-less coconut (conoidal) form using a cord-wrapped or grooved paddle against some kind of an anvil. The walls are thick and typically decorated with impressions of cord or textiles with a single row of punctates or indentations below the rim (Dyck, 1983; Syms, 1977b).

Archaeologists find pottery very useful in their investigations into past lives, though intact pots are very seldom found and clues must be painstakingly pieced together from broken sherds. Once clay has been fired it becomes very hard and will last almost forever in the earth where it provides valuable evidence for dating. The intense heat of firing releases all the energy in the form of light, or thermo-luminescence (known as TL), that the minerals in the clay (like minerals everywhere) had previously stored up. Straight from the kiln, pottery will give a TL reading of zero. But bombardment by natural radiation begins again immediately the item is cool and the amount of TL present today, calibrated against the known radiation bombardment rate for the area where it was found, will determine its approximate manufacturing date. A relatively new procedure, this method of dating can also be used on other mineral items that have been heated, including clay bricks and fire-cracked rocks used in boiling pits.

Unlike stone, clay is a plastic medium and can be manipulated until the potter has satisfied some personal or cultural standards of perfection. Pottery experts examine such things as type and amount of materials used to temper the clay, manufacturing method, shape, size, thickness, surface treatment, decorative motifs, and firing procedures and temperatures. These variables, which change in time and between groups, make pottery a valuable indicator of temporal and cultural relationships. In these respects, prehistoric pottery is far more useful than stone projectile points which were made to satisfy purely functional requirements and offered little avenue for individual creativity.

It is interesting that primitive pottery throughout the world is seldom plain. Everywhere it is textured, patterned with incised lines and figures, pinched, crimped, embossed and painted. In the American southwest, in Mexico and South America, prehistoric potters painted on their ware realistic life scenes

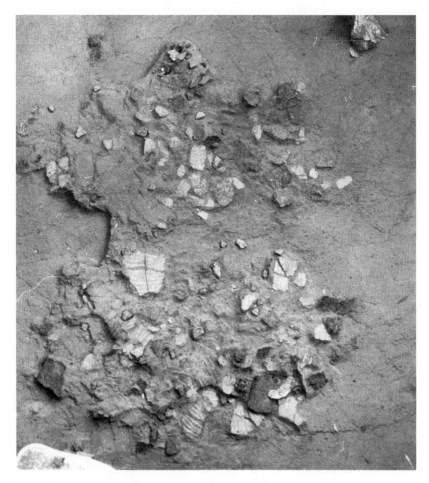

Potsherds as excavators found them at the Sjovold site, north of Moose Jaw, Saskatchewan. Archaeological detective work showed they were once part of a very large coconut-shaped pot about 60 cm tall, dating from the Avonlea period around 1,400 years ago. Courtesy of the Saskatchewan Museum of Natural History.

of people, events, plants and animals—the ancient world, often in vivid detail, made permanent by fire. Potters of the Canadian grasslands seemingly never discovered techniques for painting and glazing clay but neverthless, prehistoric Plains pottery can still provide clues to several vanished aspects of the people who made it. Much can be learned from surface treatments. In some pots, the wet clay was brushed with grass or reeds. Others bear imprints of basketry or were textured by pressing knotted or woven fabrics onto the surface, making it possible to study the textile technology of the era though the textiles

Drawings of three different kinds of prehistoric pottery found in Alberta illustrate a variety of shapes, surface texture and decorative treatment. After pottery made its appearance among the Plains tribes around 2,000 years ago it is used by archaeologists as a more useful temporal and cultural indicator than stone projectile points. Courtesy of William Byrne.

themselves have long since disintegrated. Experts can detect various types of twined yarns and several different weaving and knotting patterns, including twill and a sort of open netting. The presence of netting suggests that netted bags could have been made as containers; that perhaps nets were used to catch fish or to trap small animals. Early eyewitness accounts of Plains Indian life describe pottery being made inside a fabric mould. The fabric was later removed or burned off during the firing process but the clay impressions provide clear evidence for this method, and of the fabric itself.

At a more sophisticated level of research, pottery can also provide guides to prehistoric social patterns. Anthropologists believe that pottery was women's work and that tribal traditions of shape and pattern were carefully handed down from mother or grandmother to daughter. Pottery styles remain more constant therefore in a matrilocal society where the husband lives with the wife's family, than a patrilocal one where the wife moves in with the husband's family. Studies of decorative variation within a single site compared to that between several sites can be used to indicate the patterns of postmarital residence and the degree of intermarriage between groups (Buchner, 1983a). Any drastic alteration in social structure results in change to the ceramic patterning—a fact that archaeologists find most useful in trying to track such things as environment and lifestyle change, emigration, or population decline through disease or warfare. Admittedly such research projects (such as Deetz, 1965) have mostly studied sedentary peoples but they can be assumed to be valid for nomadic societies, too.

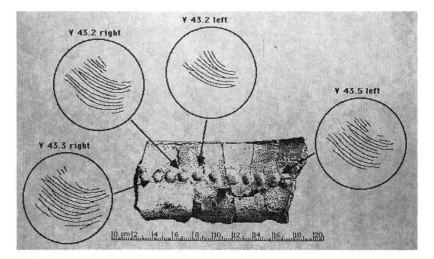

Fingerprints on prehistoric pottery offer exciting new avenues of research into the potters themselves, as well as such things as trade and intra-site settlement. Prints, illuminated under laser light, are 400 years old.

Digitized image of the interior of pottery rim section shows location of partially reconstructed fingerprint impressions. Both Courtesy of T. Gibson, Saskatchewan Research Council and S. Stratton, University of Alberta.

Another exciting avenue of prehistoric pottery research hopes to track down even the individual potters themselves. A common form of clay decoration was indentations, or punctates. These were usually made simply by pressing in with the finger to form either an inward or an outward boss and some of these punctates have been found to contain actual fingerprint impressions of the makers, baked permanently into the clay. At the University of Alberta, Terry Gibson and Sabine Stratton (1987) have been working with prints left on pottery from the ceramic-rich site of Bushfield West in east central Saskatchewan. They isolated and photographed the fingerprints using the latest in laser technology and computer enhancement methods at the RCMP crime laboratory in Edmonton and have started a fingerprint file, not of criminals but of ancient potters. If individual craftswomen can be identified through their prints, the information will be used to try to determine such things as intra-site settlement patterns and whether pottery was traded between sites. When complete, the file will be available as a reference for other pottery researchers in the area. Already the study has shown that at least one vessel was made by a very young woman with small finger tips and clear print ridges (apparently finger surfaces wear down with age) and that punctation was done using the left index finger.

Gibson reports that the Bushfield West site is unusually rich in pottery sherds with fingerprint impressions; at other prairie sites fingerprints are noticeable by their absence, or near absence. Was a single individual at Bushfield responsible for the fingerprinted ware? Or was the local clay particularly susceptible to imprinting? Both these avenues of investigation are currently being explored.

After its introduction to the grasslands during Besant times, pottery became increasingly important to all subsequent Plains peoples for cooking and storage. From a culinary point of view, its invention must have been revolutionary. Archaeologists commonly find potsherds still liberally encrusted with charred food, perhaps the remains of buffalo soup or stew, a dish that would not have been possible without pottery, except by the laborious stone-boiling method of heating water. It is interesting to speculate why the food remains are there. Did the cook burn the soup and throw the pot into the fire in disgust? Did the pot break before or after the soup was eaten? Were pots routinely washed up after meals or simply discarded? There are all sorts of domestic details that can never be known.

The women of the Besant bison hunters' camps made medium sized vessels about thirty-eight centimetres high using clays obtained locally from river banks and coulees. They mixed the clay with various types of crushed rock, sand or shells. This "temper" helped to minimize cracking in the clay during initial air drying and the later firing process. Laboratory analysis of the temper type and proportions can help to distinguish sherds belonging to one pot from those of another—very useful when technicians try to fit the jig-saw pieces together—and also reveal how the pots were fired. On the northern plains, there is little evidence of kilns; most firing was done at relatively low temperatures in an open hearth with the vessels covered with mounds of hot ashes.

While pottery fits many pieces into the puzzle of prehistoric plains lifeways, it also poses some tricky questions. Some Besant and Avonlea sites contain a little pottery, some a lot, and others none at all. Are the aceramic sites simply earlier, representing the cultures before they acquired pottery? Are the varying amounts attributable to different types of site? Pottery would be less useful and therefore less likely to be found at a kill site than in a camp or food processing site. Do sites with few sherds indicate that pottery was a scarce trade item, not manufactured on the spot? Or that the site was occupied only briefly, perhaps overnight? Does the variety of pottery distribution reflect different degrees of wealth or different seasons of occupation? Most archaeologists agree that pottery-making would have been a summer task since river clays would be frozen in winter and pots would take too long to dry.

Pottery attributable to the Avonlea culture appears to come in two basic forms: conoidal like Besant, and globular. The rounded vessels found in Alberta (Byrne, 1973) are surface textured with woven or netted fabric impressions; rims are flat or ridged and below the rims are bands of punctate decorations. In Saskatchewan and Manitoba, Avonlea pottery is generally conoidal in shape and can be net impressed with punctate decorations, spiral channelled, or smoothed (Syms, 1977b; Byrne, 1973).

When archaeologists first excavated the Avonlea type site in southern Saskatchewan (Kehoe and McCorquodale, 1961), they found no pottery that could definitely be assigned to the Avonlea people: for want of evidence, fragments of a large pot found eroding from a wind-deflated patch of field nearby was arbitrarily relegated to a later time period. But in 1984, workers from the Saskatchewan Research Council returned to the site for further investigation prior to construction of a highway realignment through the area. This time they found pottery that was definitely associated with Avonlea and the sherds bore a striking resemblance to those found in the field almost thirty years earlier. Amazingly, they were able to piece together the earlier sherds and form enough of the complete pot to show how it looked and to suggest how it was made and used. Partial reconstruction of a second almost identical pot from the later excavation was also possible.

Results of the pottery analysis show just how much day-to-day detail of domestic life long past can be deduced from simple potsherds (Hanna, 1986).

Reconstructed Avonlea pot from sherds picked up on field surface near Avonlea site in southern Saskatchewan. The pot is huge, 80 cm high and 40 to 50 cm in diameter. Inside were the carbonized remains of an ancient supper. Courtesy of Margaret Hanna, Saskatchewan Museum of Natural History.

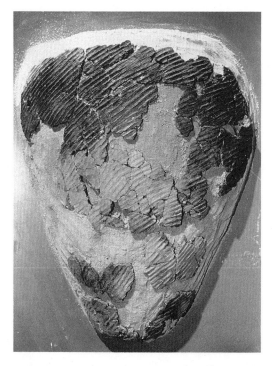

Both of the reconstructed Avonlea pots are conoidal and their surfaces check-textured with a grooved or thong-wrapped paddle. Both are large for Plains pottery, about eighty centimetres high and forty to fifty centimetres in diameter. Archaeologist Margaret Hanna could not tell exactly how they were made but suggests some combination of lump modelling and coiling. A potter herself (she has several times made duplicate Indian pottery using local clays and primitive methods of manufacture and firing) she was also able to criticize the workmanship: the clay had not been well compacted during construction. Looking at the most complete pot, Hanna found that the potter began work from the base up, paddling the exterior surface as she went. As she added clay, its extra weight flattened the still plastic base. The side cracked, an error the potter tried to mend by pinching the edges of the crack together. Microscopic examination of the granite temper showed that the vessel had been fired at a temperature of about 700 degrees Celsius, and from carbonized deposits inside, that it was used at least once to cook a meal. Why did the pot break? Hanna believes that cracks along its base, caused by firing the vessel at too high an initial temperature, eventually split the pot during use.

"Avonlea pottery may not have been the best because of its friable structure," comments Hanna. "However, it was serviceable and was used for cooking at least one meal. Perhaps this should be the important gauge against which we attempt to measure the quality of prehistoric pottery technology."

Besant Dwellings

The first archaeological dig to yield evidence of the Besant culture, a bison jump in southern Saskatchewan, also revealed distinct traces of a new type of dwelling for prehistoric bison hunters. Excavated in 1954 by Boyd Wettlaufer, the Mortlach site contained eight cultural levels in twenty-eight metres of well-stratified deposits dating from 3,400 years ago to bison kills "so recent that quantities of buffalo hair and the outside casing of the horns were still undestroyed by time" (Wettlaufer, 1955). On the same level as the signature projectile points that Wettlaufer called Besant were found a double row of shallow post hole stains in a semicircular shape, the remains of a permanent structure. While the wooden posts themselves had rotted or been removed, the holes had filled with bone and debris, making them clear to see. Several years later, postholes marking a similar complete Besant house were uncovered at the La Roche site in South Dakota. Seven by eight metres in size, this house was described as "a rude hut, probably of pole and brush construction, marked by an oval floor plan and a large fire pit" (Hoffman, 1968).

Evidence for another Besant structure was found at the Ruby site in Wyoming (Frison, 1978). Here the hunters had constructed a very successful killing machine: drive lanes and a large wooden corral built deliberately on a slope so the animals would crowd downhill. The corral's posthole patterns suggested sturdy fence construction very similar to today's. Beside the final drive lane, Frison uncovered the postholes of a bi-pointed structure some thirteen metres long by five metres wide formed by two intersecting arcs. The building was divided in half by a central dividing wall and eight male bison skulls had been positioned around its southern end. The structure was not a dwelling—there were no signs of hearths or domestic activity—and several unusual aspects, including small holes stuffed with bison vertebrae, suggested to Frison that it was religious architecture, perhaps a place where the tribal medicine man or shaman called the bison into the trap.

Despite the above evidence for different house forms, it seems that most people of the Besant culture used portable hide shelters. Throughout the grasslands, excavations at surface tipi ring sites have usually been disappointing, almost barren of artifacts, features or other signs of the people who once lived there. (A feature is anything apparently manmade that is not a dwelling or an artifact, for example, a hearth, a pile of bones, a pit, a stone cairn.) But the cluster of eighteen stone circles on the high lip of the prairie overlooking Ross Creek at the southeastern edge of Medicine Hat, Alberta, is a surprising

Excavation of tipi ring at the Ross Glen site, Alberta, showed the perimeter stones heaped into clusters probably around the tipi poles, indicating a time when the occupants had rolled up the bottom of the tipi cover to permit air to circulate. Courtesy of the Archaeological Survey of Alberta.

exception. Test-excavated in 1981 when the tipi rings were found to be in the way of a new housing subdivision, the Ross Glen site yielded generous quantities of cultural material, including tools and lithic debris, heaps of fire-broken rock, pottery sherds and forty-two well-preserved features. The richness of the site, archaeologist Michael Quigg suggests, makes this one of the most significant stone circle sites in all the northern plains. Excavation revealed not only details of general Besant lifestyles but also "significant social, cultural and individual preferences of the occupants" (Quigg, 1986).

Sixteen of the tipi rings were found to be contemporaneous and to date from around A.D. 500 (The two others, more shallowly buried, were considered to be later.) Their arrangement into two discrete groups suggested to Quigg that two separate Besant bands, a minimum of 100 people, had camped here most likely in the fall for a communal hunt. While only a meagre amount of bison bone was found (left lying on the surface, it had probably been scavenged or decayed), there was ample evidence that considerable meat and hide processing had taken place and that the people had stayed for a fair length of time. In and around the circles were large refuse heaps, piles of fire-broken rock, many small hearths, some with related postholes suggesting that hides

117

had been smoked there, and heaps of lithic debris from tool manufacture and sharpening. The locations of the finds showed that the families maintained specific activity areas, both inside and outside their lodges.

The Besant rings themselves ranged in diameter from about three to eight metres, a large disparity that Quigg thinks may reflect different social status and wealth within the groups. Four had small central postholes for the tent pegs known to have been used in historic times to tie down the tipi, particularly in windy situations. In two of the rings, the perimeter stones occurred in clusters, signs that the occupants had rolled up the bottom edges of the tents for air circulation. If, as seems likely, the displaced stones had been piled up around the tipi poles, then both tents would have had about nineteen poles.

Inside one tipi ring, directly associated with Besant artifacts, were found thirty-seven clay sherds, probably from a single vessel—the first Besant pottery to be positively identified in Alberta. The finding of pottery in only one ring prompted Quigg to ask the following questions: Does it imply elevated social status or wealth? Would the vessel have been a trade item or was it made by its owner? Did only a few Besant people know about and use ceramics? In archaeology the questions never end.

Comparisons of Besant tipi rings with those of other Plains' cultures has revealed an interesting sidelight: Besant rings, while they vary considerably in individual size, are on average far larger than others, more than six metres in diameter (at Ross Glen, the mean size was 6.4 metres) compared to a general average of 4.6 metres. What this means is ambiguous. Tipi size is generally thought to reflect the size of the family living in it. The larger tipis of Besant could indicate that they had larger families, that more than one family commonly lived together, or simply that they were very successful hunters, had hides to spare and chose to build extra large dwellings. On the other hand, the difference may only exist archaeologically: when the Besant people packed up camp, perhaps they had a way of removing the tipi that displaced the rocks more widely, leaving larger rings (Finnigan & Johnson, 1984).

Echoes of the South

A few Besant sites in Canada, scattered broadly from the aspen parklands of central Alberta to southwestern Manitoba, contain certain very different traits which seem to be strong echoes from people living along the Missouri River in the Dakotas. These traits include a small but definite difference in point style, a strong reliance on imported Knife River flint and dramatic variation in burial custom. This has prompted yet another archaeological debate. Some say these traits were physically brought north from the Missouri region by people of a different culture known as Sonota (Syms, 1977a; Neuman, 1975) while others maintain that they are merely regional cultural variations of Besant (Reeves, 1983b; Dyck, 1983). If the latter is true, as Alberta Plains archaeologist Rod Vickers has said (1986), then the Muhlbach Besant pound site near Stettler, Alberta, which shows an overwhelming preponderance of Knife River flint yet is a thousand kilometres distant from the quarries, "represents a Sonota subphase well removed from its Middle Missouri home." While not ascribing to the immigrant theory, Vickers neverthless believes that the point variation and strong lithic preference require explanation.

Perhaps the most intriguing of the Sonota traits is the burial tradition. After exposure on aerial platforms after the custom of most Plains nomads, the Sonota dead were interred in mass graves, often as many as fifty together, in subterranean log-covered chambers under mounds of earth. The mounds today are low circular domes of earth ranging in size from seventeen to thirty metres in diameter but only half to two metres high. With the burials are found ornaments of bone, West Coast marine and freshwater shells, rolled copper and native ores, the jawbones and canine teeth of grizzly bear, human palates and mandibles and quantities of projectile points and tools made from Knife River flint and Yellowstone obsidian. Hunks of red and yellow ochre and bison skulls reflect religious ceremonies—and the importance of the bison to these hunters (Neuman, 1977). The Sonota mounds seem to occur only in North and South Dakota, but as the burial trait is the only one missing from Besant/Sonota occurrences on the Canadian plains, there is still a possibility that mounds may yet be found here.

Avonlea: Hunters Nonpareil

The Avonlea hunters with their tiny, exquisitely crafted arrow points, shared the same lifestyle and environment and lived at about the same time as people of the Besant culture, from about A.D. 200 to A.D. 800, but since far fewer of their sites have been found it seems they were less numerous. Originally their culture seemed to be concentrated in the grasslands of southern Saskatchewan and Alberta but recent new evidence has shown they also ranged in eastern British Columbia and north in the parklands and mixed forests of the prairie provinces. All these peripheral sites tend to be later than the grasslands sites, suggesting an expansion or, more likely in view of their reputedly small population, displacement (Klimko, 1985).

Most Avonlea sites excavated in Canada are bison jumps and pounds. One reason for this could be archaeological visibility: often the thick tell-tale scatter of bison bones are revealed by natural erosion while other types of sites remain buried. The kill sites all show typical Avonlea attributes: good social organization and superb utilization of natural topography for the stampeding of herds of

119

bison over cliffs or into pounds for mass slaughter. Good killing sites were used over and over again. At the classic Head-Smashed-In jump in Alberta's Porcupine Hills the Avonlea people regularly drove bison over the cliffs for more than 600 years, piling up huge beds of dismembered carcasses (Reeves, 1978b, 1983a). Over the years, nothing seemed to change in their killing techniques or their success rate except for one thing: they began to burn the bone deposits, perhaps in an effort to delay the massive build up of debris below the cliffs which would effectively reduce the height of the drop—and the efficiency of the jump—or to clear away the stench of putrefaction. Many layers of Avonlea era bones are charred and sometimes completely reduced to ash. The bone beds contain quantities of the arrowheads used in the kill and many of them are in perfect condition, still sharp and unbroken. Was it easier to make new arrowheads than to retrieve the used ones?

Another classic Avonlea bison kill is Gull Lake on an escarpment of the Missouri Coteau between the Cypress and the Great Sand Hills of southwestern Saskatchewan. Here Avonlea hunters rounded up bison grazing in the knob-and kettle-plateau country to the south and drove them over an exposure of shale bedrock into a pound built at the bottom of a deep coulee. The first communal drive took place about A.D. 200. Archaeologists uncovered six Avonlea bone layers, each separated from the other by a layer of sterile earth from the continually slumping coulee wall, and each underlain by a burnt layer from site clean-up. A total of 133 Avonlea arrowheads were recovered from the two metres of bone deposits (Kehoe, 1973).

How could bison be killed en masse if there were no cliffs for a jump and no wood with which to build a pound? The Ramillies site in the relatively flat arid grasslands of southeastern Alberta shows that the Avonlea people had other methods up their sleeves. The site was discovered when archaeological survey crews found and followed a series of stone drive lane cairns to a small natural depression, about four by eight metres in size, on the edge of a large deep coulee. Excavations by John Brumley (1976) showed that Avonlea people had used this basin as a pound, building not a fence but an earth and rock wall along the coulee edge to confine the animals. The pound itself contained few bones or projectile points and at first this was a puzzle. Later, Brumley discovered that the hunters had cleaned out the basin after each use and had thrown the debris over the pound wall to land on the slope below. If this had not been done, then the depression would have quickly filled up with bones, ruining it for future use. The pound depression could hold, at best, twenty to thirty animals at a time. Brumley wondered why the Avonlea people would have spent so much time and effort to build the earth containment wall and the long drive lanes for what was, essentially, a very small trap. But it must

The eroded rocks which huddle beside the Milk River give Writing-on-Stone park an eerie beauty. Prehistoric Indians revered the site and came here for vision quests. Courtesy of Jack Bryan.

Peigan tipis at the 1989 Head-Smashed-In Pow wow. The designs are traditional but modern canvas has replaced bison hides. Courtesy of the author.

The jump cliffs at Head-Smashed-In Buffalo Jump in Alberta. The sandstone escarpment tops the southeastern edge of the Porcupine Hills. Courtesy of the author.

Rare primary burial from the Gray site in Saskatchewan, a graveyard used for more than 2,000 years by people of the Oxbow culture. Courtesy of J.F.V. Millar.

Probably the best preserved of the Manitoba mounds, this one at Westbourne, now tufted with trees, was originally in the shape of a long-tailed muskrat. It has not yet been scientifically excavated. Courtesy of the author.

The medicine wheel atop Moose Mountain in Saskatchewan was built between 2,500 and 3,000 years ago. Courtesy of the author.

have been a successful one for it was used again and again for several hundred years, both by Avonlea and the people who came afterwards.

Campsites of the Avonlea people seem rare, at least few have been found and investigated to provide insights into lifestyles. The Balzac site on Nose Creek north of Calgary, Alberta, considered one of the best, is deeply stratified, another rarity for the wind-swept western plains. Here, periodic flood deposits not only regularly buried the site but separated the different periods of occupation. Excavations showed the Avonlea camp had been occupied from winter to spring and that extensive butchering and meat processing had taken place there. On the Avonlea living floors, occupied between A.D. 550 and A.D. 750, different kinds of artifacts were distributed by area. The pottery was all in one excavated block, the fleshing tools in another, a separation that seemed to continue over time. This suggested to archaeologist Tom Head that specific parts of the site had been set aside for different domestic activities. Among the interesting items found here were cut beaver incisor teeth (they were used as chisels in the forests of the north and east) and the lower jaws of badgers, also probable tools (Head, 1985).

The Fishermen

Most Canadian Plains sites are rich repositories of butchered bison bones; there are also the bones of deer, antelope and a few smaller mammals, but the sheer volume of bison is undeniable proof that bison meat was the mainstay of all the Plains peoples. There are virtually no grinding stones for the processing of grains or seeds, and fish bones are rare. It was primarily a hunting economy. However, one plains site shows that, at least seasonally, some grassland residents explored a different subsistence strategy. In the valley of the Qu'Appelle River, a large glacial spillway that has carved a deep trench three kilometres wide and 400 kilometres long through the prairies of southern Saskatchewan, the ponding of the river behind alluvial fans has created a string of long freshwater lakes and extensive marshes. Beside one of the lakes, archaeologist Brian Smith excavated a campsite (known as the Lebret site) that had been occupied regularly for the past 3,000 years.

Amazingly, at all the different occupation levels, he found very few bison remains but fish bones in abundance. The Avonlea level, for example, contained only scraps of bison bone but nearly 4,000 fish bones, the remains of pike, walleye, perch and whitefish. Also found were many stone projectile points that seemed to have broken during manufacture, well-used bone fleshers and awls, and other bone artifacts. From these clues, Smith reasoned that a small regional band had camped at the site in early spring to catch fish as they swam upriver to spawn, perhaps building weirs and using spears and nets. While they waited for the grass to green and for the bison to venture out again onto the grasslands, the men spent their time manufacturing spear and arrow points while the women worked hides. Fish provided valuable protein during the months when their winter supplies of preserved meat and pemmican had likely run out (Smith, M.A. thesis, The University of Saskatchewan.)

The End of Avonlea/Besant

While Avonlea was a long-lived culture, its distinctive style of arrowhead eventually faded away and by about A.D. 800 it began to be replaced by different forms of side-notched point. These later arrowheads became standard throughout the grasslands and lasted, without significant change, for more than a thousand years, until the bison and the indigenous Plains way of life were gone. The new type of projectile point is known in Alberta as Old Women's from the type site but in Saskatchewan as Late Side-Notched, sometimes divided sequentially into Prairie and Plains Side-Notched. To complicate things, several cultural complexes within the era of the side-notched point are distinguished in Manitoba and parts of Saskatchewan mainly on the basis of ceramic variations. As you can see, from here on even the nomenclature becomes complex.

Not surprisingly, archaeologists cannot decide what happened to Avonlea and Besant, nor where the Late Side-Notched tradition came from. The latest theory seems to be that the new culture owes it existence, in part, to both former traditions, perhaps Besant evolving into Prairie Side-Notched and Avonlea into Plains. Certainly there are distinct differences between the two subtypes, both in workmanship and notching. The Prairie notches are always very close to the base, sometimes even touching it, while the Plains notches are higher up. The Plains is also more skillfully made, its well-balanced beauty and smaller, more regular flakes strongly reminiscent of Avonlea, as several archaeologists have noted (Kehoe, 1966; Dyck, 1983). Ian Dyck sees affinities between Prairie Side-Notched points and those from the Eastern Woodlands, and sees the Plains type as typical of those used in the Middle Missouri.

To confound the issue, points of both Avonlea and Old Women's cultures appear to be contemporary in some Plains archaeological sites. One of these is Estuary Pound in southwestern Saskatchewan, a trap at the head of a large riverside coulee that was used at least three times by Avonlea and Old Women's hunters. (It is not clear whether Prairie or Plains Side-Notched points, or both, were involved.) Archaeologist Gary Adams found here that a series of postholes marking the north edge of the pound were stuffed longitudinally with bones thought to be supports for the corral posts. He also found a semicircle of postholes that suggested a separate structure, probably a shaman's shed similar

Assortment of Old Women's points excavated from Head-Smashed-In Buffalo Jump, Alberta. Courtesy of the Archaeological Survey of Alberta.

to the Besant example at Ruby and placed in an identical position next to the pound entrance. But the interesting thing from the point of view of cultural chronology is that in the earlier levels Avonlea and Old Women's points are clearly mixed yet contemporary, while 100 years later, all the points are Old Women's. Does this suggest a melding of two different cultures or one culture changing? A very similar scenario is found at the Bakken-Wright jump site on the Frenchman River south of Estuary Pound. Here, sandwiched between a pure Avonlea and pure Old Women's are three occupation levels where the cultures appear to mix (Adams, 1977).

Until about A.D. 800, the cultural history of the grasslands of the three prairie provinces remains remarkably uniform. The influx of different peoples and influences from the west and the east seemed to affect them equally. All the prehistoric peoples of the Plains were bison hunters, tied to the movements of the herds and disciplined by the harsh weather and the limited resources. After A.D. 800, however, the eastern edges of the plains—eastern Saskatchewan and southwestern Manitoba—diverge from the mainstream because of strong southern influences. Here there was an explosion of new ideas, new peoples, new trading patterns, perhaps even new lifestyles. So A.D. 800 marks a kind of watershed in the human history of the Canadian Plains: the first cultural rift between east and west.

SEVEN

The Western
Way of Life

I n the summer of 1952, a torrential rainstorm over Alberta's Porcupine
Hills resulted in a flash flood which tore through Squaw Coulee northwest of the village of Cayley, ripping out a deep gulley and "leaving
a white sheet of bones on the meadow below" (Forbis, 1962). Archaeologists
were alerted to examine and protect the site and excavation of the buffalo
jump began six years later. The jump is noteworthy for a number of reasons.
It is one of the few archaeological sites on the Canadian plains that is identified in Indian folk history; it is the type site of the Old Women's cultural
complex; and from its multi-layered deposits and rich treasure trove of projectile points archaeologist Richard Forbis, then of the Glenbow Foundation in Calgary, established a typological sequence of side-notched point
changes for the northwestern plains that has remained unchallenged.

There are several versions of the Blackfoot legend but all of them identify a location in Squaw Coulee. The humourous story of the first marriage
between men and women involves a character called Napi or Old Man who
plays a large part in Blackfoot mythology; notorious for his trickery, he was
also revered as the creator of many things. (Alberta's Oldman River is named
for him.) The events, as related to Glenbow archivist Hugh Dempsey by an
aged member of the Blood tribe, are told like this:

"In the early days of the world the men and the women used to travel
in separate camps. The men had their chief and the women had theirs. One
day Napi called the men together and said: "Why should we live apart from
the women? If we all live together, then we can spend our time hunting and
going to war, while the women can do the cooking and tanning of hides.

"The men thought this was a good idea so Napi went in search of the
women. He found them near the foothills where they all lived in a large camp.
Nearby they had a buffalo jump which was their main source of food. This
was the Women's Buffalo Jump near Cayley.

"Napi met the leader of the women and told her the plan. The woman chief agreed and asked Napi to bring the men to her camp so that each woman could choose a man to be her partner. Napi returned to the men and told them the news. He had noticed many beautiful women at the camp and made plans to get the best one for himself. When the men moved to the Women's Buffalo Jump, Napi stole from the camp and, dressing himself in women's clothes, he went to the women's camp and decided which woman was the most beautiful.

"Before he had time to return to the men, they arrived and the women began to choose their partners. The woman of Napi's choice saw a man she liked but Napi intercepted her and told her to choose him. The woman, however, wanted the other man and bypassed Napi in favour of him.

"Napi then went to the next most beautiful woman and the same thing happened. Finally, when all the choosing had been done, Napi was the only one without a woman. In anger he went to the buffalo jump and changed himself into a pine tree. And there he stood, alone, for many, many years."

John Yellow Horn, a chief of the local Peigan band, later recalled that a pine tree was growing at the site when he passed it in 1900 (Forbis, 1962).

Old Women's Buffalo Jump (the term old applies to the jump, not the women, as Forbis has noted) is also recorded in white people's history: it was one of a list of Blackfoot place names prepared by geologist George Dawson for the Geological Survey of Canada in 1881. It is rare that folk mythology, history and archaeology converge in a single spot.

When it was excavated, the jump site was found to contain bone beds some seven metres deep and twenty-nine different cultural layers. These could be divided into two distinct chronologies: the ones at the bottom with spear or atlatl points and the ones at the top with arrow points. The change in technology appeared to take place around A.D. 600. After that date, the side-notched arrow points which Forbis called Old Women's continued through many different levels until the jump was abandoned around A.D. 1600. During these thousand years, however, Forbis found that the style of the points gradually changed, and he was able to divide them into seven distinct sub-types representing seven different time periods, an exercise known to archaeologists as seriation. Application of Forbis's typology/chronology sequence has since been tested and found valid at other Alberta sites and serves to delineate fine slices of time within the Old Women's cultural sequence.

Another site important to the story of Plains archaeology also lies at the foot of the Porcupine Hills just a few kilometres to the south of the buffalo jump. Used by prehistoric people for more than 2,000 years, the Morkin camp-site was found to be unusually rich in potsherds. Here, archaeologist William

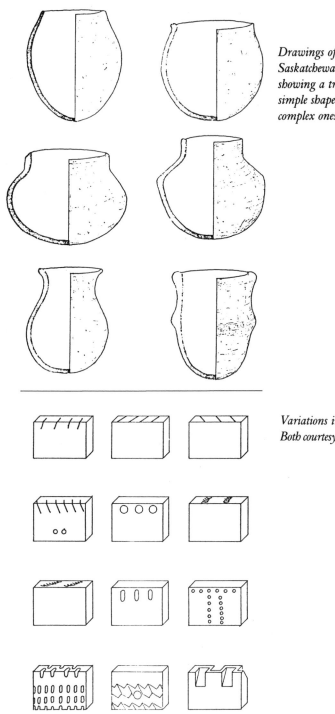

Drawings of reconstructed Saskatchewan Basin pots, showing a transition from simple shapes to more complex ones.

Variations in rim decorations. Both courtesy of William Byrne.

Byrne excavated lithics (stone points) diagnostic of Besant, Avonlea and Old Women's cultures and nearly 4,000 pieces of clay pottery, more than half of which, representing a minimum of seventy-one individual vessels, were suitable for analysis. Using these sherds and another 3,200 sherds (118 pots) from eighteen other Alberta sites, he conducted the first major study of prehistoric Alberta ceramics (Byrne, 1973). On the basis of several distinct attributes, he divided the pottery into two kinds: a local, long-lived tradition which he called the Saskatchewan Basin Complex and split into two variants, Early (Avonlea) and Late (Old Women's), and a subsequent intrusive Cluny complex. No pottery was found that could be directly related to Besant.

Throughout its 1,200 year tradition, Saskatchewan Basin pottery was found to change substantially in form, finish and decoration. Earlier pots tended to be of both globular and coconut shape, their surfaces textured by fabric or net impressions and with rich decorations in the form of punctate rows and finger pinching. As time went on, shapes gradually became more complex, with narrow necks and shoulders, flared rims and thickened lips. More pots had their surfaces smoothed over before firing and there was generally less decoration, although a new type, bands of short vertical incisions, made its appearance. Later still, vessels began to show signs of paddling by cord-wrapped implements.

However, Byrne concluded that these modifications did not represent major cultural change but merely continuous development within a single, technologically stable ceramic industry which seemed to be linked to the pottery traditions of the southeastern Manitoba Woodlands. He suggested that the design traits, perhaps even the idea of pottery-making itself, filtered west from this origin and that the actual passing over of ideas may have taken place in southern Saskatchewan since much of the pottery found there is typologically transitional.

With all this emphasis on pottery changes, one interesting human detail of the Morkin site tends to be overlooked. On one packed earth floor, near fire hearths and upright bison bone tent pegs, Byrne found several lenses—they had once been small piles—of light grey clay, seemingly prepared and ready for the potter's use, proof indeed that pottery was made in Alberta, not imported. Evidence of pottery manufacturing also came to light at the Mortlach site in Saskatchewan (Wettlaufer, 1955). Here was found a rough quartzite chopper with a quantity of clay baked onto one side. Archaeologist Boyd Wettlaufer believed that it had been used to break up and work the potter's material. Afterwards, still daubed with clay, it fell into the campfire where evidence of its use was preserved. "Seldom do we have such an opportunity to reconstruct the actions of an individual living in this remote time period," said Wettlaufer.

The findings of Forbis and Byrne both seem to indicate a long period of stability for the inhabitants of the western plains of Canada. The climate changed: a thousand years ago, the grasslands were warmer and moister than today; six hundred years ago there was a great drought which lasted for nearly two centuries, and following this a period of cool summers and cold autumns (Dyck, 1983). But in the west, neither the climatic variations nor the cultural turmoil in the east seemed to have affected the lives of the western bison hunters to any great extent. They changed their arrow points and their pottery only to vary the style; there were apparently no technological innovations. After 11,000 years of occupation, the bison hunters were supremely well adapted to life on the harsh, demanding plains.

Archaeological sites examined so far in this investigation have provided clues only to the surface lives of the Plains nomads. From this fragmentary evidence, we think we know how and where they lived, how and where and what they killed, even how they cooked and preserved their meat. We know they worked leather for shelter and clothing, made beads and hung pierced shells and teeth for adornment and played at games of chance. We can monitor their technological developments, from thrusting spear to atlatl to bow and arrow and from stone boiling pit to pottery. But their inner or spiritual lives remain closed to us. From burial sites, we glimpse only a few of their thoughts about death and the afterlife, and from the stone constructions they left scattered on prairie prominences we can only infer their efforts to understand the workings of the sky and the seasons. However, archaeological sites that date from the Late Side-Notched or Old Women's period provide not only substantiation of previous evidence but further clues to the intangibles of thought, belief and even social status. And all these help to clear the hazy pictures of the first prairie peoples in the years before the impact of the European presence in North America.

Intimate Portraits

One of the most electrifying places in all the prairie provinces is Writing-on-Stone provincial park in southwestern Alberta. Here torrents of glacial outwash from melting mountain glaciers have sliced into the ancient sedimentary bedrock of the ancestral Milk River valley to form a deep, wide canyon. Thousands of years of wind and water erosion have worked the layered sandstone of the canyon sides into a wilderness of fantastic pinnacles and arches, turrets, capped hoodoos and caves: an eerily beautiful landscape sculptured from stone the warm colour of honey and overlooked by the three conical points of Montana's Sweetgrass Hills which spear the southern horizon. Through this beautiful labyrinth, the river, today as meek as its name, meanders gently through groves of cottonwoods on a wide valley floor. The scenery alone is enough to make this a very special and exciting place.

If you were there when the alchemy of an October sunset turns the contorted stone to gold, and a hawk, alone in the immense and darkening sky, cries warning above the sibilant grass, then you could not escape its aura of strange sanctity. Moonrise above the rocks and the fast-falling blackness of night bring feelings of irrational unease, almost of fear, despite the unearthly beauty of the place. This powerful and dramatic landscape must have had a deep effect on the native peoples of the plains, for here it seems they tried to communicate with the spirit world by drawing pictures on the cliff faces. Some of these figures stand alone; others are massed into panels containing hundreds of individual motifs and several complete and detailed life scenes— the prehistoric world, seen through ancient eyes.

At first glance, the simple, almost childish representations of men and animals seem easily dismissed, an alien iconography that is charming, but incomprehensible. Yet these pictures, more than anything else, can draw us closer to past realities, to changing times and changing peoples. Above all, they document, sometimes with startling clarity, confrontation with the culture that ultimately destroyed theirs, bridging the period between prehistory and history, from the bow and arrow to the horse and gun.

The Milk River cliffs contain the largest single concentration of rock art in all of Canada, much of it protected within the boundaries of Writing-on-Stone provincial park, so called because early settlers believed the motifs to be a form of primitive picture writing. The site has been known since the turn of the century and at that time the local Blackfoot and Peigan Indians, who shunned the place, said the pictures were of supernatural origin, although mounted police scout Jerry Potts, himself half Indian, seemed to think that most of them were simply war records.

Archaeologists believe that the protected river valley with its curious rock formations was a sacred location reserved for the vision quest, a spiritual event which traditionally entailed a solitary visit to an isolated place. Here a young man would stay for several days and nights, fasting and praying, hoping to encounter the world of mysteries. If a spirit guide made itself known to him and answered his requests, when the vision was over, he often recorded the symbols of the spirit's message on the rocks: dreams turned to stone to outlast the dreamer. The weird hoodoo fields and high cliffs of the Milk River certainly provide the right atmosphere for such an experience.

Archaeological investigations at Writing-on-Stone (Brink, 1979) seem to verify the vision quest theory, for they reveal a pattern of many very brief occupations. Even in prime riverside camping areas, the sites found were

Two of the petroglyphs at Writing-on-Stone Provincial Park, Alberta. Battle scene with both shield-bodied and V-necked warriors. Figures (left centre) have been interpreted as a woman giving birth and an attendant midwife.

Deeply incised man, three horses and a tipi. Note incurved hoofs, perhaps an indication that the horses were shod. Both courtesy of Jack Bryan.

Excavations at the foot of the glyph cliffs at Writing-on-Stone gave a picture of many brief visitations during the past 3,000 years, exactly what one would expect of a vision quest site. Some of the artists' tools, sharpened bones showing signs of sandstone abrasion, were found. Courtesy of the Archaeological Survey of Alberta.

described as visitations rather than encampments—a shallow hearth, a few scattered artifacts. From excavations directly beneath the picture cliffs searchers even found some of the artists' tools, including three sharpened bones showing signs of use on a hard, abrasive surface, likely the sandstone above. (More than ninety percent of the glyphs at Writing-on-Stone are incised petroglyphs rather than painted pictographs.) Carbon 14 dates from several locations showed that the area had been visited, presumably for religious and artistic purposes, throughout the past 3,000 years.

While the primary purpose of many of the drawings may have been to record spiritual experiences, the thousands of individual motifs that make up the Writing-on-Stone anthology also give vivid glimpses of life on the plains, from pedestrian days through to the first horses and guns of the trading era, then to the wagons and forts of the white settlement period. Much of what is portrayed validates and embellishes the findings of the archaeologists; here are Indian tipis, arranged in camp circles; here are bows and arrows (there are no atlatls), spears and clubs; the animals they hunted, the enemies they slew, the tribal battles they fought. Then, about A.D. 1740, the horse arrives on the plains, at first awkwardly drawn—the rider on its back even more awkward—as if the artist had never himself seen the strange new beast, let alone ridden one. Later, drawn with surer strokes, whole herds of horses ride into the pictures, with bridles and saddles—and cattlemen's brands on their flanks. And everywhere there are the people themselves, seven hundred of them, drawn in several different ways. Some hide their torsos behind large round shields; others have rectangular bodies and V-necks; others have bodies and legs in the shape of an X.

Careful examination of this rock portfolio reveals two distinct art styles which have been attributed to different periods of time and to separate peoples. James Keyser, who has done the most exhaustive studies of the Milk River glyphs (1977), identifies the earlier style as Ceremonial. Here, the human forms are all either shield-bodied or V-necked and the animals are boat-shaped, conventions that probably span the period between A.D. 500 and A.D. 1740, from the introduction of the bow and arrow to the first horses, though he places the introduction of the "shield-bearing warrior" motif more specifically at around A.D. 1300. The Ceremonial art, typical of vision quest records throughout the Northern plains, is carefully drawn on some of the smoothest slabs but with a stiff and stilted hand. There is neither action nor vivacity even in hunting and combat scenes—seemingly the artists were striving for symbolism not realism—although the detailing is rich. The shield-bodies are decorated with many different heraldic emblems; the men themselves wear headdresses of horns and sunbursts and single feathers, their arms and legs sometimes fringed, suggestive of buckskin. Some carry objects that look like rakes, believed to be symbols of supernatural power, and weapons that are not only drawn in great detail but are often grossly oversized, perhaps an indication of magic powers or a kind of primitive wishful thinking. (One weapon unique to Ceremonial style glyphs is the bow-spear, a large bow with a projectile point on one end.) Animal features such as bison humps, deer and antelope horns and hooves are carefully drawn and the X-ray technique fairly common in primitive art sees the depiction of ribs and heartlines on both humans and animals.

During the first half of the eighteenth century, the later years of the Ceremonial artists' use of Writing-on-Stone, the horse made its way north from Spanish settlements in New Mexico. The petroglyphs document its arrival in Canada and establish that it came before the Indians of the Western Plains obtained fur-trade guns from the northeast: ceremonial combat scenes show men on boat-shaped horses fighting with spears and bows and arrows. Other drawings show horses wearing leather armour, a protection known to have

Examples of Ceremonial art, typified by boat-shaped animals and shield-bodied and V-necked humans. Adapted from Keyser, 1977 by the author.

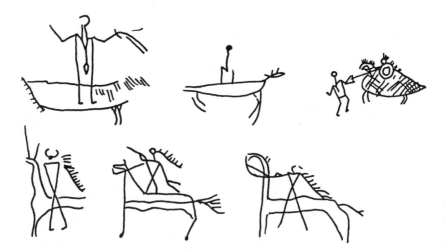

Early drawings of horses are boat-shaped; one wears armour, a Shoshone trait (top). In the later Biographic art style, men have X-shaped bodies and the horses are drawn with more realism (bottom). Adapted from Keyser, 1977 by the author.

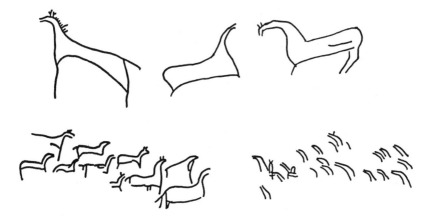

James Keyser saw in these "shorthand" renderings of horses at Writing-on-Stone the beginning of writing. Adapted from Keyser, 1977 by the author.

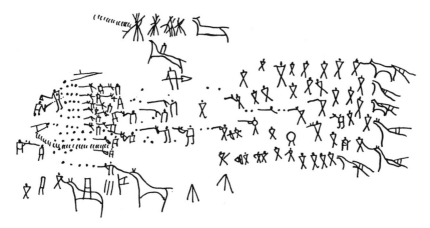

Part of the large battle scene at Writing-on-Stone. Notice the different body styles of the warriors, the use of guns, bows and arrows and an axe. Bullet trajectories are shown by lines of dots. The horses on the right drag travois. Adapted from Keyser, 1977 by the author.

been used by only one Plains tribe, the Shoshone. Because of this, and because several of the characteristic art motifs have been clearly identified with this tribe, James Keyser suggests that the Shoshone used the lands of the Milk River, at least for vision quests, until 1750. Then they moved or were forced away and different people came down to the river to write on the sandstone pages, a people who by this time were already in the grip of cultural change.

Sometimes overwritten on the records of the Shoshone vision quests is a graphically very different kind of art that Keyser calls the Biographic because most of it seems to depict the real, rather than the supernatural world. From an artistic point of view this later art, let loose from the stilted traditions of magic, is freer, more fluid; there is much more action and vitality. Some of the large pictures are so detailed they can be read almost like stories. And one can see, through the use of stylistic conventions and even a kind of shorthand rendering, the beginnings of writing: a herd of horses is represented only by a group of flowing necks, warriors by their guns.

This Biographic Art is distinguished by drawings of people with X-shaped bodies, a convention found elsewhere only in the art of the Eastern Canadian Woodlands, where it dates to early prehistoric times. This seems to suggest either artistic influence from the northeast, or, as Keyser believes, direct immigration from that direction by Blackfoot, Cree and Gros Ventre Indians. Other humans are represented by rectangular bodies, a form common everywhere, and there are many guns and many horses, the latter drawn in an artistically knowledgeable, free-flowing form epitomizing movement and grace.

Some of the large battle scenes are fascinating. In one, a force of seventy-one men armed with flintlock rifles attacks a camp circle of twenty-four tipis. Inside the circle are three defensive pits and a single large tipi, all with men inside, and the ground is strewn with spent bullets. A line of fourteen sharp-shooters, in most cases represented simply by their guns, mounts a sturdy defence, the paths of all the bullet trajectories marked by dots and dashes. In the centre of the action, a man with a hatchet battles with a rifleman. The attackers alone, it seems, possess horses, and several of these are shown pulling travois. Another combat scene, painted in red ochre, is on a smaller scale: Eight men, four of them mounted, fight five pedestrians. Five men have guns, the rest use bows and arrows, a spear and what looks like a sword. Horse tracks indicate the route of the riders from the tipi village where four weaponless figures (captives? women?) stand in a row. In the centre, a horseman spears a fallen rifleman and the man with a sword strikes a rider. Both these battle scenes are thought to date to the mid-1800s because of the numbers of horses and guns.

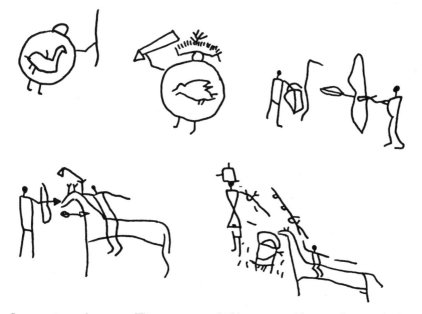

Contrasts in combat scenes. The warriors use shields, spears and bows and arrows (top); Tribesmen have acquired horses, metal axes and guns (bottom). Adapted from Keyser, 1977 by the author.

Another telling scene shows two men hanging from gallows near a rectangular fort. There are other figures nearby, one driving a horse-drawn wagon, and two of them have crosses for heads, the stylistic convention for hats and therefore white men. While most of the pictures at Writing-on-Stone denote male machismo, one glyph has been interpreted as portraying the female act of giving birth. A woman lies with legs open and another kneels before her, arms outstretched to receive the baby whose head is just beginning to emerge.

The Milk River art provides raw data for many studies of change, social as well as technological. James Keyser, for example, uses it to show how the introduction of horses and guns drastically altered both the nature of warfare and the ways of conferring individual social status (Keyser, 1979). Prehistoric combat, heavily armed and armoured behind giant shields, was like most warfare conducted primarily for group economic gain. Individual battle honours were not awarded; social status was achieved solely through the possession of spiritual power acquired during a vision quest. (The emblem of a warrior's spirit helper emblazoned on his shield was believed to protect more than the shield itself.) When the horse arrived on the plains, mounted soldiers at first still carried shields, although logically these became far smaller, and for a while, the purpose of battle was still material advantage.

But the arrival of firearms, which perhaps made killing too easy, changed the essence of Plains Indian warfare. Now involving only small, highly mobile groups of lightly-armed or unarmed men, it became an opportunity for personal glory, not for group economic gain. At Writing-on-Stone there are several depictions of warriors striking better-armed or mounted opponents, or taking away their weapons. In the well-documented Plains exercise of "counting coup," a warrior won the respect of his community through such acts of reckless, and often ridiculous, bravery—typically riding unarmed into an enemy camp to steal a horse or strike an opponent on the cheek—and it is just this type of deed that Keyser says is typical of combat scenes in the Biographic Art era. Status achieved by real deeds of bravery had supplanted the spiritual triumphs of the vision quest (Keyser, 1979).

Writing-on-Stone park acquired its name because of an abiding local belief that the petroglyphs were some form of Indian writing akin to the hieroglyphics of Egypt. James Keyser's continuing studies of rock art on the American Plains have convinced him that this early belief was correct. It is more writing than art, he says, because the content was more important than the aesthetics; the artists were communicating vital aspects of events and their efforts should be considered "brief narrative vignettes rather than static illustrations." To help others read the stories on the rocks, he has compiled a lexicon of artistic conventions along with meanings derived from explained historic period art painted on hides and in the margins of books which he says constitute a sort of Rosetta Stone for rock art. The lexicon provides important clues for recognizing such things as future and past tenses, distances, directions and quantities, as well as the subtle nuances of battle and distinctions between different types of men and horses (Keyser, 1987).

The Milk River glyphs are so numerous and so interesting, a densely-packed palimpsest of prehistoric expression, that other sites tend to be overlooked. Yet rock art is found occasionally elsewhere in the grasslands: on large glacial erratics along the Foothills Belt in Alberta and on rock outcrops such as the one at St. Victor's in Saskatchewan. All are priceless relics of the past but sadly, some have suffered much at the hands of vandals with knives or cans of spray paint.

The Vision Quest

The vision quest, which likely inspired much of this prehistoric art, remained an important part of life well into the historic era and it has been well described, often by the participants themselves. The ancient practice seems recently to have been revived and is said to take place even today, though perhaps it never truly came to a halt (Hughes, 1986). Writing-on-Stone, unquestionably a most

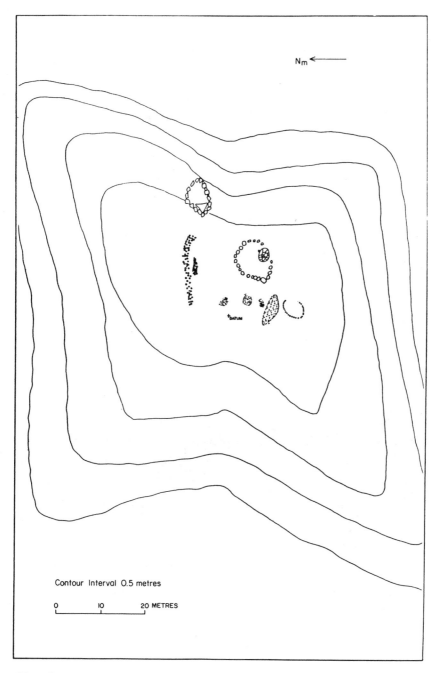

Contour Interval 0.5 metres

0   10   20 METRES

Plan of vision quest on the highest elevation of the southeastern escarpment of Alberta's Porcupine Hills, above Head-Smashed-In Buffalo Jump. Courtesy of the Archaeological Survey of Alberta.

Human and animal figures shown in abstract association are typical vision quest renderings. Adapted from Keyser, 1977 by the author.

Porcupine Vision quest site enjoys a fine view west to the Rocky Mountains. Courtesy of the author.

magnificently illustrated site of many individual religious experiences, is not a typical vision quest location. Found throughout the plains, though not in large numbers, other sites are difficult to authenticate because commonly all that remains is a small oval or semicircle of locally obtained rocks, sometimes with built-up walls to provide some shelter. Most of these are found in high, inaccessible places; there are several in the Rockies and in Montana's Sweetgrass Hills. Elsewhere on the plains they occupy other kinds of exposed situations: a rocky tor, the rim of a river valley, the edge of a coteau. All the known sites are isolated and enjoy splendid views. Johan Dormaar, a research scientist in Lethbridge, has found in fact that all the sites he has visited in southwest Alberta and Montana have views focussed on one of several mountains, including Crownest and Chief mountains, which were believed to be seats of spiritual power. Typically, offerings of material goods, including ribbons, feathers and tobacco, were left at the sites, a practice that sometimes continues today (Conner, 1982; Hughes, 1986).

One of the few vision quest sites that have been studied archaeologically is on the highest point of the same escarpment of the Porcupine Hills as Head-Smashed-In Buffalo Jump. Overlooking to the east the flat plains of southern Alberta and to the west the snow-tipped skyline of the Rockies, the hilltop contains several structures including a deeply buried small stone semicircle open to the east, a larger stone circle with a small cairn, an oval, walled structure with a sandstone slab or pillow at one end, and two linear arrangements of small rocks, like ladders. When Chris Hughes mapped, surveyed and test-excavated the site in the summer of 1984 a length of purple ribbon was found tied around a cobble at the base of the cairn.

Two small test pits yielded little in the way of artifacts but several were recovered from the surface of the site. These included small pieces of bone, seven stone projectile points, many stone flakes and fragments of weathered beer bottle. One of the points was a Late Side-Notched arrowhead and a piece of the stone that had been flaked from it was also found, suggesting that the weapon tip, which had never been hafted for use (its basal edges were not ground smooth) had been sharpened here before it was left, probably as a votive offering. Hughes thought the ribbon at the base of the cairn was also an offering. Excavation inside the large circle revealed two burnt matches, some stone flakes and two empty pop cans.

Hughes' studies showed that the site appeared to contain two different vision quest structures: the walled oval, which seemed large enough for a man to lie down in, his head on the pillow facing east, and the large stone circle. The latter had been cannibalized to build the cairn, perhaps, suggests Hughes, at the same time that the pop cans were buried. The purpose of the small, buried semicircle was not determined.

Detailed mapping and laboratory study revealed that the linear arrangement, first believed to be some kind of an effigy, spelled out the words "Nelson Small Legs," the name of a prominent leader of the American Indian movement who killed himself on the nearby Peigan Reserve to protest the plight of his people. This, says Hughes, suggests that the Porcupine vision quest site also served a memorial function.

At a suspected vision quest site in Saskatchewan, archaeologist David Burley found only one construction, a U-shape 2.5 metres wide with low walls of piled-up rocks. While its location was high and it commanded a 360-degree view over the Souris River plain, at one time it had not been isolated since a cluster of tipi rings lay nearby. The opening of the structure was found to face northeast and its interior had been scooped out into three side-by-side oblong depressions, like giant footprints leading out of the doorway. Burley concluded that the site was likely used for vision quests because all other possibilities could be easily eliminated. The construction was far too small for a fortification which typically held a group of men, though it might conceivably have been a look-out post for the nearby village. And the pits were too shallow to trap eagles. Eagle feathers were prized beyond measure by the Plains Indians and they were not easily obtained. To catch a bird a hunter would go alone to a high and solitary spot and dig a pit to hide himself, pulling brush over the top as camouflage and baiting the trap with a small live animal. Hours or even days later, when an eagle came to snatch the bait the man below would grab it by the legs and wrestle it down. A man could hardly hide in a pit thirty centimetres deep, said Burley, let alone subdue a golden eagle (Burley, 1985)!

Evidence from the Grave

While vision quests provide some insight into one aspect of the Plains Indians' spiritual nature, how they treated their dead reveals another: belief in an afterlife. Did burial traditions change very much on the western plains as the Indian way of life came crashing towards the historic era?

In 1968, chance erosion of a human bone revealed a burial at the foot of the cliffs in Writing-on-Stone park. Excavated almost at once by Ronald Getty, the burial became known as Many Snakes: three rattlesnakes were found here within as many days. The skull of the dead person was missing, believed kicked loose by cattle from the eroding slope, but from the rest of the bones Getty was able to determine that the skeleton was of a man aged between forty and fifty-five years. He had been buried in a flexed position, lying on his right side, with his head to the east. Pathological studies showed the man's teeth to be badly worn and coated with so much tartar that the gums had shrunk, loosening the teeth in their sockets. The man had osteo-arthritis of the lower back, as well as crippling rhumatoid arthritis probably precipitated by an infection of the left leg which was severely incurved. Shortly before his death he had received a blow on his right side heavy enough to crush shoulder blade and ribs, a massive injury that indirectly killed him, although actual cause of death was probably pneumonia.

Buried alongside the body were twenty-four items which Getty called "offerings." These included four bone flakes, an antler hammer, six projectile points and several other stone tools and flakes, plus a single shell bead. Except for the bead, all were items associated with traditional male activities of flint-knapping and hunting. This was an old man by the standards of the time (around A.D. 1600) and a cripple, a burden to his people, yet he was given full primary burial with offerings, a deviation from the norm. Plains nomads of the late prehistoric period customarily left the bodies of their dead exposed to the air to disintegrate. Was it possible, mused Getty, that the buried man had great spiritual power and had been recording a vision on the sacred rocks of Writing-on-Stone? Perhaps he had built a wooden scaffold to reach high up on the rock face. Did the scaffold slip and did he try to save himself by hanging onto the rocks with his arthritic hands? And was he buried here as a mark of respect (Getty, 1971)?

Another unusual burial was located near the former whisky trader's fort called Conrad's Post now on the Blood Indian reserve west of Lethbridge. The three individual graves were well known and had not been robbed: it was believed they belonged to white whisky traders, killed in a skirmish. However, they were later found to lie in the path of a planned highway realignment and they were then excavated by archaeologists. Inside the graves were found not white men but a native woman and two children aged about two and four. The children had been carefully buried, one wrapped in a beaded blanket and one covered by pole and rush matting. Both were accompanied by massive amounts of personal ornaments and other goods. They wore earrings, bracelets of brass, and many-stranded bead necklaces, and both had leather pouches filled with such things as cartridge cases, bullets, wooden spools, glass bottles, pieces of tin cans and other items of European manufacture. The woman, who had died in her early thirties, had been wrapped in a heavy wool blanket and also wore many brass bracelets and rings. It was clear she had died in childbirth because a full-term fetus was still in the birth canal. From manufacturing dates stamped on the rifle cartridges and from preserved fragments of a newspaper, the *Sioux City Daily Journal*, the burials could be dated fairly securely at around 1873.

Aerial view of Ellis medicine wheel, located among thirteen tipi rings on promontory overlooking the South Saskatchewan River. According to John Brumley, this medicine wheel is the remains of a Blackfoot burial lodge.

Archaeologists guess—and it is only a guess—that the woman who died giving birth was the mother of the other two children. They also say, since Indian burials of this era are rare, that white men must have been involved. Was the woman the "wife" of one of the traders, and were the dead children his children? No-one will ever know. The bodies and all the artifacts were reburied on the reserve safe from further encroachment by civilization (Reeves et al., 1984).

Burial in the ground was not the only way that the Plains Indians honoured their dead. Particularly among the Blackfoot, a chief or great warrior was often lain in state inside his tipi, then the tipi was tightly closed and abandoned. Sometimes this "death lodge" was identified by radiating lines of stones, a practice that has confused today's evidence, for what is left on the prairie after the tipi and its contents have gone is not a simple tipi ring but a construction resembling a medicine wheel. Archaeologist John Brumley drew attention to this confusion in his study of the Ellis medicine wheel, one of several inside the Suffield Military Reserve near Medicine Hat (Brumley, 1985). The wheel

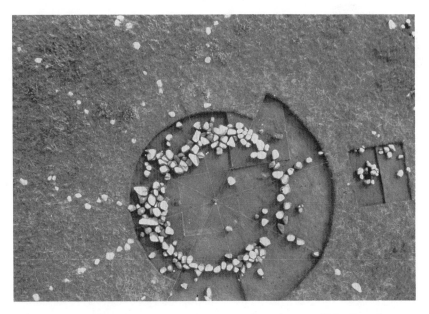

Close-up of Ellis medicine wheel during excavation. Both courtesy of John Brumley.

is located among thirteen ordinary tipi rings on a prairie promontory overlooking the deep valley of the South Saskatchewan River. Excavations inside the wheel's circle uncovered the fragmented bones of an old man and the remains of a sharpened oak stake, painted turquoise blue and driven into the ground in the centre. The bones were as deeply buried as the stones of the surrounding circle, suggesting that they had been placed on the earth at the same time, and they were well preserved. Brumley studied several past ethnographic accounts of burials inside tipis and found "striking and irrefutable similarities" between them and the archaeological evidence from Ellis. He believes that this "medicine wheel"—like sixteen others of a similar design found on the western prairies—was a Blackfoot burial lodge; the bones were those of an honoured chief and owed their well-preserved state to the protection of the lodge cover. The wooden stake had been used to tie down the centre of the tipi.

EIGHT

Infusions

U ntil hit by the shock wave of European influence, the lifestyles of
the nomadic bison hunters on the western plains of Canada remained
basically unaltered for thousands of years. On the eastern fringes,
however, it was a different story. A sudden vibrant flowering of cultures in
the Mississippi/Missouri basin to the south led to tribal displacement and
the sudden infusion into Canada of new peoples, practices and ideas that
shattered the age-old patterns. The impetus for this change was a growing
reliance on the new (to North America) practice of agriculture, a way of life
commonly seen as a necessary step on the path to civilization.

However, contrary to general opinion, the deliberate planting and
harvesting of edible crops offers no immediate benefit to a people reliant on
hunting and gathering. It is far more labour intensive and offers no definite
assurance of a stable food supply, nor of better quality food. Domesticated
crops, removed from their natural habitat and thus altered genetically in ways
often detrimental to their hardiness, can, and still do, fail for a number of
reasons. The total crop failure of a wild species gathered over a large area
of native habitat is far less likely. Nutritionists have found, too, that
domesticated plant foods contain far less protein than wild varieties. Agriculture
does offer the advantage of increased yield: a hectare of cultivated farmland
can produce more food than a hectare of wilderness—but this is hardly
something of immediate concern to small bands of people living in and
off an immense expanse of country. There was no shortage of land. So
how and why did agriculture begin? And why did it take such a hold on the
story of humanity?

Scientists believe it must have started in areas where wild food supplies
were marginal, though it could not have been successful (and therefore
probably would not have begun), in times of drought or scarcity, for a starv-
ing people do not voluntarily set aside stores of seed for future planting. Perhaps
agriculture had something to do with population growth. Hunter-gatherers
had to range over large areas to provide enough food for the survival of the
group. When the group increased in numbers, it would have to forage over

146

far greater areas, spending most of its time travelling—and there are obvious limits to this equation. In primitive societies, most groups simply splintered when they became too big, but agriculture provided another solution: it made it possible to increase the food supply without the need for increased range. Whatever the impetus, it seems that in most of Europe and Asia, mankind turned early to farming for life support, at least on a part-time or seasonal basis. Remains of clearly domesticated species of wheat and barley dating back to 18,000 years ago have been excavated in the Nile Valley (Festinger, 1983).

On the American continent agriculture came far later and it is interesting to ponder why. First, it is believed that the population in prehistoric times was small; and it is certain that the land they occupied was immense. Drastically different ecological zones encouraged various kinds of lifestyles, many of them comfortably self-sufficient without agriculture. The Indians of Canada's West Coast, bottomless larders lapping at their feet, did not need it, and neither did the hunters of the game-rich northern plains who in any case occupied land only marginally suitable. But in the semideserts of the south, where people had early on adopted a hunting-gathering regime, the planting and harvesting of crops to augment the wild food supply was a likely survival strategy once populations reached a critical level.

Search for the First Corn

Archaeologists believe that American agriculture began first in the highlands of Central Mexico where the staple crop, maize (*Zea mays* or corn-on-the-cob) originated. Fossil pollen from what is believed to be wild corn was found in a drill core at a depth of seventy metres below Mexico City in deposits dating to around 80,000 years ago (Coe, 1984). Corn has been domesticated for so long that no wild forms still exist, and so completely that it can no longer reproduce itself without human help to strip away the tough, seed-enclosing husks. The search for its ancestors has occupied botanists as well as archaeologists for generations. Initially, the cereal was thought to be a hybrid of teosinte, a grass that even today grows wild in the land of the Maya, but current botanical theories (Mangelsdorf, 1983) suggest that it originated as a hybrid of three other similar plants, including a podcorn and a popcorn, and that natural muta-tion resulted in larger cobs with the seeds imprisoned in thick husks. In the wild, these mutants would have died out. But in their quest for food, human foragers likely chose the large cobs to take back to camp; stripped from their husks, some of the seeds undoubtedly ended up on the garbage heap to sprout, take root and be harvested again. When people deliberately began to plant the seeds (for creatures of their brain size this is not such a fantastic feat as many think) they unconsciously started a long process of artificial selection and genetic inbreeding that completely altered the original stock. By the time Columbus arrived in America at the end of the fifteenth century, seven hundred species of "Indian corn" were flourishing, proof of many independent plant breeding experiments.

Though corn was perhaps the most important of the early American crops it was not by any means the only or even the first plant to be domesticated. The most ancient cultigens were not food plants at all but bottle gourds, good only as containers. Not native to America, they originated in the Old World and were first domesticated in Africa. Since their seeds remain viable even after long periods of immersion in salt water, it is thought that they could have floated across the Atlantic to land on a New World shore (most likely the bulge of Brazil) where they were found, opened and ultimately planted. This may seem far-fetched, but at the moment it is the only likely explanation. Bottle gourd seeds have been found in levels dating back to 8,000 years in a rockshelter in Northeastern Mexico (Coe, 1984). Above the gourd seeds, Canadian archaeologist Richard MacNeish, who has devoted many years to tracking down signs of the first American agriculture, found a sequence of other domesticated plants, including pumpkin, beans, chili peppers and squash, but no maize; only the tiny cobs of a kind of popcorn.

Later, in cultural deposits dating between 9,000 and 7,000 years ago in another rockshelter, this one in the arid Tehuacan Valley south of Mexico City, MacNeish found signs of avocados and bolls of domestic cotton, apparently the world's first. Also in the site were traces of bottle gourds, beans and squash—and the earliest cultivated corn yet found in America. Interestingly, found along with this corn were tiny cobs believed to be of wild maize, and these closely resembled one of the hypothetical corn ancestors of the botanists' theories. This momentous discovery of 1960 appears to fix both the time, before 7,000 years ago, and the place, central Mexico, for the domestication of corn. Before MacNeish's finds, the earliest archaeological evidence of this cereal, which was to have such a "civilizing" effect, came from Bat Cave in south central New Mexico. Here, the tiny charred cobs, still smaller than a little finger, were found with artifacts of a hunting-gathering culture dating to about 4,500 years ago. Also found were popped kernels of a wild popcorn— perhaps the start of an American indulgence that has continued to this day.

In North America, the transition from hunting and gathering to farming undoubtedly took place gradually, perhaps even accidentally. The nomads of the semidesert south simply threw out a handful of seeds near one of their habitual campsites and happened to return at harvest time. Then they made this planting and gathering a regular part of their seasonal round. It was only later they found that regular tilling of the soil and the addition of water during dry periods significantly increased the size of the yield. Archaeologists refer to these early efforts as gardening, not agriculture, because they did not significantly change the economic base or the lifestyles of the people.

Nevertheless, the shift from nomad to even part-time farmer was an important one, one that sowed the seeds of today's urban civilization. Clearing fields, planting and harvesting involved considerable time, energy and community cooperation—and also raised the new notions of land ownership and fixed residence. People began to stay by their fields, along with their heavy grinding stones and large storage pots, for at least the critical months of planting and harvest. And even short-term settlement encouraged the building of permanent dwellings and the organization of a home base or village. As villages grew in size, the sheer numbers of people living together initiated such things as civil government, trade specialization and status determination based on material success. The settled life also ultimately provided more leisure time for arts and games, politics and religion—the "cultural" components of a society. And as population grew, straining the resources of village farmlands, splinter groups moved out to settle and cultivate new lands. It was this territorial expansion, often at the expense of the indigenous hunter-gatherers in the area, that had such an effect on Plains nomads far to the north.

Agriculture Moves North

From its origins in middle Mexico, agriculture and the new agrarian way of life spread south into Central and South America and north into the United States, infiltrating first the semidesert areas where hunter-gatherers were its most likely beneficiaries, then the river valleys. By 3,000 years ago, it had spread into the southern Mississippi Basin where the Indians grew squash, gourds, sunflowers, knotweed and goosefoot in riverside fields beside their villages of round post-and-wattle houses. At first they could not grow beans or corn, for both are essentially tropical plants and it took thousands of years for hardy strains able to withstand cold climates to be developed.

In the Ohio Valley about 2,700 years ago the first tentative farmers were of the Adena tradition and they also planted native tobacco. Archaeologists have found not only the carved stone pipes they smoked it in, but even the tiny seeds themselves, preserved through charring in hearths. (The practice of smoking, which is believed to have originated in South America, gradually spread throughout most of the Western hemisphere and had reached into Canada some time before the Europeans arrived.) The Adena civilization and the more successful, more artistic Hopewell one that came later, both flowering from the roots of agriculture, extended their influence into all the major tributaries of the Mississippi. These people built huge earthworks that were

149

probably religious enclosures rather than defenses, and buried their dead accompanied by masses of rich grave goods in large log tombs under mounds of earth. Their mortuary ceremonies were elaborate and led to a tradition of increasing conspicuous consumption based on status: the more important the deceased, the larger the quantities of rare and beautiful objects buried with them. To fill the demand for these luxury grave goods, talented craftsmen became full-time specialist artisans. And there began an insatiable quest for large quantities of new and exotic materials. Hopewell trading tentacles stretched far and wide, to Lake Superior for copper, to the Gulf of Mexico for shells and sharks' teeth, to the western mountains for grizzly bear claws and to localities as distant as Ontario and Wyoming and half a dozen places in between for fine cherts and chalcedonies, sheet mica, galena and silver. It was a trading empire the like of which North America had not seen before—and its influence was strongly felt in the eastern fringes of the Canadian Plains.

However, beginning about A.D. 600, a far larger, more influential culture, named for the river that was its artery, came to power in the southeastern United States. The Mississippi culture's rise to prominence was due not to trading ability or superior weaponry but to the development of a hardier strain of corn, one that ripened early and could tolerate cooler temperatures. No longer limited by climate, the Mississippi farmers surged north to plant and occupy the bottomlands of all the major river systems of the American heartland. The soft, rich, well-watered valley soils were easily tended with simple digging sticks but to make cultivation easier still, the people invented a new implement, the bone hoe, made from the large, strong shoulder bones (scapulae) of bison. Their corn fields flourished. Soon beans were added to their crop list of corn, squash, and sunflowers (including the variety of sunflower we know as the Jerusalem artichoke). Well-nourished, and with huge reserves of stored food, the population exploded, concentrating into villages of large, multi-family houses with thatched roofs and walls of woven osiers cemented with clay. The group developed a complex social hierarchy headed by a caste of spiritual and political rulers who lived in separate ceremonial centres, their houses and temples built on the summits of large earthen mounds reminiscent of the pyramids of Mexico. When members of this elite class died they were buried in similar mounds along with all their treasures. All this opulence and social stratification was supported by a spreading network of smaller towns, villages and farms—and underpinning everything was a growing reliance on part-time agriculture or horticulture.

As these Mississippi peoples moved north, commandeering all the land suitable for horticulture, they displaced other cultures, a domino effect which reached ultimately as far as Canada. People as well as ideas were on the move.

They filtered up the valley of the Missouri River into today's North and South Dakota where some nomadic hunters, like others before them, exchanged their bows and arrows, at first only seasonally, for hoes and digging sticks. Adopting many of the traits of the influential Mississippian culture, they built semipermanent homes, large earth-covered lodges supported by timber framework, and settled down in villages beside their corn fields,

This transition to farming or gardening in the north was made possible by an important shift towards a warm but moister climate conducive to corn agriculture, during a period known as the Neo-Atlantic, which lasted from about A.D. 900 to A.D. 1200 (Dyck, 1983). These three hundred years of ideal growing conditions fostered a rich corn-dependent culture that later climatic deterioration—to drought and then to cold—was to seriously disrupt.

Perhaps because of the novelty of the agricultural tradition or the fact that they were geographically transitional between the shortgrass plains and the eastern woodlands, most of the Plains Villagers of the Dakotas were only part-time farmers who left their valley homes in spring after the crops were planted, spent the summers on the high plains in pursuit of bison, returned in time for the harvest, then went off again to the fall hunt. The larger villages became trading centres and here there was no need for the men to hunt. Buffalo nomads from the north, including eastern Saskatchewan and southwest Manitoba, were eager to barter. They brought their surplus meat and hides along with other goods—stone from faraway quarries, teeth of the mountain grizzly bear and shells from distant oceans—and exchanged them for the products of the Dakota fields and items that had been traded up the Mississippi from points south. This symbiotic trade relationship lasted for hundreds of years and ultimately had a grave impact on both ways of life.

The Blackduck

At about the same time that this southern influence was sweeping up into Canada, another culture began encroaching from the east. The indigenous peoples of the Minnesota and southern Ontario woodlands had established a stable way of life based on the hunting of small game and the collecting of wild rice from the marshes. However, introduction of corn agriculture south of the Great Lakes produced a violent displacement effect: the woodlanders were pushed north and west from their home territory into the aspen parklands of Manitoba. Here, known archaeologically as the Blackduck people, they became bison hunters, though they retained some of their woodland preferences for river clams, small game, wild fruits and plants.

Archaeologists identify the Blackduck people, who spread throughout southern Manitoba and into southern Saskatchewan, by their distinctive

Partially reconstructed Blackfoot pot from the Lord Site, Manitoba, typically globular with a textured surface. Bands of cord impressions and a row of punctates decorate the neck. Courtesy of Leigh Syms, Manitoba Museum of Man.

pottery. Large, globular and thin-walled, it was probably formed inside twined textile containers which imprinted the surface, then it was decorated with bands of cord impressions (Syms, 1977b; Buchner, 1983a). The people who made the pottery also constructed burial mounds, smoked tobacco in tubular stone pipes and made flutes or whistles from the leg bones of birds. No trace of their dwellings has yet been found but archaeologists believe they lived in wigwams similar to those of the historic Algonquians. These were oval structures framed with bent saplings and covered with matting of birch bark or woven rushes. Like other people to venture onto the plains, the Blackduck were nomads and archaeologists believe it did not take them long to adopt the traditional Plains tipi, an architecture that was more easily erected and dismantled, and far more suited to the windy grassland environment.

Canadian Clues

Archaeologists working in southern Manitoba and the Saskatchewan fringe find signs of these foreign or intrusive influences from south and east in the

A typical prehistoric Indian camp, below the jump cliffs at Head-Smashed-In, Alberta. The scene is as authentic as possible: it was re-enacted for a government of Alberta movie. Courtesy of the Archaeological Survey of Alberta.

Glyphs scratched into sandstone bedrock above Head-Smashed-In Buffalo Jump in Alberta. Some believe the star and crescent, a combination which occurs frequently throughout Western America, to be a record of the Crab Nebula explosion which took place in A.D. 1054. Courtesy of the Archaeological Survey of Alberta.

Richly beaded Indian leather bag from North Dakota. The artistic traditions of the Plains Indians were easily adapted to the European imports of brightly-coloured glass beads and metal. Courtesy of the author.

Effigy of a turtle constructed of glacial boulders sits on a Saskatchewan hilltop. The outline stones were covered with white flour to make mapping easier. Courtesy of the Saskatchewan Museum of Natural History.

A fall sunset turns the Milk River cliffs to gold and mule deer step out of the shadows to feed on the young willows. The cliffs beside the river display the largest concentration of prehistoric rock art on the Canadian prairies. Courtesy of Jack Bryan.

Moonrise above the spectacular sandstone cliffs in the Milk River canyon at Writing-on-Stone Provincial Park, Alberta. Courtesy of Jack Bryan.

sudden proliferation of many new types of pottery and in the appearance of such new traits as burial mounds (there are several types) and storage pits. However, agriculture itself, the one occupation that might have revolutionized the plains way of life, was never practiced here, except for one brief episode on the eastern periphery. The prairie landscape lacked the wide, flooding river valleys that were easy to cultivate (the tough prairie sod itself was never broken except, much later, by the iron plough) and in any case the growing season was too short for the varieties of corn, squash and beans then known. What would have happened if conditions had been right for corn agriculture? Would the Blackduck—and others—at least have tried the new agricultural lifestyle? We shall never know. Ourselves the beneficiaries of a long-lived Old World agrarian heritage, we take it for granted that, given the choice, the bison hunters would have settled down to farming and would ultimately have enjoyed all the cultural and social developments that urban life encouraged. But it is just possible that in the days of bison plenty they would have been content to stay as they were. When the horse caused a sudden and intense florescence of the nomadic way of life, it is known that there were several agricultural tribes who abandoned their villages for the glamour and ease of life on the wild prairie. And certainly there must have been others, ground down with the drudgery of farm chores and community politics, who envied the bison hunters' egalitarian independence.

The only instance of prehistoric horticulture so far found on the Canadian plains is at Lockport on the Red River north of Winnipeg, definitely an area peripheral to the main grasslands focus. Yet in the past it was grassland and excavation showed that 3,000 years ago, towards the end of the long drought known as the Altithermal, the riverside camp at Lockport was occupied by bison hunters. Subsequent occupations clearly showed that variation in climate favoured the growth of forests and that this environmental change prompted a major shift in the economy of area inhabitants. The hunting camp became a fishing camp occupied initially by people of the Laurel tradition, the first to use pottery in the plains, then the Blackduck. Vast quantities of fish bones from half a dozen different species were excavated at both time levels.

Conclusive signs of horticulture were found in later deposits dated to around seven hundred years ago and attributed to an as-yet unnamed culture. Here were hoes made from the scapulae of bison and deer, grinding stones for milling flour and large bell-shaped underground storage pits similar to those used by corn farmers in the Dakotas. Even more convincing were actual charred corn kernels, found in one of the pits. These people had definitely been farmers—or at least horticulturalists—the first on the Canadian prairies. But the agrarian revolution here was short-lived. Around A.D. 1500 the North

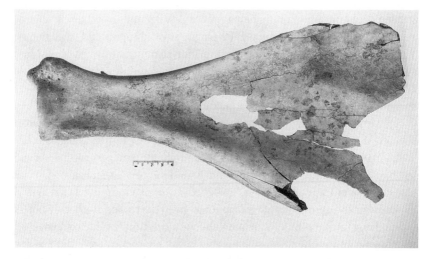

Gardening hoe made from bison scapula was one of the signs that corn-growing people had once occupied the Lockport site on the Red River north of Winnipeg. Courtesy of the Manitoba Historic Resources Board.

American climate changed for the worse and in northern latitudes it became impossible for corn to ripen before the first frosts. With no other crop to fall back on, native horticulture on the plains was abandoned and the people seemingly reverted to the mixed hunting-and-gathering economy of the woodlands/plains edge. Agriculture here was not tried again until the late eighteenth century (MacNeish, 1958; Buchner, 1986).

Some of the Lockport storage pits were located using a fairly new device, a proton magnetometer, an instrument used by geologists to measure the changing strength of the earth's magnetic field. In doing this, the device also reveals subsurface anomalies and soil disturbances such as large pieces of metal, masonry walls, fire hearths, and pits. The magnetometer survey of the river flat was used to indicate likely areas for the archaeologists to dig, and proved tremendously accurate.

The Grave Robbers

When the first Europeans arrived on the plains of Manitoba they found some areas hillocky with low mounds of earth. Some of the settlers, not bothering to ask what these bumps might be, simply ploughed them over or dug them out for root cellars, tossing aside any old bones they found. Others paused,

Artist's reconstruction of one of two pots found in the horticultural level of the Lockport site. Courtesy of the Manitoba Historic Resources Board.

perhaps compared them to the tumulus burials or "barrows" of England and also started to dig — for treasure. They found under the soil several kinds of chambered tombs with skeletons of men and bison. And buried with the bones were other things: arrowheads and stone tools, large marine shells beautifully engraved with weeping faces, bone and stone beads, pipes and whistles, necklaces, copper ornaments, birch-bark containers, pottery cups — not quite the gold and silver treasures they had hoped for but keepsakes nonetheless.

The mounds in Manitoba were mostly solitary and small, rarely more than three metres high, but south of the United States border they seemed to grow in numbers, size and complexity, reaching their zenith in the American Midwest states of Ohio, Illinois, Indiana and Missouri, though they spread as far south as the Gulf Coast. Some of the southern mounds were huge, more than thirty metres high and they were of different types: some conical, others formed into truncated pyramids or into effigy figures of animals and snakes, still others in giant lines like raised roadbeds. In addition to the mounds, huge earth embankments formed hilltop fortifications while on the lowlands there were giant geometric enclosures that were patently nonmilitary. Just what these constructions were and who had built them provided much grist for the "scientific" mill.

Several learned men, the "archaeologists" of the day, dug into the mounds, not merely for treasure but with the serious intention of finding out who had made them. After all, they reasoned, the sophisticated constructions and the artistic works inside could not possibly be the work of local Indian "savages." The Mound Builders (always capitalized as if to give substance to supposition) must have been a long-lost race from the Old World who had occupied America a long time ago and then had vanished, perhaps at the hands of the present indigenes. Who were they? There were many competing theories: they were Greeks, Romans, Celts, Vikings, Phoenicians, the Lost Tribes of Israel, or the inhabitants of the mysterious continent of Atlantis. The similarity of some of the southern mounds to the pyramids of Mexico did not escape notice: perhaps the North American master builders had come up from Mexico, they suggested, or perhaps, since the mounds seemed to show a north-south improvement, the Old World immigrants had arrived first in the north then made their way south, refining their architectural skills as they went. There were also a few scholars who argued, quietly, that the mounds were simply the products of the local Indians, built at a time of past cultural strength, but their voices went largely unheard (Silverberg, 1968).

While many of these early scientific investigators wrote papers about their discoveries and often turned over the "loot" to museums, in many ways they were as plundering as the Sunday diggers. They hired teams of men with picks and shovels and earth-scrapers pulled by cart-horses. And in their search for knowledge they did more than tamper with the evidence: they destroyed it. They made no notes, kept no records, made no sketches. All they wanted, it seems, were artifacts to bolster their theories. As mitigation for their deeds, it should be remembered that what they were doing was acceptable practice. In the Old World, the burial tumuli of the Bronze Age as well as the great tombs of Egypt received just as short a shrift.

In the story of archaeology on the Canadian plains, the early saga of the Manitoba mounds is one of opportunity lost. Where are the mounds today? Mostly plundered, ploughed back into the earth, tramped down by cattle, built on, bulldozed. Few mounds remain intact for scientific excavation. And archaeologists trying to make sense of the scrambled evidence of new peoples and new traditions on the eastern plains must make do with musty museum collections and the scribbled diaries of Victorian antiquarians. The what and

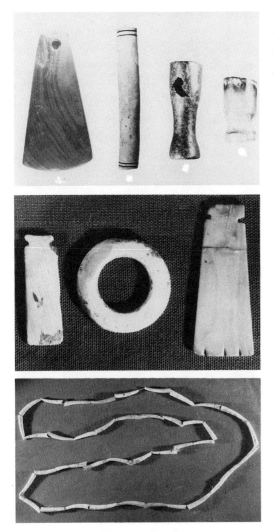

Typical artifacts from burial mounds in Manitoba include a) left to right: drilled and polished axe-shaped pendant, bone tube and tubular stone pipes

b) shell pendants and "washer"

c) dentalium shells, native to Canada's West Coast, here reconstructed into a necklace. Courtesy of the Manitoba Historic Resources Board.

the where of the mounds may be recorded, but the evidence for when, how and why has gone.

While the accounts of the early diggers' exploits are not much use to archaeologists, they are fascinating documents of Victorian attitudes. George Bryce, President of the Historical and Scientific Society of Manitoba, refused, like others of his era, to believe that the mounds were of Indian origin. In his article "The Mound Builders," published in the *Society Transactions* in 1885, he states: "Whoever built the mounds had a faculty not possessed by modern Indians. Building instincts are hereditary. The beaver and the muskrat build a house. Other creatures to whom a dwelling might be serviceable, such as the squirrel, obtain shelter in another way. And races have their distinctive tendencies likewise. It never occurs to an Indian to build a mound." Later: "The making of pottery is the occupation peculiarly of a sedentary race and hence of a race likely to be agriculturalists. As it requires the building faculty to originate the mounds, so it requires the constructive faculty to make pottery. In constructive ability our Indians are singularly deficient."

Bryce opened—plundered—several mounds in southern Manitoba, amassing a wealth of artifacts. He came up with several different notions regarding the origins of the builders. In 1885 he concluded that they were Takawgamis, a people descended from the Toltecs of Mexico who had emigrated north in the eleventh century A.D. and who lived in Manitoba until they were destroyed "with fire and sword" three hundred years later by the Aztecs (Bryce, 1885).

Two years later Bryce explored the southwest corner of the province around the Souris River. Here he noted "a group of remarkable earthworks, running from north to south respectively 125, 100, 150 and 75 yards in length and arranged in a sort of echelon. These are each from five to ten yards wide, some three or four feet high and have much the appearance of a railway grade on the prairie." What he had found in fact were simply different kinds of linear burial mounds—and thank goodness he did not stop to loot them all. Instead he transferred his attention to other conical mounds in the area. The first that he dug into were empty: he found no bones, no artifacts. These, he states with assurance, must have been built merely for observation purposes. A "promising-looking mound" nearby proved more rewarding. Here was exhumed a nearly complete skeleton wearing a headband of flattened copper; two pottery cups, one almost intact, a bird bone whistle, nine bead bones, a conjuror's sucking tube, a breast ornament of perforated shell, two red stone pipes, three round gaming pieces, two stone hammers and pieces of birch bark. A rich haul, indeed, one that seems to have clinched the latest of his origin theories: the mound-builders were Mandans, "an agricultural, pottery making, earth-dwelling tribe" who lived on the Missouri River in North Dakota (Bryce, 1887).

In 1904, Bryce changed his theory yet again and this time his flights of fancy soared. He described a mound excavated twenty-five years earlier in which he found more than thirty skeletons whose bones, lying in "red warpaint," seemed to be those of warriors. Because no utilitarian objects were found with them, he deduced that these people were of "a higher faith than that of the savage who thinks he is but transferred to another hunting ground when death overtakes him." The presence of sea shells and the "fewness" of the bodies made him believe that the remains were those of "sea-faring adventurers" who had come from another continent.

In the same article (Bryce, 1904) he mentions another theory of the day: that the mound builders were Welsh, descendants of an expeditionary force sent out by Prince Madoc in the twelfth century. Ten boatloads of people were believed to have crossed the Atlantic, infiltrated the American interior and settled on the Missouri River where they were known as the Mandans or Magdawys, followers of Madoc. The Mandan tribe furnished "proof" of this connection, for many had white skin and blue eyes and their round boats were identical to Welsh coracles. Even many of their words were similar. Bryce, however, remained sceptical of the Welsh connection, though for the rest of his life he continued to believe that the mound builders were immigrants, probably from North Europe.

Another researcher intent on solving the identity of the mysterious builders was Henry Montgomery, a professor at the University of North Dakota who carried out his investigations mainly throughout the Dakotas, though he did make some surveys in Manitoba, Saskatchewan and Ontario. While his reports were far more descriptive than those of Bryce and others and he deposited his Canadian finds in the Royal Ontario Museum, he too shoved aside any pretence at scientific method and excavated hastily and, alas, untiringly, with shovels and earth-scrapers. He left his trademark everywhere: deep central pits that turned mounds into doughnuts. Because of the volume of his twenty years' work on the plains he probably did more damage than any other single mound digger. In most cases, not even the geographic locations of the plundered mounds were recorded. Many of the mounds contained several graves, often at different levels, yet no attempt was made to map their positions or even to keep the contents of each burial separate. Artifacts from possibly different time periods and cultures were all lumped together simply as Mound Builders' artifacts.

The sad thing is that Montgomery unearthed in Manitoba what would have been splendid evidence for today's scientists: different kinds of burial pits with skeletons in sitting and flexed positions as well as in bundles; the presence of large stones or "bowlders"; bison bones, mostly skulls and scapulae; heaps of charcoal and fragments of charred wood; different kinds of pottery, engraved shells, stone pipes, copper ornaments, and artifacts of stone and bone. He also noticed semicircular layers of "calcareous earth" separating different burials within the same mound. This led him to speculate that some of the mounds grew to their finished size by the cumulative effect of multiple burials over the course of many years. In this case, he was right.

One of the largest mounds that Montgomery excavated was Calf

Shell gorget recovered from turn-of-the-century excavation of Calf Mountain burial mound near Darlingford, Manitoba. The artistic motif, perhaps even the finished item itself, originated in the Lower Mississippi Valley. The clamshell is native to the Gulf of Mexico. Courtesy of the Royal Ontario Museum, Toronto.

Mountain mound near Darlingford, Manitoba. More than three metres high and nearly thirty metres in diameter, this contained nine different burials and took thirty days to excavate. Though Montgomery began his excavations as early as 1909, this mound had already been robbed: he reckoned that at least two or three other burials had been removed.

Again, from an archaeological point of view, the "treasure trove" was considerable, the evidence ruined.

The Scientists

In 1912, W.B. Nickerson was sent by the National Museum of Canada on a reconnaissance mission into the plains of southern Manitoba to record and excavate the burial mounds. By the standards of the day, Nickerson had a passion for systematic investigation and recording. His painstaking fieldwork took three years to complete and his notebooks of detailed measurements and descriptions were so precise that, edited and published more than fifty years later (Capes, 1963), they provide some of the best archaeological data on the mounds, an invaluable reference source even today.

After Nickerson's work, nothing more was done officially to explore the Manitoba mounds—they had mostly all been looted anyway—until the investigations of archaeologist Richard MacNeish in the 1950s. The burial mound he excavated lay on a high lip of the Assiniboine River valley northwest of Brandon (MacNeish, 1954). Unlike many others, the Stott mound had been protected from vandalism by the landowner. It was also different because while most burial mounds are away from habitation sites, this was directly above a village or campsite on the river flats below. Originally about 1.5 metres high and 12 metres in diameter, the mound contained three deep burial pits originally roofed with poles of oak and cedar. Two of the pits were occupied by ochre-stained burials of women and children, some apparently placed in a seated position. With them were found bison skulls and a few grave goods, including a bird bone flute and several shell artifacts. A separate pair of articulated arms without hands, which had been placed vertically against the pit wall, added a baffling, macabre touch.

Surprisingly, the third burial pit contained only a puppy, found in a curled up position as if asleep, its nose pointing towards the east. Was this a favourite family pet sent to accompany its owner into the afterworld? Or was it some sort of a sacrifice? Two small fires, perhaps for ceremonial purposes, had been built on the original burial surface. Some time later, another grave had been dug into the mound, this time for a child found with a necklace of sea shells.

In the village site below the mound MacNeish located a compact layer of bison bones (the site of a pound), several fire pits and many side-notched and triangular arrowheads, scrapers and bone tools—at first glance a typical nomadic bison-hunters' camp. However, included among the artifacts was a rolled copper bead, some beaver-tooth gouges and clay sherds from decorated, globular pots. The pottery was a clear give-away: it was Blackduck, indicating that the people originally came from the Eastern Woodlands. Many of the

Diagrams showing the arrangement of bones in the Stott Mound burial pits, and the stone, earth and wood coverings. Note the bison skulls and the separate burial of a dog. Courtesy of the Canadian Museum of Civilization.

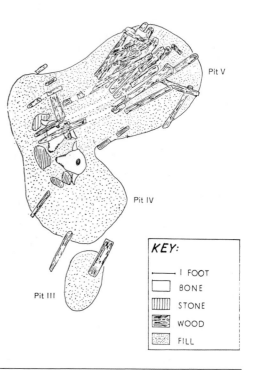

Pit V

Pit IV

Pit III

KEY:

├──┤	1 FOOT
▭	BONE
▥	STONE
▨	WOOD
▦	FILL

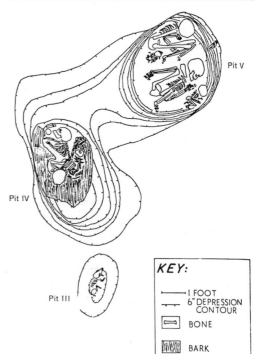

Pit V

Pit IV

Pit III

KEY:

├──┤	1 FOOT
─┬─	6" DEPRESSION CONTOUR
▭	BONE
▨	BARK

lithic artifacts were of quartzite from north and east Manitoba, but several were of Knife River flint and obsidian and the presence of these exotics, plus shells which had originated in the Gulf of Mexico, suggested to MacNeish that the Blackduck immigrants to Manitoba were already participating in a well organized trading network. The Stott mound was later carbon dated at around A.D. 600.

The only other intact burial mound on the Canadian plains that has been scientifically excavated lies far removed from the general area of mound construction (a good 160 kilometres from the Souris River concentrations) and thus escaped the notice of turn-of-the-century grave-robbers. Discovered in 1951, it was protected by the landowner until the Saskatchewan Museum of Natural History began excavations in 1968 (Hanna, 1976). On the crest of the high north rim of the Qu'appelle Valley, an enormous glacial spillway in southeastern Saskatchewan, the Moose Bay burial mound commands a truly beautiful view of the whole river trench with Crooked Lake and the resort community of Moose Bay directly below. It was found to have been built around A.D. 1040 as a repository for nine secondary burials. Two were of men (one an ancient of more than eighty years), the rest of children. All the bones had been liberally smeared with red ochre and placed directly on the prairie soil. A low, tipilike structure of logs had been built as a roof over them, then earth had been mounded up over the top. When the logs had decayed, the earth had fallen in, crushing some of the bones.

Artifacts buried with the dead included birchbark containers so well preserved that archaeologists could discover exactly how they had been made, cut from a single piece of bark, then folded and stitched with spruce root. There were also round clay concretions, fragments of the shell or carapace of a Western Painted turtle (some of the fragments fitted together to form a gorget), pipes, pottery sherds and projectile points. Found with the old man was a curved bone knife identical to those traditionally used for cutting squash in the agricultural villages along the Missouri River. Was this proof that the man was a farmer and that his people practiced agriculture? Margaret Hanna doesn't think so. Gathering squash was traditionally women's work. The knife was more likely a personal talisman, obtained through trade.

Some time after the burial mound had been constructed a pit had been dug into the centre for the interment of a tenth individual, a girl of about fourteen years who had been buried with a large number of very fine grave goods. These included a beautiful intact pottery vessel engraved with turtles, two birchbark baskets, stone and clay pipes, scrapers and bone awls.

The only other known burial mound in Saskatchewan, an X-shaped linear construction near Halbrite in the extreme southeast, was also investigated by

Excavation trench through the Moose Bay burial mound on the north rim of the Qu'Appelle Valley in southeastern Saskatchewan. Repository for nine secondary burials, the mound is around 1,000 years old. Courtesy of Saskatchewan Heritage Resources Board.

Excavation of the Moose Bay mound unearthed a late intrusive burial of a young girl along with a) some well preserved birch bark containers holding ceramic pipes and a sandstone polishing tool

b) An intact ceramic vessel was discovered underneath the birch bark. Vessel was inscribed with four turtles, the symbol for fertility.

Turtle pot, cleaned up

Close-up of turtle motif. All courtesy of the Saskatchewan Museum of Natural History.

Folded and stitched from a single piece of birch bark, this container is one of several found in the older central burial chamber of Moose Bay burial mound; it contained two projectile points and a knife. Courtesy of the Saskatchewan Museum of Natural History.

the Saskatchewan Museum but the wooden roofed burial pit had been so thoroughly plundered by grave robbers (Montgomery was one of them in 1907) that only a few bones were recovered. However an intriguing intact burial was discovered in the mound fill. This consisted only of a single, flexed human arm that archaeologists guess was all that could be recovered of a warrior or a hunter killed in action. The artifacts and bones known to have been removed from the main burial pit have disappeared and the affiliations of the people remain unknown (*Saskatchewan Archaeology Newsletter*, October 1964).

The Mounds Today

There are several different types of mounds and examples of all of them can still be found in Manitoba. Most are simple, symmetrical low heaps of earth covering a single grave. Others are accumulative, constructed over a period of time and containing more than one interment; each time a burial took place, more earth was added to these multi-storey graveyards until many of them reached sizable height.

Occasionally the covering earth was fashioned into the form of an animal effigy figure. The most spectacular example of this type is the Serpent Mound in Ohio, a curvy snake of incredible size (four hundred metres uncoiled) carrying an egg in its mouth. The Manitoba effigy mounds are nowhere near as dramatic, or as well preserved. Star Mound near Snowflake (excavated by Nickerson and others) is said to have been originally in the shape of a beaver (Capes, 1963). On top of a hill thirty metres high and with a view over the plains in all directions, it was known to the local Indians in the mid-nineteenth century as "Dry Dance Hill." Today it is worth a visit mainly for its scenic location: the mound where Nickerson unearthed several ancient burial pits is only a low grassy knoll of indistinguishable shape in the middle of a old school playground. A flagpole has been planted, like a stake, in the mound's heart. Another effigy mound appears to be in the shape of a long-tailed muskrat. This, one of the best preserved of all the Manitoba mounds, lies on the Whitemud River just outside the community of Westbourne. Well protected inside a local resident's front garden, the mound has a tuft of tall trees growing along its back. For years it was believed to have been looted, but there are indications that a deep and undisturbed burial still awaits investigation (Syms, 1978).

Perhaps the most intriguing mounds of all are the linear constructions, most of which are found in the Souris area of southwestern Manitoba. Running like railway embankments often for considerable distances across the prairie, only a few have burial mounds on one or both ends and they are frequently organized into geometric groupings. It is easy to understand the simple heaping up of earth over a grave, for this is a European tradition of long standing, but what was the purpose of these long earth causeways? While often only about half a metre high, these range in width up to seven metres and in length to more than two hundred and fifty metres. The amount of effort needed to complete these monumental works must have been prodigious and protracted, requiring the labour of many people equipped only with simple digging sticks and with baskets to carry the earth. A linear mound one hundred metres long, ten metres wide and half a metre high contains five hundred cubic metres of earth. Just to move the earth into position would take the unceasing work of fifteen people, each carrying about half a cubic metre of earth a day, for more than sixty-six days.

It has been suggested (Syms, 1978) that for prehistoric peoples the building of any mound was more than a practical burying of the dead; that it served to bring people together for group ceremonies, a show of solidarity between allies. Archaeologists point to the presence of small fires on the burial surface and the inclusion of exotic materials and artifacts as evidence of a ritual importance far beyond the physical need to cover bodies with earth. Research has even shown that this outward show of cooperation grew at times of cultural stress, when populations were expanding or climatic changes forced a shift in lifestyles. Perhaps, it is argued, this group expression of togetherness prevented the aggression that might otherwise have broken out between peoples competing for the same niche. If this is indeed so, then the labour-intensive linear mounds would indicate a time of upheaval in the Eastern plains, and this corroborates other archaeological findings.

There is another theory about the linear mounds that is perhaps even more fascinating. Most of them are oriented roughly thirty degrees askew of the cardinal points and many incorporate a right angle. The general absence of burials and the regular orientation suggest the possibility of astronomical significance. Experiments in the planetarium of the Manitoba Museum of Man and Nature have shown that at A.D. 1000 and A.D. 1500 the constellation Sagittarius and two bright stars, Pollux, one of the twins, and Beta Tauri would have been in rough correlation with an east-of-south sighting line. The same sighting line could have been used to locate and commemorate the unnamed star which exploded into a supernova then diminished to create today's Crab Nebula, one of the most beautiful telescope sights of the night sky. The Crab Nebula's gigantic nuclear explosion, as recorded by Chinese scholars, took place on 4 July, A.D. 1054. Astronomers have computed that this dazzling event would have been visible throughout the western plains of North America where it would have formed a spectacular conjunction with the waning crescent moon just before sunrise, its light refusing to fade even at high noon, a sight that would have awed and mystified and lingered long in folk memory (Buchner, 1983a). Graphic combinations of super star and crescent moon have been found portrayed on several rock art sites in the American southwest, including one exceptionally clear version in Chaco Canyon, New Mexico (Williamson, 1984). Several star and crescent motifs are also to be found among the glyphs on the sandstone rocks above Head-Smashed-In Buffalo Jump, Alberta. Could these glyphs be records of the Crab Nebula explosion? Might the linear mounds be signposts to celestial history? Like the stone medicine wheels on the plains farther west, could they be some kind of astronomical observatories? No-one will ever know. Apart from some burial function, the true purpose of these monumental earth lines, if they had one, has been lost.

Fitting the Pieces Together

Archaeologists have struggled to piece together all the evidence from the looted as well as the scientifically-excavated mounds on the northeastern plains of North America and have so far managed to divide them, on the basis of burial

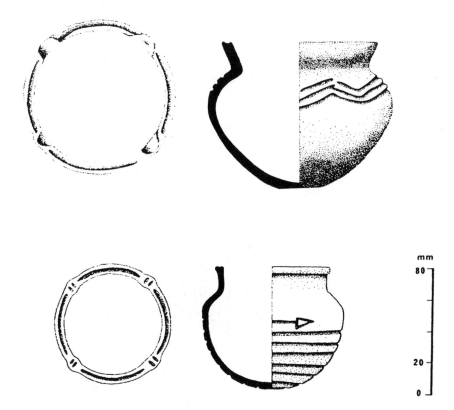

Drawings of two small pots associated with late period burials in Saskatchewan; pot with wavy parallel lines was found near St. Victor (top). Pot with spiral arrow design was found near Silton (bottom). Both vessels are divided into four sectors by indentations on the rim. Courtesy of the Saskatchewan Archaeological Society.

methods and kinds of artifacts, particularly pottery, into six distinct complexes. Ironically, the Moose Bay mound, which has by far the most satisfactory evidence in Canada, does not fit clearly into any of them. Most of the Canadian plains burial mounds seem to belong to only two of these complexes: the Blackduck (or Manitoba), and the Devil's Lake-Sourisford (Syms, 1978). Blackduck mounds are mostly found in the woodlands of southern Ontario and northern Minnesota; in Manitoba, only the Stott mound appears to belong, far removed from the rest, though it seems clear, from the amount of Blackduck pottery found elsewhere in southern Manitoba, that people with strong links to the Woodland cultures, if not the Blackduck peoples themselves, had entered the grasslands and had adopted the nomadic hunters' way of life.

Most of the Manitoba mounds have been assigned to the Devil's

Fragments of a small vessel found in a mass grave near Reston, Manitoba, were inscribed with a thunderbird, a motif common to the Devil's Lake-Sourisford burial complex. Courtesy of Leigh Syms, Manitoba Museum of Man.

Lake-Sourisford complex which seems to have been directly influenced from the south at the time (around A.D. 900) of the expansion of the Mississippian culture. This burial complex is known for its use of deep subsurface pits with primary burials placed in sitting or flexed positions. Accompanying grave goods include distinctive incised miniature pots, decorated gorgets made from the shells of large marine snails from the Gulf Coast (often with a weeping face motif), stone tubular pipes and other items. However, the people who built these mounds have so far been identified only by their burial traits. Their village sites have yet to be found (Syms, 1979a). Again, there is a suggestion of a culture in transition: many of these burials are accompanied by bison skulls, evidence of a new veneration, perhaps a new dependency, that people to the south did not have.

However, it seems that not all the Manitoba Devil's Lake people were buried in mounds, a discovery that suggests differences in social or economic status within the population. In December 1967, workers at a municipal gravel pit in a glacial outwash ridge near the village of Reston, Manitoba, uncovered a frozen mass of human bones. Analysis of the remains by archaeologists from the University of Manitoba revealed at least nine individuals, their ochre-stained bones tangled with pieces of wood. Also found were sherds of diminutive "mortuary ware" decorated with the tell-tale incised lines, figures and spiral grooving of the Devil's Lake-Sourisford Burial complex, plus Plains Side-notched projectile points and a bird skull (Bradell et al., 1970). A second nonmound burial, dating to around A.D. 1080, was unearthed near Estevan, Saskatchewan. The Woodlawn site contained, along with the bundled burial of a forty-five-year-old woman and two extra bones, a pendant made from the central column of a Gulf Coast whelk shell, a definite Devil's Lake trait. This burial was of great medical interest, for the dead woman's bones showed that she had suffered from tuberculosis, the first evidence for this infection on the Western Canadian plains. Investigating archaeologist Ernie Walker suggested that the disease, which is common in the overcrowded, unsanitary confines of a large city, was transmitted through contact with the densely populated Mississippian centres to the southeast (Walker, 1983). The southern influence was not always a benign one.

While pottery is the main diagnostic used to track movement of peoples and ideas after about A.D. 1000 in the eastern Canadian plains, the people continued to make and use stone tools and weapons right up into the Historic era. Projectile point typology therefore continues to be useful. The point style in general use during most of the ceramic eras throughout the Canadian plains is known as the Late Side-notched or Old Women's and this has been divided into two distinct subseries, the earlier (from 1,200 to 700 years ago) Prairie Side-notched type, and the later (550 years ago to Historic) Plains Side-notched (Dyck, 1983). Archaeologist Ian Dyck has noticed that the apparent 150-year gap in Canadian radiocarbon dates between the two types coincides with the Pacific period drought which devastated the lives of the Plains horticultural villagers of the Missouri, causing many settlements to be abandoned. Perhaps, says Dyck, the drought also caused depopulation in the northern grasslands and the gap in the archaeological record is a real one in terms of people. When the drought ended, the Missouri villagers began a pattern of increased trade and contact with outside groups, and their typical stone points, the Plains Side-notched, first appeared in Canadian bison hunters' camps, indicating, or so Dyck suggests, strong connections between the two groups at this time.

Villagers

Did these connections include actual immigration of Missouri villagers into Canada? Did they build their distinctive earth-lodges here and try to grow corn? No-one can say for certain but there are enough intriguing hints of

Reconstruction of a Mandan earthlodge in On-a-Slope Indian Village in North Dakota. Courtesy of the author.

their presence, both historical and archaeological, to suggest that this may be so. The homes of the Missouri villagers were circular in perimeter and domed in appearance, but their construction was based on a square inner framework of massive posts and beams, with roof and walls of wooden poles and an external covering of earth or sod. Peter Fidler, one of the first of the fur traders to visit southwestern Saskatchewan, may have seen some of these circular earth lodges on his journeys. In the fall of 1800 he was travelling up the South Saskatchewan River to the trading post of Chesterfield House at the mouth of the Red Deer River. His diary entry for 20 September includes the following:

a little below in this reach 3 Mud Houses on this side amongst a few poplars, they are in a circular form about 9 feet diameter and 4 1/2 high, they appear to be nearly 20 years old, they are said to have been built by a small war party from the Missouri River who live in these kind of habitation (quoted by Russell, 1982).

Archaeologists have searched for this site in vain; it is believed to be submerged under the impounded waters of Lake Diefenbaker. (For that matter, no trace has ever been found of the three separate fur-trading posts known to have been built nearby.)

Fidler also reported digging into one of Manitoba's earth mounds near the mouth of today's Gainsborough Creek:

On a point between a small brook and the river we found a number of conical mounds and the remains of an intrenchment. Our half-breeds said it was an old Mandan Village; the Indians of that tribe having formerly hunted and lived in this part of the Great Prairies. We endeavoured to make an opening into one of the mound and penetrated six feet without finding anything to indicate that the mounds were the remains of Mandan lodges (quoted by Syms, 1978).

W.B. Nickerson was the first to find intriguing hints of an earthlodge in an archaeological excavation. Digging in the Heath burial mound in southwest Manitoba he uncovered enough burnt earth and charred wood to suggest "that some kind of a round mud-plastered hut was destroyed here by fire and the mound built over its ruins" (Capes, 1963). Signs were also found at the Long Creek Site in southeastern Saskatchewan in 1957. Here at least two circular depressions about four metres in diameter were noted just east of the main excavation. When work at the site was over for the season, the first skiff of snow clearly outlined a series of postholes inside the depressions, tantalizing archaeologists with the possibility that here lay "the first indication of late prehistoric house types in Saskatchewan" (Wettlaufer, 1960). No further work was done at the site, and the house-pits—if that is what they were—were never excavated.

The Enigmatic Cluny Site

By far the best proof of southern immigration is the Cluny site which lies east of Calgary, nearly 650 kilometres to the northwest of the Missouri villages. Here, near an important ford on the Bow River known as Blackfoot Crossing, archaeologist Richard Forbis (1977) found what appeared to be the remains of a village of earth houses inside a log palisade and a semicircular ditch. In general appearance it is convincingly similar to the remains of a fortified Missouri village and pottery sherds from the site show clear parallels. But in total, Cluny does not fit neatly into the Missouri mould. It is an enigma: like, but yet maddeningly different.

The ditch was originally 2.5 metres wide and one metre deep and described half of an oval 120 metres in diameter, with a former river cutbank at its open end completing the village defences. Several metres inside the ditch cottonwood logs had once been embedded in a trench to form a protective palisade; they stood on end, leaning slightly inwards and were supported on the inner

173

Aerial view of supposed earthlodge village discovered near Cluny, Alberta. Village fortification ditch and palisade were semi-circular: the high bank of the Bow River at the time of occupation completed its defenses. W.D. Marsden photo, courtesy of the Glenbow Foundation.

Part of the Cluny site towards the end of excavation shows one of the "house pits", palisade support posts and trench. Courtesy of Richard Forbis.

side by larger posts. Between the ditch and the palisade were eleven roughly circular pits that in the North Dakota villages would have marked the remains of the slightly subterranean earth-lodges, their roofs supported on four internal posts and with a central fire hearth. But the Cluny pits were only about four metres in diameter, far smaller than the smallest known Missouri house and excavation of two of them revealed no roof posts or hearths and only scant evidence of domesticity. Their location, too, was wrong. For maximum protection, they should have been inside, not outside, the palisade. Perhaps, said Forbis, trying to explain the discrepancies, the pits had not been houses at all but part of the fortification system and the villagers had lived in tipis on the flat land inside the palisade. Certainly most of the artifacts were found here, along with numerous hearths.

There are other mysteries, too. If the Cluny inhabitants were immigrants from the farming villages on the Missouri, where were their squash knives, their scapula hoes and other digging implements? Why did they not excavate their traditional deep storage pits, and why were there no remains of domesticated plants? Forbis suggests that the lack of evidence for farming could mean that the villagers found the Alberta climate too cold for the growing of crops and had been forced to become bison hunters like the people around them. But even this hypothesis is problematical—he found hardly any butchering tools or hide scrapers and only a few bison bones, certainly not enough to feed a number of people for any length of time. The bison bones had all been shattered and scraped clean to extract every scrap of nutrient and there were other signs of very lean times: three of the eight domestic dogs found appeared to have been butchered.

In addition to Missouri-type pottery, the artifacts left by the mysterious residents included chipped and ground stone tools, bone and shell beads, flat discs of shell and baked clay that might have been gaming pieces, and a varied inventory of bone tools including porcupine quill flatteners (flattened quills were dyed and used like beads to decorate items of clothing), fleshers, knife handles and awls. An unusual find was a tool clearly manufactured for stamping pottery: the notches cut along one edge of a bone splinter were found to correspond exactly with the toothlike patterns on a piece of pottery found nearby.

When was the Cluny site occupied? A radiocarbon date from charcoal set the limits: between A.D. 1730 and 1890. The earlier date seems more reasonable, Forbis suggests, since the site was generally similar to a Middle Missouri Village, a pattern of habitation that spread north into North Dakota between 1675 and 1780, and the pottery showed definite Missouri traits. The near-absence of white trade goods—only two copper or brass knives were found—and the presence of only two horse bones also suggest an early occupancy. (Horses reached the northern plains from the south about 1730.) Projectile point seriation, based on Forbis's Old Women's study, inferred only a date later than the Old Women's Buffalo Jump, which was last used around A.D. 1600.

The occupation of Cluny by foreigners from the south is still remembered in local Blackfoot oral history and this has helped to substantiate both a fairly late date and the identity of the inhabitants. Still, the puzzles persist. The number of artifacts found at the site suggests only a very brief occupation, a couple of months at the most, not much longer than it would have taken to build the village earthworks. Archaeologists found the earth of the river bench "compacted and highly calcareous," in other words, tough digging; how much tougher it must have been for the original builders with their simple bone, wood and stone tools. If the earth were frozen, construction would have been impossible, said Forbis and he therefore suggests that the village must have been built between May and November; a few of the other faunal remains also suggest the site was occupied between spring and fall.

Why, after the considerable labour of building the village, did its occupants leave so soon? The most obvious reasons, that they were all wiped out by disease or by enemy invaders, are negated by the absence of any human bones. Perhaps they simply packed up and went home, or left to join the buffalo nomads. Both hypotheses are impossible to substantiate, though the latter shows the most promise as the pottery analysis shows.

More than 2,000 small, mostly shattered sherds of typically grey "Cluny" pottery were recovered, most of them from the flat area inside the fortifications thought to be the most likely living area. Rim sherds of at least twenty-four different vessels were found and some of the pieces could be fitted together to show shape, size and decorative treatment of individual pots. The Cluny vessels were all globular and wide-mouthed, with neck constrictions just below a thickened lip. They appear to have been lump modelled, perhaps of clay from a local nearby hillside, then finished by the paddle-and-anvil technique. Some still showed the characteristic "check-stamping" from the grooved paddle but most were later smoothed to obliterate the paddling marks then decorated about the neck, rim and shoulders by incising, punctation, pinching, impressing with knotted cords and stamping. Firing likely took place in an open hearth.

William Byrne's analysis of prehistoric Alberta ceramics (Byrne, 1973) found that until about A.D. 1700 all pottery belonged to a single local tradition known as Saskatchewan Basin. Then there appeared a clearly new type of pottery which Byrne placed into a cultural phase called One Gun after the Indian who first led investigators to the Cluny village site. Cluny pottery was

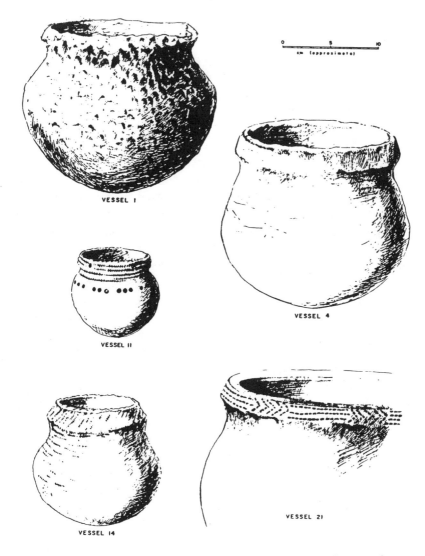

Reconstructions of some of the pottery found at the Cluny village site. Courtesy of Richard Forbis.

not confined, however, to the village: stray sherds were also found at several other archaeological sites in southern Alberta and southern Saskatchewan. The largest concentrations were recovered at the Morkin site below the eastern slopes of the Porcupine Hills where the top two cultural levels (carbon-dated to after A.D. 1700) also contained other typical Missouri village traits: a large

177

bell-shaped cache pit of 115 centimetres in diameter, several rectangular bison scapulae "squash knives" and pitted grinding stones.

Comparing the Cluny complex ware with that from the Middle Missouri, Byrne found "both striking similarities and potentially significant differences." The pottery was alike in size and shape and both wares had bands of repeated patterns positioned between neck and shoulder. But while every motif on the Cluny pottery could be matched with those on southern sherds, missing were important Missouri design elements such as cord impressions and elaborate triangular, rectangular and rainbow patterns.

Neverthless, the similarities were enough to convince Byrne that the Cluny pottery was derived from a ceramic tradition centred in the Middle Missouri and that it had arrived in southern Alberta as a direct result of population movement. The emigrants had likely followed the river valleys through northeastern Montana into southern Saskatchewan. This would neatly explain the possible house pits at Long Creek and the ones that Fidler reported near the mouth of the Red Deer River. However, Byrne does not suggest a single mass exodus but rather a series of small migrations over a period of time. The fact that the people were no longer in Canada when the first fur-traders and explorers came through would seem to suggest, he says, that by then either the people had returned to their homeland or merged so completely into the resident population that they were no longer discernible.

Why did the Missouri peoples, comfortably settled in earthlodge villages beside their garden plots, leave home in the first place? And why did they travel so far north—650 kilometres—into alien country impossible for agriculture? Archaeologists have proposed the following speculative scenario. The treks took place about 1740 when the Spanish in the south and the English and French to the north and east were starting a sort of pincer movement towards the plains and the domino effect of tribal displacement had already begun. It is also possible that the villagers along the Missouri were feeling the effects of the deadliest, if accidental, weapon in the European arsenal: disease. The aboriginal populations of America had lived so long in isolation from the rest of the world that they had no natural immunity even to such childhood maladies as chicken pox and measles, much less to the ravages of smallpox. Once introduced, disease spread like a prairie grass fire, particularly in the crowded urban centres of the south. Fleeing from the mysterious sicknesses, Indians spread the contagions farther afield, so that tribes hundreds of kilometres from the source were quickly infected.

Everywhere on the North American plains at the beginning of the eighteenth century, people were on the move, abandoning their home territories because of disease and because of warfare, both attributable to

Petroglyph of horse and rider and a bison, one of the very few representations of this animal so vital to prehistoric plains cultures, can be seen at Writing-on-Stone. Courtesy of the Archaeological Survey of Alberta.

European encroachment. From the south they migrated up the Missouri where the well-stocked villages provided obvious take-over targets. With numbers and courage perhaps sapped by disease, the villagers offered no resistance. They fled north upriver, towards country they knew to be occupied only lightly by nomadic bison hunters.

They were likely aided in their escape by another dramatic Spanish import, the horse, which offered a revolutionary means of transportation. With this new animal to ride and pull their travois, the long journey to Cluny was made easier and faster. Reconstruction of the northward spread of horses on the plains suggests that the Missouri villages were at the extreme northern end of a horse-trading chain that began in the Spanish colonial city of Santa Fe, New Mexico; horses were definitely in the Dakotas by about A.D. 1720, though they were not common in Canada north of the Missouri Coteau until after 1750. The fact that the Plains villagers possessed horses and the nomads of Alberta and Saskatchewan did not may have been another factor in the villagers' choice of a northward destination. Horses gave them a distinct advantage over the resident tribes, not just for transportation, but in the hunt. And perhaps the immigrants knew that on the northern plains they would have to depend on the hunt as never before.

This disaster scenario may be the most likely, but there are other possibilities. Forbis suggests that since the eighteenth century was the acknowledged heyday of the Middle Missouri villages there could have been a population explosion and not enough farmland to support everyone. Like later pioneer settlers in the prairies, the southern immigrants might have come north simply for more room, to build a better life for themselves. Too, there could have been some kind of civil or religious upheaval among the villages that caused a rift serious enough to impel dissenters away.

Whatever the reason for their uprooting, people from the Middle Missouri do appear to have travelled north, perhaps over a period of years, to settle on the northern grasslands. One group came to the banks of the Bow River at Cluny where they built a rough replica of the village they had left. They did not have an easy time of it: judging from the amount of food bones found at the site, they faced starvation. Perhaps this was why they moved out so soon, to follow the bison herds on their annual round. They dropped their different lifestyles and merged with the indigenous bison hunters to become in Forbis' words, "archaeologically invisible." Pottery was one tradition they seem to have kept, at least for a while, for the distinctive Cluny ware is found in sites throughout Southern Saskatchewan and Alberta; perhaps it was traded; perhaps introduced through intermarriage. Certainly, in time, it was like all native pottery supplanted by the iron kettles of the fur traders.

NINE

Slipping into History

C luny lies on the very lip of prehistory, unrecorded and therefore not a part of history, yet obviously affected by the wash of European encroachment. If we knew nothing about the upheavals along the Missouri which prompted the Cluny immigration, the two little horse bones found with the camp refuse would be sure signals of intervention from the south. Well before European traders and explorers trod the prairie grass in person, the Indians had felt the hot breath of an alien culture at their backs. First came disease, then the horse and gun, then whisky and other material goods from a technologically superior civilization, goods that were ultimately bought most dearly: at the cost of an independent way of life that had sustained human life on the grasslands for 12,000 years.

The transition zone between prehistory and history is a bit like a tide line, varying in time and place and dependent on distant surges. It was nearly two hundred years between Henry Kelsey's journey through the plains of Saskatchewan in 1691 and the march of the mounted police into the unexplored grasslands of southwest Alberta in 1874, and even as the fur traders and explorers were scribbling in their journals, change was accelerating all around them. What they recorded was soon obsolete as the Indians entered into the crucible of European trade and influence, shifting their territories, adopting new life-styles, coping with changes in resource supplies.

Archaeologists call the period immediately before documentation the Protohistoric. At best, it is an uneasy junction, difficult to identify and to reconstruct. The only sure signs of change and influence that can be excavated are material things—horse bones, scraps of European iron, a spent cartridge, a handful of glass beads. Alterations to the patterns of a society leave little imprint in the dust. To learn about these, witnesses need to be called. In this respect, North America is fortunate; other countries must recover their prehistoric past solely from the archaeological record, but we have eye-witness reports, both verbal and visual, though of varying utility. The written evidence from traders, explorers, missionaries and soldiers was usually only peripheral to the writer's purpose and is often infuriatingly clipped and incomplete, its record confined to the reaches of the great rivers which were the arteries of European trade and travel. Nevertheless, it helps to piece together the details of protohistoric life—and to validate the findings of the archaeologists. Luckily, several artists came to North America with the main intention of recording the scenery and the people. And from these documentaries come the vivid details of everyday Indian life that often the fur traders were too preoccupied to notice—or too tired at the end of a day to record. Paintings by such artists as Karl Bodmer and George Caitlin summon the spirit of the age and the people as no written account can; they have given immortality to a vanished way of life.

Another very important source of testimony lies with the Indians themselves. Their oral histories and legends often provide excellent glimpses into the mechanics of prehistoric Indian society and its ideas about the real and spiritual worlds. Together, history, art and ethnography provide us with many details of life on the plains at the beginning of the historic era and this enables archaeologists to pad out the evidence of prehistory. A circle of stones and a hearth becomes a hide tipi with fur blankets and backrests; a pile of bones and a few postholes becomes a bison pound; a clutch of rocks in the earth, a boiling pit. Human skeletons can be clothed in deerskin decorated with porcupine quills and beads; arrowheads can be fixed to feathered shafts; scrapers to bone and wood handles; dogs and horses to travois. In a wink, dust and bones and stones have become life.

However, most art, history and oral memories portray a Plains society transformed by the horse, an import that had enormous and almost instantaneous impact. It was impressed eagerly and completely into the cultural fabric and soon became part of tribal image, folklore and even memory. In the span of a few decades, the Plains Indians became one of the greatest equestrian cultures the world has ever known and to achieve this distinction many early customs of the "dog days" had to be cast off. The horse improved existing hunting strategies and introduced new ones; it changed residence patterns, altered the nature of warfare, fostered a new sense of territorial imperative and led to much intertribal stress. Itself a symbol of wealth and prestige, it also made feasible the accumulation of material goods by providing easier transport for them, though dogs also continued to be used right up until historic times. Increased efficiency in the hunt and on the move afforded more leisure time, time for such things as politics, arts and crafts, religion and ceremony— even warfare. All of these changes took place amazingly swiftly, it seems, just as soon as horses reached the plains. And on their backs, the nomad bison hunters reached a cultural crescendo, a tremendously bright flowering, like the last fierce light from a guttering candle. Ironically, this took place only a few years before the end of it all.

Any rudimentary discussion of the effect of the European presence on the Indian populations of the grasslands must make allowances for geography. To the east and the north, the major influence was the fur trade out of Hudson Bay where English traders established posts by A.D. 1670 and introduced the black magic of gunpower to the Stone Age inhabitants of the northern woodlands. The Cree Indians were likely the first to possess this powerful new weapon and they, becoming traders themselves, introduced the gun gradually southwestward onto the plains. Soon after 1700, the Assiniboins in Manitoba and central Saskatchewan also possessed firearms.

The early English and French fur traders to the northeast did not use horses—they would have been useless in the trackless forests—nor did they permit the trading of alcohol. Their great contribution to change was the gun. By contrast, the first European import to reach the lands of the western bison hunters came from the south; the horse was a creature ideally suited to the shortgrass plains and travelled fast from Spanish settlements in New Mexico through trade and theft (which became an honourable Indian pursuit). No guns came up from this direction however, for the Spanish, perhaps fearing for their own skins, steadfastly refused to use them as items of trade. For a while, then, the grassland tribes of the protohistoric era were divided: those in the northeast possessed guns and those in the southwest owned horses. And presumably there were others between them who possessed neither. This dichotomy was shortlived, for both the horse and the gun ultimately became widely distributed but there must have been times when the possession of one or the other was a distinct advantage.

David Thompson, an explorer for the fur trade who visited the Peigan Indians of southern Alberta in 1786, was told a tale of confrontation between the two new "weapons" which he believed had taken place about 1730. It seems that for a long time the Shoshone tribe of the south was the only one in the area to possess horses and with them it had gained the upper hand over all the other horseless tribes of the area, including the Peigan. Tired of constant harrassment, the Peigans sought the aid of their neighbours the Cree and the Assiniboins who brought into the fray ten fur trade muskets. At the next battle the Shoshone galloped in as usual among the pedestrian Peigans, wielding their stone battle clubs—only to be surprised and quickly dispatched by new and terrifying weapons, weapons that belched deadly fire and ear-splitting noise. Overwhelmed by fear, the Shoshone fled. This time the gun was proved superior to the horse (Thompson, 1916).

While all the Plains tribes coveted guns for warfare (a standard trade price for a gun was three silver fox pelts or five buffalo robes), in the southwest the early acquisition of the horse kept the fur trade at bay. Distanced by geography and with an independence bred of centuries of self sufficiency, the Indians of the far western grasslands had few furs to trade and could get along very well without the white man's goods. The first guns, clumsy muzzle-loading muskets, had their limitations. They were heavy, awkward for a horseman to hold and slow to reload. The Indians soon learned to shorten the barrel for equestrian use, a practice that made the weapon deadly, but only at close range. In the hunt, guns had other drawbacks: the sound of a single shot could stampede a whole bison herd and unless the first shot hit its mark, there was seldom enough time for a second. Bows and arrows were silent, more dependable, usually more accurate and a whole volley of arrows could be fired in the time taken to reload a musket. Even when guns became widespread among the bison hunters, many still preferred traditional hunting weapons.

At first then, the Indians of the grassland were far less dependent on the traders than the Indians of the northern forests. They did not need hunting ammunition: they continued to make their own stone arrowheads (though they preferred metal points, when they could get them). They did not need imported blankets or food supplements: the bison provided all. When the desire for guns, metal goods and tobacco finally induced them to trade they refused to make the long trek north through the woods but dealt instead with Cree middlemen until trading posts were established in the south. Even then, it was not furs that the plains people traded—there were precious few fur-bearing animals on the grasslands—but dressed bison hides and pemmican, the nutritious dried-meat-and-berries that the voyageurs had come to depend on during their long canoe trips to trade headquarters.

Did this mass manufacture of bison pemmican start the species tumbling into its disastrous decline? Certainly it must have had an effect. For the first time, Indians were slaughtering bison for more than their own immediate needs. An increasing supply of efficient breech-loading repeating rifles made this killing easier, so easy that often the carcasses were ripped only for their tongues (the greatest delicacy) or the foetal calves and the rest of the meat abandoned. And the Indians were not the only hunters. By the end of the eighteenth century they were joined by bands of Metis, the offspring of Indian women and English or French fur traders, who mounted enormous fall hunts, tearing across the prairie in their creaking Red River carts and killing huge numbers of bison for pemmican and hides. It is a pity that so few of the Metis were literate: the journals of such a people astride two cultures could have told us much.

However, the chief culprits in the demise of the bison are thought to be

184

the Americans. When they entered the fur trade—they came late, reaching the Canadian grasslands only in the 1830s—they wanted principally bison hides for leather and robes. These were bulky items, too costly for Canadian traders to transport by the long northern overland route to market. But the Americans had a great and easy highway to the industrial centres of the southeast: the Mississippi River system. Heavy bundles of hides could be put on a boat and simply floated down at little or no cost. So lucrative was the hide business that thousands of slaughtered bison were skinned where they lay and the meat left to rot. The plains reeked with putrefaction. It was an example of profligate waste that has never been equalled—and it led to the near extinction of a species that had thrived on the grasslands since the Ice Age.

Interestingly, the need for large numbers of bison robes for trade may have increased the prestige of women. A single bison hide took several days for a woman to work and dress properly, a procedure entailing nine sequential and time-consuming steps; a man needed many wives just for this job alone. Women became valuable assets, often worth many horses in bride price.

The Americans' principal item of Indian trade was liquor, mostly home-brewed or adulterated into cheap and often deadly potions that were never-thless highly desired. But the Indians' physical system was as defenceless against alcohol as it was against European diseases; even watered-down products fomented much mental and social unrest and the swift decline of the bison only accelerated the problems. To keep the peace on the Canadian grasslands the North West Mounted Police marched west to Fort Macleod, Alberta, in 1874—but this and everything to follow have been well documented. The eras of pre- and protohistory were over. Once the great herds of free-roaming bison were gone, the way of life that had sustained so many people on the grasslands for so long a time disintegrated. It exists today not even in memory, for time and swift upheaval have all but erased the old prehistoric ways. The native bison hunters have been hurtled headlong into an alien and highly technological society: almost overnight, they have made the transition from the Stone Age to the Space Age.

For a while, it seemed the ancient cultures were indeed dead and buried. But much can be reconstructed through the work of archaeologists and other scientists; they dig up the shattered sherds of culture and rebuild it, piece by piece, if incompletely. And today's Plains Indians, the Black-foot, Blood, Peigan, Sarcee, Assiniboin (Stoney), Cree and Dakota Sioux, living on reserves allotted them by the government, are also keeping alive the traditions of their ancestors: languages, songs and legends, arts and crafts, dances and religions have all been revived, often with the help of early ethnographic accounts. But again, the revivals reflect the short-lived

The arts and crafts of the Plains Indian are still very much alive.

Richly beaded moccasins (Dakota) and Cree saddle illustrate Indian flair for design. Courtesy of the Saskatchewan Museum of Natural History.

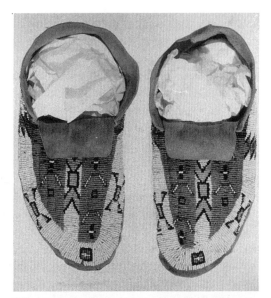

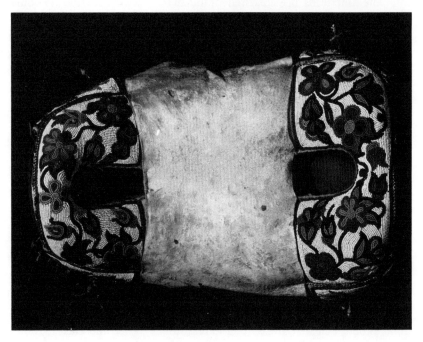

Photos taken at the 1989 Peigan Pow wow at Head-Smashed-In Buffalo Jump. A traditional camp circle, mostly of tipis, is arranged around a dance pavilion walled with poplar branches from the Oldman River Valley.

Traditional tipi designs and a dancer with a feathered mask and bustle. Both courtesy of the author.

heyday of the equestrian Plains Indian; much of the life of the dog nomads lies for ever obscured.

From History to Prehistory

In theory, the written records of history can be used as tools to dig into the dust of prehistory. A native site described by early European visitors (such as the earthlodges in Saskatchewan mentioned by Peter Fidler) should be able to be located. It could then be excavated and assessed to see if the traditional archaeological reading of the site corresponds with its actual use, a valuable check for the validity of all archaeological interpretation on the plains, much of which is only intelligent guesswork.

However, few of the prehistoric sites documented in the early literature of the Canadian grasslands have been found, though there have been several attempts. One site in particular was well identified and intrigued the archaeologists because it was unlike anything they had seen before. In December 1792, Peter Fidler travelled on foot with a group of Peigan Indians through Alberta's foothills region. Beside the banks of the Oldman River where it carves a steep and narrow canyon through the limestone wall of the Livingstone Range, he stopped to examine an unusual arrangement of stones. On New Year's Eve he drew a plan of it and wrote in his journal:

> It is a place where Indians formerly assembled here to play at a particular Game by rolling a small hoop of 4 inches diameter and darting an Arrow out of the hand after it & those that put the arrow through the hoop while rolling along is reckoned to have gamed. This is on a fine level grass plain, very little bigger than the enclosed space. One side is within 10 yards of the river & the direction of this curiosity is directly one North & south. All those peaces that compose the outer and inner parts are small stones set close together about the bigness of a person's fist above the ground & they are so close set and so neatly put together that it appears one entire ledge of stones. There are 11 piles of stones, loosely piled up at regular distances along the outside, 14 inches Diameter and about the same height. These I imagine to have been places for the Older men to sit upon to see fair play on both sides and to be the umpires of the game. (Quoted in McGregor, 1966.)

The sport described by Fidler seems to have been a version of the hoop and arrow game played in historic time by many different tribes, including the Missouri villagers.

Fidler's diary entry continues:

188

On my enquiring concerning the origin of this spot, the Indians gave me a surprising and ridiculous account. They said that a white man came from the south many ages ago and built this for the Indians to play at, that is different nations whom he wished to meet here annually & bury all anemosities betwixt the different tribes by assembling here and play-ing together. They also say that this person made the Buffalo, on pur-pose for the Indians. They described him as a very old white headed man and several more things very ridiculous.

Archaeologists found mention of this same intertribal ball court in early geologists' records, including that of George Dawson who explored the area in 1882 to 1884 and reported the "obscure remains of a couple of rectangles formed of larger stones . . . named . . . 'the Old Man's Playing Ground.'" Long-time ranchers in the area were also familiar with it and archaeologist Brian Reeves reports seeing cairns there as late as 1965. But when archaeologists went back more recently to investigate, all traces had vanished. From Fidler's report, the site lay beside the Oldman River where it runs due north/south, about a kilometre below its confluence with Racehorse Creek. Several flat river benches fitted the description and all had plenty of fist-shaped stones, but searchers found no cairns, no alignments. The ball park must have been destroyed when the road through the canyon was put through.

This attempt to marry history and archaeology failed, but this does not negate the validity of the principle and in fact the exercise itself has proved useful. When a similar arrangement of stones was later discovered in the Crowsnest Pass, excavations proved only that the rock constructions were not part of a bison pound. Without the record of history, archaeologists would have been nonplussed to explain the site. Now, thanks to Fidler, a ball game court is high on their list of probabilities (Ronaghan, n.d.)

CONCLUSION

Investigations at the Old Man's Bowling Green exemplify the extraordinary efforts that are taking place to recreate, as fully as possible, the lost lives of the prehistoric hunters of the prairies. The work of science goes on, in the field and in the laboratory, and every turn of the spade, every microscopic examination of the shreds of recovered evidence reveal additional minute details to help in the reconstructions. Archaeology has often been likened to a giant jig-saw puzzle, one where the finished picture as well as all the pieces have been lost and scattered. An individual piece of any puzzle, though interesting enough, is often meaningless until fitted together with one or two others and it is only then that a tiny fragment of the final picture emerges. Another analogy that has been used—and one which appears frequently in this book—is that of the detective, patiently searching for clues, sifting through evidence, listening to witnesses, following hunches in an attempt to piece together past events. In the case of the buffalo hunters the trail of evidence has long grown cold and archaeologists know that only a very few clues will ever be found and explained. They also admit the impossibility of ever capturing the reality of the past, for it is not a single picture, not a single truth of people and events, but a complex chiaroscuro, bent by perspective and coloured by vastly different perceptions. How can Space Age humanity ever begin to understand the workings of Stone Age mind?

In the long run, then, the story of the prehistoric native peoples of the Canadian plains, a story of supremely successful adaptation to an environment and its resources, will never fully be known. This book is merely an attempt to synthesize present knowledge and beliefs as revealed by the work of archaeologists. There are visible gaps in the story and undoubtedly many inaccuracies. Both these shortcomings may be alleviated as more information develops from current research—but then there will be new questions to ask, new contradictions to explain, new possibilities to raise. And so the work goes on.

As each new shovelful of prairie soil reveals more details of the lives of the first prairie inhabitants, our respect for them is bound to increase. For what is emerging, even as you read this, is a picture of people ever resourceful, ever tenacious, with a far richer culture than we have previously imagined. For at least as long as 12,000 years they have clung fiercely to a land not generous in its bounty, surviving the rigours of climatic and environmental change and inventing for themselves a way of life that sustained them, both

191

physically and emotionally, without the need for constant innovation and without negative impact to the natural environment. It is perhaps the unchanging nature of their lives that seems most alien to the present day urban technological society. Conditioned to expect accelerated progress in things material we tend to think of the relatively static prehistoric way of life as "primitive." But if you look closely at the evidence of archaeology, the Indians of the Canadian plains were progressing, though at a snail's pace compared to recent rates. Given time, and left alone in their bright new land, would the native peoples of North America have ultimately worked their way up into urban industrial societies? Would they too have misused and polluted the natural environment so that the very future of life on earth was in jeopardy?

Somehow, I think not.

BIBLIOGRAPHY

Adams, G.F.

1977 The Estuary Bison Pound Site in Southwest Saskatchewan. National Museum of Man Mercury Series, Archaeological Survey of Canada Paper No. 68, Ottawa.

1978 Tipi Rings in Southern Alberta: The Alkali Creek Sites, Lower Red Deer River. Archaeological Survey of Alberta Occasional Paper No. 9.

Adovasio, J.M. and R.C. Carlisle.

1984 Meadowcroft Rock Shelter. Scientific American 250:5.

Adovasio, J.M., J.D. Gunn, J. Donahue, R. Stuckenrath, J.E. Guilday, K. Lord

1978 Meadowcroft Rock Shelter. In Early Man in America, ed. A. Bryan. Department of Anthropology, University of Alberta Occasional Paper No. 1.

Adovasio, J.M., J.D. Gunn, J. Donahue, R. Stuckenrath, J.E. Guilday, K. Volman

1980 Yes, Virginia, It Really Is that Old: A Reply to Haynes and Mead. American Antiquity 45:3.

Arthur, G.

1975 An Introduction to the Ecology of Early Historic Communal Bison Hunting among the Northern Plains Indian. National Museum of Man Mercury Series, Archaeological Survey of Canada Paper No. 37.

Beebe, B.F.

1980 A Domestic Dog of Probable Pleistocene Age from Old Crow, Yukon Territory. Canadian Journal of Archaeology 4.

Brace, G.I.

1987 Boulder Monuments of Saskatchewan. Ph.D. Dissertation, University of Alberta.

Bradell, D.C., C. Minty, M. Tamplin

1970 A Prehistoric Burial near Reston, Manitoba. In 10,000 Years: Archaeology in Manitoba, ed. W. Hlady. Archaeological Society of Manitoba.

Brennan, L.

1959 No Stone Unturned. An Almanac of American Prehistory. New York: Random House.

Brink, J.

1979 Excavations at Writing-on-Stone. Archaeological Survey of Alberta Occasional Paper No. 12.

Brink, J. and S. Baldwin

1988 The Highwood River Burial. Canadian Journal of Archaeology 12.

Brink, J. and R. Dawe

1986 An Introduction to the Archaeology of the Grande Cache Region in the Northern Alberta Rocky Mountains. In Eastern Slopes Prehistory: Selected Papers. Archaeological Survey of Alberta Occasional Paper No. 30.

Brink, J., M. Wright, R. Dawe, D. Glaum

1986 The Final report of the 1984 Season at Head-Smashed-In Buffalo Jump, Alberta. Archaeological Survey of Alberta Manuscript Series No. 9.

Briuer, F.

1976 New Clues to Stone Tool Function: Plant and Animal Residues. American Antiquity 41.

Brown, R., H. Andrews, G. Ball, N. Burn, Y. Imahori, J. Milton

1983 Accelerator C 14 Dating of the Taber Child. Canadian Journal of Archaeology 7:2.

Brumley, J.

1975 The Cactus Flower Site in Southeast Alberta: 1972-74 Excavations. National Museum of Man Mercury Series, Archaeological Survey of Canada Paper No. 46.

1976 Ramillies: A Late Prehistoric Bison Kill and Campsite located in Southeast Alberta. National Museum of Man Mercury Series, Archaeological Survey of Canada Paper No. 55.

1985 The Ellis Site: A Late Prehistoric Burial Lodge/Medicine Wheel in Southeastern Alberta. In Contributions to Plains Prehistory. Archaeological Survey of Alberta Occasional Paper No. 26.

1986 Medicine Wheels on the Northern Plains: A Summary and Appraisal. Paper prepared for the Archaeological Survey of Alberta.

Bryce, G.

1885 The Mound Builders. Historic and Scientific Society of Manitoba Transaction No. 18.

1887 The Souris Country: Its Monuments, Mounds, Forts and Rivers. Historic and Scientific Society of Manitoba Transaction No. 24.

1904 Among the Mound Builders' Remains. Historic and Scientific Society of Manitoba Transaction No. 66.

Buchner, A.

1980 Archeo-Astronomical Investigations of the Petroform Phenomena of South East Manitoba. In Directions in Manitoba Prehistory, Manitoba Archaeological Society.

1983a Introducing Manitoba Prehistory. Papers in Manitoba Archaeology, Popular Series No. 4.

1983b A Survey of South East Manitoba Petroforms. In Studies in Manitoba Rock Art. Papers in Manitoba Archaeology, Dept. of Cultural Affairs and Historic Resources.

1985 The Prehistory of the Lockport Site. Historic Resources Branch, Manitoba Culture, Heritage and Recreation.

1986 Kenosewun Centre and Lockport Site. Information sheet, Kenosewun Centre, Lockport, Manitoba.

Burley, D.

1985 Evidence for a Prehistoric Vision Quest in Saskatchewan: The Roughbark Creek Overlook Site. Saskatchewan Archaeology 6.

Byrne, W.

1973 The Archaeology and Prehistory of Southern Alberta as Reflected in Ceramics. National Museum of Man Mercury Series, Archaeological Survey of Canada Paper No. 14.

Calder, J.

1977 The Majorville Cairn and Medicine Wheel Site. National Museum of Man Mercury Series, Archaeological Survey of Canada Paper No. 62.

Capes, K.

1963 W.B. Nickerson Survey and Excavations 1912-15 of Southern Manitoba Mounds Region. National Museum of Canada Anthropology Papers No. 4.

Carter, D.

1967 The Manyberries Cairn. Manuscript at Archaeological Survey of Alberta, Edmonton.

Choquette, W.

1980 The Role of Lithic Raw Material; Studies in Kootenay Archaeology. B.C. Studies 48.

Cinq-Mars, J.

1979 Bluefish Cave: A Late Pleistocene Eastern Beringian Cave Deposit in the Northern Yukon. Canadian Journal of Archaeology 3.

Coe, M.

1984 Mexico. New York: Thames & Hudson.

Coe, M., D. Snow, E. Benson

1986 Atlas of Ancient America. New York: Facts on File Publications.

Conner, S.

1982 Archaeology of the Crow Indian Vision Quest. Archaeology in Montana 23:3.

Deetz, J.

    1965   The Dynamics of Stylistic Change in Arikara Ceramics. Illinois Studies in Anthropology No. 4. University of Illinois Press, Urbana.

Dempsey, H.

    1956   Stone Medicine Wheels: Memorials to Blackfoot War Chiefs. Journal of Washington Academy of Science 46:6.

Dillehay, T.

    1984   Monte Verde Site, Southern Chile. Scientific American 251:4.

    1987   By the Banks of the Chinchihuapi. The First Americans series, Natural History No. 4.

Dillehay, T. and M. Collins

    1988   Early Cultural Evidence from Monte Verde in Chile. Nature 332, 10 March.

Doll, M.

    1982   The Boss Hill Site. Provincial Museum of Alberta. Human History Occasional Papers No. 2, Edmonton.

Dormaar, J.

    1976   Effect of Boulderflow on Soil Transformation under Tipi Rings. Plains Anthopologist 21.

Driver, J.

    1976   Dogs from Archaeological Sites in Alberta. Paper in fulfillment of Archaeology 602, The University of Calgary. Manuscript on file at the Archaeological Survey of Alberta, Edmonton.

Dyck, I.

    1977   The Harder Site: A Middle Period Bison Hunter's Campsite in the Northern Great Plains. National Museum of Man Mercury Series. Archaeological Survey of Canada Paper No. 67.

    1981   Wild Man Butte Effigy. Saskatchewan Archaeology 2:1 and 2.

1983 The Prehistory of Southern Saskatchewan. In Tracking Ancient Hunters: Prehistoric Archaeology in Saskatchewan, eds. Epp & Dyck. Saskatchewan Archaeological Society.

Ebell, S.

1980 The Parkhill Site. Pastlog, Manuscript Series in Archaeology and History No. 4. Saskatchewan Culture and Youth.

Eddy, J.

1974 Astronomical Alignments of Bighorn Medicine Wheel. Science 184:4141.

1977 Medicine Wheels and Plains Indian Astronomy. In Native American Astronomy, ed. A.F. Aveni. University of Texas Press.

Epp, H. and I. Dyck (eds.)

1983 Tracking Ancient Hunters: Prehistoric Archaeology in Saskatchewan. Saskatchewan Archaeological Society.

Fagan, B.

1986 People of the Earth. New York: Little, Brown.

1987 The Great Journey. The Peopling of Ancient America. London and New York: Thames & Hudson.

Fedje, D.

1986 Banff Archaeology, 1983-85. In Eastern Slopes Prehistory, Selected Papers. ed. B. Ronaghan. Archaeological Survey of Alberta, Occasional Papers No. 30.

Festinger, L.

1983 The Human Legacy. New York: Columbia University Press.

Finnigan, J.

1982 Tipi Rings and Plains Prehistory. A Reassessment of their Archaeological Potential. National Museum of Man Mercury Series, Archaeological Survey of Canada Paper No. 108.

Finnigan, J. and E. Johnson

1984 The Elma Thompson Site. A Besant Phase Tipi Ring in the West Central Saskatchewan Plains. Saskatchewan Archaeology 5.

Fladmark, K.

1978   The Feasibility of the Northwest Coast as a Migration Route for Early Man. In Early Man in America, ed. A. Bryan. Department of Anthropology, University of Alberta, Occasional Paper No 1.

1986a British Columbia Prehistory. Archaeological Survey of Canada, National Museum of Man.

1986b Getting One's Bering. In The First Americans series, Natural History No. 11.

Fladmark, K., J. Driver, and D. Alexander

1988   The Paleoindian Component at Charlie Lake Cave, British Columbia. American Antiquity 53:2.

Forbis, R.

1962   Old Women's Buffalo Jump. Contributions to Anthropology 1960 Part 1. Bulletin 180, National Museum of Canada.

1968   Fletcher: A Paleo Indian Site in Alberta. American Antiquity 33:1.

1970   A Review of Alberta Archaeology to 1964. Publications in Archaeology No. 1. National Museum of Man, Ottawa.

1977   Cluny: An Ancient Fortified Village in Alberta. Department of Archaeology, University of Calgary. Occasional Paper No. 4.

Friberg, T.

1974   The Manyberries Cairn. Manuscript at Archaeological Survey of Alberta, Edmonton.

Frison, G.

1978   Prehistoric Hunters of the High Plains. New York: Academic Press.

Getty, R.

1971   The Many Snakes Burial. Calgary: Unileth Press.

Gibson, T. and S. Stratton

1987   In Search of the Individual in Prehistory; Analyzing Finger-prints from Selkirk Pottery from Saskatchewan. Paper given at Canadian Archaeological Association Meeting, Calgary.

Gryba, E.

1975   The Cypress Hills Archaeological Site. Manuscript on file at Archaeological Survey of Alberta, Edmonton.

1980   Early Side-Notched Point Tradition in the Central and Northern Plains. In Directions in Manitoba Prehistory, Archaeological Society of Manitoba.

1983   Sibbald Creek: 11,000 Years of Human Use of the Alberta Foothills. Archaeological Survey of Alberta Occasional Paper No. 22.

1985   Evidence of the Fluted Point Tradition in Alberta. In Contributions to Plains Prehistory. Archaeological Survey of Alberta Occasional Paper No. 26.

Guilday, J.

1967   Differential Extinction during Late Pleistocene and Recent Times. In Pleistocene Extinctions: The Search for a Cause. Eds. Martin and Wright. New Haven, CT: Yale University Press.

Haack, S.

1987   A Critical Evaluation of Medicine Wheel Astronomy. Plains Anthropologist 32:115.

Hanna, M.

1976   The Moose Bay Burial Mound. Saskatchewan Museum of Natural History Anthropological Series No. 3.

1986   An Examination of Vessels from the Avonlea Type Site. Saskatchewan Archaeology 7.

Harington, C., R. Bonnichsen, and R. Morlan

1975   Bones Say Man Lived in the Yukon 27,000 Years Ago. Canadian Geographic Journal 91.

Haynes, C.

1964   Fluted Projectile Points: Their Age and Dispersal. Science 145:3639.

Head, T.

1985 The Late Prehistoric Period as Viewed from the H.M.S. Balzac Site. In Contributions to Plains Prehistory. Archaeological Survey of Alberta Occasional Paper No. 26.

Hill, M.

1948 The Atlatl or Throwing Stick. Tennessee Archaeology 4:4.

Hlady, W. (ed.)

1970 10,000 Years; Archaeology in Manitoba. Altona: Friesen & Sons.

Hoffman, J.

1968 The La Roche Site. River Basin Surveys, Publications in Salvage Archaeology No. 11, Smithsonian Institution.

Hughes, C.

1986 DkPj-21: A Description and Discussion of a Vision Quest Site in the Porcupine Hills, Alberta. In Final Report of the 1984 Season at Head-Smashed-In Buffalo Jump, Alberta. eds. Brink, Wright, Dawe and Glaum. Archaeological Survey of Alberta Manuscript Series No. 9.

Husted, W.

1969 Bighorn Canyon Archaeology, River Basin Surveys. Publications in Salvage Archaeology No. 12, Smithsonian Institution.

Irving, W.

1987 New Dates from Old Bones. In The First Americans series. Natural History No. 2.

Irving, W, J. Mayhall, F. Melbye and B. Beebe

1977 A Human Mandible in Probable Association with a Pleistocene Faunal Assemblage in Eastern Beringia: A Preliminary Report. Canadian Journal of Archaeology 1.

Jennings, J. and E. Norbeck (eds.)

1964 Prehistoric Man in the New World. Chicago: University of Chicago Press.

Joyes, D.

1970　The Culture Sequence at the Avery Site at Rock Lake. In 10,000 years; Archaeology in Manitoba. ed. W. Hlady.

Kehoe, A. and T. Kehoe

1979　Solstice-Aligned Boulder Configurations in Saskatchewan. National Museum of Man Mercury Series. Canadian Ethnology Service Paper No. 48.

Kehoe, T.

1966　The Small Side-notched Point System of the Northern Plains. American Antiquity 31:6.

1973　The Gull Lake Site: A Prehistoric Bison Drive Site in Southwest Saskatchewan. Publications in Anthropology and History No. 1. Milwaukee Public Museum.

Kehoe, T. and B. McCorquodale

1961　The Avonlea Point: Horizon Marker for the N.W. Plains. Plains Anthropologist 6:13.

Kelly, R.

1987　A Comment on the Pre-Clovis Deposits at Meadowcroft Rock Shelter. Quaternary Research 27.

Kennedy, M. and R. Steinhauser

1985　Conservation Excavations at DkPf-2, a major site complex on the Blood Reserve. Alberta Transportation Project S.R. 509. Lifeways of Canada Ltd.

Keyser, J.

1977　Writing-on-Stone: Rock Art on the N.W. Plains. Canadian Journal of Archaeology 1.

1979　The Plains Indian War Complex and the Rock Art of Writing-on-Stone, Alberta. Journal of Field Archaeology 6.

1987　A Lexicon for Historic Plains Indian Rock Art. Increasing Interpretive Potential. Plains Anthropologist 32:115.

King, D.

    1961   The Bracken Cairn. A Prehistoric Burial. The Blue Jay 19, March.

Klimko, O.

    1985   New Perspectives on Avonlea: A View from the Saskatchewan Forests. In Contributions to Plains Prehistory, Archaeological Survey of Alberta Occasional Paper No. 26.

Kopper, P.

    1986   The Smithsonian Book of North American Indians Before the Coming of Europeans. Washington, D.C.: Smithsonian Books.

Lahren, L. and R. Bonnichsen

    1974   Bone Foreshafts from a Clovis Burial in S.W. Montana. Science 186:4159, 11 October.

Lee, R.

    1983   The Botched Debunking of the "Taber Theory." Anthropological Journal of Canada 21.

Loveseth, B.

    1976   Lithic Source Survey in the Crowsnest Pass Area. In Archaeology in Alberta 1975. Archaeological Survey of Alberta Occasional Paper No. 1.

Loy, T.

    1983   Prehistoric Blood Residues: Detection on Tool Surfaces and Identification of Species of Origin. Science 220:4603.

Maclean, J.

    1896   Canadian Savage Folk. Toronto. (self-published).

MacNeish, R.

    1954   The Stott Mound. National Museums of Canada Bulletin No. 132, Ottawa.

    1958   Introduction to the Archaeology of Southeast Manitoba. National Museums of Canada Bulletin No. 157, Ottawa.

McGregor, J.

1966 Peter Fidler: Canada's Forgotten Surveyor. Toronto: McClelland & Stewart.

Mallory, O.

1977 Archaeological Monitoring Report on the Liebenthal, Mortlach and Moosomin Loops, Saskatchewan and Portage La Prairie Loop, Manitoba and Trans Canada Pipelines Ltd. Toronto: F.F. Slaney & Co. Ltd.

Mangelsdorf, P.

1974 Corn: Its Origins, Evolution and Improvement. Cambridge: Harvard University Press.

1983 The Mystery of Corn: New Perspectives. Proceedings of the American Philosophical Society 127:4.

Martin, P.

1967 Prehistoric Overkill. In Pleistocene Extinctions. The Search for a Cause, eds. Martin & Wright. New Haven CT: Yale University Press.

Matthews, J.

1979 Beringia during the Late Pleistocene: Arctic Steppe or Discontinuous Herb-Tundra? Geological Survey of Canada, Open File Report No. 649.

Mead, J.I.

1980 Is It Really that Old? A Comment about the Meadowcroft Rockshelter "Overview." American Antiquity 45:2.

Millar, J.

1972 The Gray Burial Site. In The Southwest Saskatchewan Archaeological Project. Napao 3:2.

1978 The Gray Site: An Early Plains Burial Ground. Parks Canada Manuscript Report No. 304.

1981a The Oxbow Complex in Time and Space. Canadian Journal of Archaeology 5.

1981b Mortuary Practices of the Oxbow Complex. Canadian Journal of Archaeology 5.

Moffat, E. and I. Wainwright

1983 Protein Concentrations in the Taber Child Skeleton. Canadian Journal of Archaeology 7:2.

Morgan, R.

1979 An Ecological Study of the Northern Plains as seen through The Garratt Site. Department of Anthropology, University of Regina. Occasional Papers No. 1.

Montgomery, H.

1908 Prehistoric Man in Manitoba and Saskatchewan. American Anthropologist 10:1.

1910 Calf Mountain Mound in Manitoba. American Anthropologist 12:1.

Nelson, D.E., R. Morlan, J. Vogel, J. Southon, C. Harington

1984 New Dates on Northern Yukon Artifacts: Holocene not Upper Pleistocene. Science 232, May.

Neuman, R.

1975 The Sonota Complex and Associated Sites on the Northern Great Plains. Nebraska State Historical Society Publications in Anthropology No. 6.

Olsen, S.

1985 Origins of the Domestic Dog: The Fossil Record. Tucson: University of Arizona Press.

Ovenden, M. and D. Rodger

1981 Megaliths and Medicine Wheels. In Megaliths to Medicine Wheels: Boulder Structures in Archaeology. Proceedings of the 11th Annual Chacmool Conference. Archaeological Association of The University of Calgary.

Palter, J.

1976 A New Approach to the Significance of the "Weighted" Spear Thrower. American Antiquity 41:4.

Pettipas, L.

1985 Recent Developments in Palaeo-Indian Archaeology in Manitoba. In Contributions to Plains Prehistory. Archaeological Survey of Alberta Occasional Paper No. 26.

Pohorecky, Z., and J. Wilson

1968 Preliminary Archaeological Report on the Saskatoon Site. Napao 1:2.

Quigg, J.

1986 Ross Glen: A Besant Stone Circle Site in S.E. Alberta. Archaeological Survey of Alberta Manuscript Series No. 10.

Reeves, B.

1969 The Southern Alberta Paleo-Environment Sequence. In Post-Pleistocene Man and His Environment on the Northern Plains. Archaeological Association, The University of Calgary.

1973 The Concept of an Altithermal Cultural Hiatus in Northern Plains Prehistory. American Anthropologist 75:5.

1978a Men, Mountains and Mammals. Paper delivered at the Plains Conference, Denver.

1978b Head-Smashed-In: 5500 Years of Bison Jumping in the Alberta Plains. Plains Anthropologist Memoir No. 14.

1983a Six Milleniums of Buffalo Kills. Scientific American 249:4, October.

1983b Culture Change in the Northern Plains 1000 B.C. to 1000 A.D. Archaeological Survey of Alberta Occasional Paper No. 20.

Reeves, B., M. Kennedy and O. Beattie

1984 Alberta Transportation Project, Proposed SR 509 Alignment. DkPf-2 burials. Final Report. Lifeways of Canada.

Ronaghan, B.

n.d. Early Historic Records Provide Clues for the Archaeologist. Unpublished paper.

Roe, F.

1951   The North American Buffalo. Toronto: University of Toronto Press.

Russell, D.

1982   The Ethnohistoric and Demographic Context of Central Saskatchewan to 1800. In Nipawin Reservoir Heritage Study, Vol. 3; Saskatchewan Power Corporation.

Schroedl, A. and E. Walker

1978   A Preliminary Report on the Gowan Site. Napao 8:1 and 2.

Silverberg, R.

1968   Mound Builders of Ancient America. The Archaeology of a Myth. New York: New York Graphic Society Ltd.

Slaughter, R.

1967   Animal Ranges as a Clue to Late Pleistocene Extinctions. In Pleistocene Extinctions: The Search for a Cause. eds. Martin and Wright. New Haven, CT: Yale University Press.

Smith, B.

1987   The Lebret Site. M.A. Thesis, The University of Saskatchewan.

Snow, D.

1980   The Archaeology of North America. London and New York: Thames & Hudson.

Stalker, A.

1983   A Detailed Stratigraphy of the Woodpecker Island Section and Commentary on the Taber Child Bones. Canadian Journal of Archaeology 7:2.

Stanford, D.

1987   The Ginsberg Experiment. In The First Americans series. Natural History No. 9.

Steinbring, J.

1970 The Tie Creek Boulder Site of Southeastern Manitoba. In 10,000 Years: Archaeology in Manitoba. ed. W. Hlady. Manitoba Archaeological Society.

1980 An Introduction to Archaeology on the Winnipeg River. Papers in Manitoba Archaeology No. 9, Manitoba Dept. of Cultural Affairs and Historical Resources.

Syms, E.

1977a Cultural Ecology and Ecological Dynamics of the Ceramic Period in S.W. Manitoba. Plains Anthropologist Memoir No. 12.

1977b Pottery in Prehistoric Manitoba. The Beaver, Outfit No. 308, No 1, summer.

1978 Aboriginal Mounds in Southern Manitoba. Research Report, Parks Canada.

1979a The Devil's Lake—Sourisford Complex. Plains Anthropologist 24:86.

1979b The Snyder Dam Site, Southwest Manitoba. Two New Ceramic Components. Canadian Journal of Archaeology 3.

Thompson, D.

1916 David Thompson's Narrative of His Explorations in Western America 1784—1812. Ed. J.B. Tyrrell. Toronto.

Turner, C.

1987 Tell-Tale Teeth. In The First Americans series. Natural History No. 1.

VanDyke, S. and S. Stewart

1985 The Hawkwood Site: A Multi-Component Prehistoric Campsite on Nose Hill. Archaeological Survey of Alberta Manuscript Series No. 7.

Verbicky-Todd, E.

1984 Communal Buffalo Hunting Among the Plains Indians. Archaeological Survey of Alberta Occasional Paper No. 24.

Vickers, J.

1986 Alberta Prehistory: A Review. Archaeological Survey of Alberta Occasional Paper No. 27.

Vogt, D.

1983 Medicine Wheels: Boulder by Boulder. Proceedings of the 1st International Ethnoastronomy Conference, Washington, D.C.

Walker, D. and G. Frison

1982 Studies on Amerindian Dogs, 3: Prehistoric Wolf/Dog Hybrids from the Northwestern Plains. Journal of Archaeological Science 9.

Walker, E.

1982a The Bracken Cairn: A Late Middle Archaic Burial in Southwestern Saskatchewan. Saskatchewan Archaeology 3:1 and 2.

1982b The Graham Site: A McKean Cremation from Southern Saskatchewan. Plains Anthropologist 29:104.

1983 The Woodlawn Site: A Case for Inter-regional Disease Transmission in the Late Prehistoric Period. Canadian Journal of Archaeology 7:1.

Wedel, W.

1961 Prehistoric Man on the Great Plains. Norman: The University of Oklahoma Press.

Wedel, W., W. Husted and J. Moss

1968 Mummy Cave. Science 160:3824.

Wettlaufer, B.

1955 The Mortlach Site in the Besant Valley of Central Saskatchewan. Anthopology Series No. 1, Dept. of Natural Resources, Regina.

1960 The Long Creek Site. ed. W. Mayer-Oakes. Anthropology Series No. 2, Saskatchewan Museum of Natural History, Regina.

Wheat, J.

1972 Olsen-Chubbock Site: A Paleo-Indian Bison Kill. Memoirs of the Society for American Archaeology No. 26.

Williamson, R.

1984 Living the Sky: The Cosmos of the North American Indian. Boston: Houghton-Mifflin Co.

Wilson, I.

1987 The Pink Mountain Palaeo-Indian Site. In Archaeology in Alberta, 1986. Archaeological Survey of Alberta Occasional Paper No. 37.

Wilson, M.

1975 Local Fauna in the Cactus Flower Site. In The Cactus Flower Site in Southeastern Alberta, J. Brumley. Canada Museum of Man Mercury Series, Archaeological Survey of Canada Paper No. 46.

1977 Archaeological Studies in the Longview/Pekisko area of Southern Alberta. Report at Archaeological Survey of Alberta, Edmonton.

1981 Sun Dances, Thirst Dances and Medicine Wheels: A Search for Alternative Hypotheses. In Megaliths to Medicine Wheels. Proceedings of the 11th Chacmool Conference, The University of Calgary.

Wilson, M., D. Harvey, and R. Forbis

1983 Geoarchaeological Investigations of the Age and Context of the Stalker (Taber Child) Site, Alberta. Canadian Journal of Archaeology 7:2.

Wormington, H. and R. Forbis.

1965 An Introduction to the Archaeology of Alberta. Proceedings No. 11, Denver Museum of Natural History.

Zegura, S.

1987 Blood Test. In The First American series. Natural History 7.

INDEX